John James Stevenson

House architecture

John James Stevenson

House architecture

ISBN/EAN: 9783337150723

Printed in Europe, USA, Canada, Australia, Japan

Cover: Foto ©Andreas Hilbeck / pixelio.de

More available books at **www.hansebooks.com**

CAROLINEN-STRASSE, NUREMBERG.

HOUSE ARCHITECTURE.

BY

J. J. STEVENSON,

FELLOW OF THE ROYAL INSTITUTE OF BRITISH ARCHITECTS.

IN TWO VOLUMES.

VOL. I.

ARCHITECTURE.

London:
MACMILLAN AND CO.
1880.

LONDON:
PRINTED BY WILLIAM CLOWES AND SONS,
STAMFORD STREET AND CHARING CROSS.

PREFACE.

I BEGAN this book ten years ago during an interval in the practice of my profession. Many causes have delayed its completion, foremost among which was a sense of the inadequacy and imperfection of what I had written. The constant engagements of an architect made it difficult for me to give to the book the time needed to make it satisfactory. At the same time I was unwilling to lose the labour and the cost already expended. A consequence of the time the writing of the book has occupied is that many of the views it advocates, which were unusual when they were written, are now current and fashionable. I believe that the book may still be useful. Though inadequate, it is not, I hope, misleading. Throughout it, while stating my own opinions, I have tried to give the reader data for judging for himself.

The illustrations have been one cause of the delay in publishing. They are all from wood blocks, which give more satisfactory results than some modern processes, not being liable to the imperfect printing of the lines in parts which is apt to occur in these. Most of the illustrations have been drawn on the wood by Mr. H. W. Brewer, some from my own sketches, but the greater part from his. The illustration of the Colosseum at Rome was drawn on the wood for me by Mr. Mac Whirter, A.R.A.

The drawings have been cut on the wood by several engravers, including Mr. Cooper, Mr. Walmsley, Mr. Morison, Miss MacLaren, and Mr. Pitt, Miss Bateman, and some others on the staff of the 'Graphic,' to all of whom I feel under obligation for the careful way in which the cuts have been executed. I venture to think that some of them deserve a high place among modern examples of the art of wood engraving.

I am indebted for the use of a number of the cuts to the kindness of the Proprietors of the 'Graphic,' to Mr. George Godwin of the 'Builder,' and to Mr. James Parker of Oxford for those from his father's work on 'English Domestic Architecture in the Middle Ages,' and the examples of the Orders from Rickman's 'Gothic Architecture.' In two or three cases where the same cut illustrates different parts of the text, I have repeated it to save the reader the trouble of looking it up in a different part of the book.

THE RED HOUSE, *Bayswater Hill*,
    December, 1879.

CONTENTS OF VOL. I.

CHAPTER I.
INTRODUCTORY .. ..   PAGE 1

CHAPTER II.
WHAT CONSTITUTES GOOD ARCHITECTURE?   25

CHAPTER III.
THE CONDITIONS NECESSARY FOR PRODUCING GOOD ARCHITECTURE ..   70

CHAPTER IV.
WHAT STYLE OF ARCHITECTURE IS MOST SUITABLE FOR OUR HOUSES? ..   119

CHAPTER V.
GOTHIC ARCHITECTURE   123

CHAPTER VI.
GREEK ARCHITECTURE   185

CHAPTER VII.
CLASSICAL OR RENAISSANCE ARCHITECTURE   199

CHAPTER VIII.
THE RENAISSANCE IN FLORENCE AND SIENNA   217

CHAPTER IX.

The Renaissance in Rome 222

CHAPTER X.

Venetian Renaissance 225

CHAPTER XI.

The Renaissance in France 238

CHAPTER XII.

The Renaissance in Germany and the Low Countries 258

CHAPTER XIII.

The Renaissance in England 284

CHAPTER XIV.

The Renaissance in Scotland 350

CHAPTER XV.

Conclusion 380

LIST OF ILLUSTRATIONS TO VOL. I.

FIG.		PAGE
	Carolinen-Strass, Nuremberg .. .. *Frontispiece.*	
1.	Shed for ladders at Höchberg, near Würtzburg..	22
2.	Tilquhillie Castle, Aberdeenshire..	28
3.	Rock-hewn Architecture, Petra	30
4.	Houses at Münster	36
5, 6, 7 and 8.	Different modes of architectural treatment of the front of a House	38, 39
9.	House opposite the Cathedral at Augsburg	40
10.	Old House in the High Street, Glasgow	41
11.	House near the Town Hall, Nuremberg..	42
12.	Towers on the Walls at Nuremberg	45
13.	Borthwick Castle	46
14, 15, 16 and 17.	Architectural Ornaments: fret, chevron, lines and dots	47
18.	Wall decoration in Chapter House, Burnham Abbey	50
19.	Egyptian Architecture.—Temple of Karnac	52
20.	Greek Architecture.—Temple at Pæstum, Magna Grecia	56
21.	Roman Architecture.—The Colosseum at Rome.—From a drawing by J. Mac Whirter, Esq., A.R.A.	59
22.	Gothic Architecture.—View in Westminster Abbey.—From a drawing by R. J. Johnson, Esq., F.R.I.B.A.	62
23.	Renaissance Architecture.—Church of St. Étienne du Mont, Paris ..	66
24.	Gable at Nuremberg	118
25, 26.	Sections of round and pointed Waggon Vaults	128
27, 28 and 29.	Round and pointed Domes, plan and sections	128
30.	Church roofed with pointed Waggon Vault	129
31.	Church with Groined Vaulting	130
32.	Plan of Vaulting, square in plan	131
33, 34.	View and plan of Vaulting, oblong in plan in Nave, and square in Aisles	132
35.	Round-headed window under pointed Vault	133
36.	Groining without ribs	137

FIG.		PAGE
37.	Romanesque House at Boppart on the Rhine.—From the 'Builder'	144
38.	Goliath House, Ratisbon	145
39.	Gothic Street in Ratisbon	148
40.	House of the Musicians at Rheims	150
41.	Markenfield Hall, Yorkshire.—From Parker's 'English Domestic Architecture of the Middle Ages'	151
42.	Decorated Window, under level Cornice	152
43.	Perpendicular Window, under level Cornice	152
44.	House of Jacques Cœur at Bourges	154
45.	Plans of Vaulting showing development	160
46.	Vaulting of the Crossing, St. George's Chapel, Windsor.—From the 'Graphic'	161
47.	Morton Hall, Cheshire	165
48.	Corner Oriel at Augsburg.—From the 'Builder'	169
49.	Gothic House at Boppart on the Rhine.—From the 'Builder'	176
50.	The Nassauer House, Nuremberg	177
51.	Hohenzollern	184
52.	Grecian Doric.—Temple of Theseus, Athens. (For the use of this and the other illustrations of the Greek and Roman Orders from Rickman's 'Gothic Architecture,' I am indebted to Mr. James Parker, of Oxford.)	186
53.	Grecian Doric.—Temple of Apollo at Delos	187
54.	Grecian Ionic.—Erechtheum, Athens	189
55.	,, ,, Temple on the Ilissus	189
56.	The Corinthian Order.—Temple of Vesta, Tivoli	190
57.	,, ,, Temple of Jupiter Olympus, Athens	190
58.	The Composite Order.—Arch of Septimius Severus, Rome	191
59.	The Erectheum, Athens	194
60.	Arch of Hadrian, Athens	204
61.	The Custom House, King's Lynn	206
62.	The Black Gate, Treves	207
63.	Roman Capital carved in brick	208
64.	Amresbury, principal front	209
65.	Roman Doric.—Theatre of Marcellus, Rome	210
66.	Roman Ionic.—Aqueduct of Hadrian, Athens	211
67.	,, ,, Temple of Fortuna Virilis, Rome	211
68.	Nicollini Palace, Florence	219
69.	House in Via d'Bianchi, Rome	223
70.	Small Gothic House at Venice	226
71.	Vandramini Palace, Venice	228

LIST OF ILLUSTRATIONS TO VOL. I.

FIG.		PAGE
72.	Cornaro Palace, Venice	230
73.	Staircase in the Ducal Palace, Venice	232
74.	Pesaro Palace, Venice	234
75.	Château de Thery	239
76.	Jacques Cœur's House at Bourges, plan of Ground-floor	243
77.	Château d'Azy-le-Rideau, Indre-et-Loire	245
78.	House at Orleans	248
79, 80.	Gables at Nuremberg	259
81.	Houses at Münster, Westphalia	261
82.	Street in Landshut, Bavaria	264
83.	Houses on the Pegnitz, Nuremberg	266
84.	Oriel Window at Freiburg in Breisgau	267
85.	Inn at Kriegshaben, near Augsburg	268
86.	Bishop's House, Würzburg	269
87.	New Münsterhof Würzburg	272
88.	House at Würzburg	273
89.	Tower of the Rathhaus, Mannheim	274
90.	Wooden House at Hildesheim	275
91.	Houses in the Market Place, Brussels	281
92.	Old House at Lucerne	283
93.	Longleat, Wiltshire.—From an old print	286
94.	Interior in old House in Lime Street.—From the 'Graphic'	291
95.	Chimney-piece in old House in Lime Street.—From the 'Graphic'	293
96.	York Gate, a Landing-place on the Thames	299
97, 98, 99 and 100.	Amresbury, plans and elevations	301–5
101.	St. John's College, Oxford, second quad	308
102.	Market-Cross, Peterborough	312
103.	Steeple of St. Magnus, London Bridge (designed by Sir Christopher Wren)	318
104.	Old Merchant Taylors' School, designed by Wren, Street Front.—From the 'Graphic'	319
105.	Merchant Taylors' School, Playing Court.—From the 'Graphic'	320
106.	School-room of Merchant Taylors' School.—Ditto	321
107.	Old Bedlam, Central block	327
108.	St. Catherine's College, Cambridge	329
109.	Drapers' Almhouses, Margate	330
110.	Kew Palace	333
111.	Cowper's House at Olney.—From the 'Graphic'	335
112.	Redington Rectory	337
113.	Town Hall, South Shields	338

FIG.		PAGE
114.	Custom House, King's Lynn	339
115.	Montague House—the old British Museum	340
116.	Old Street in London	341
117, 118 and 119.	Doorways in Essex Street, Strand	342-3
120.	Tilquhillie Castle, Aberdeenshire	352
121.	Courtyard of House at Linlithgow	353
122.	Borthwick Castle	358
123.	Old House in High Street, Glasgow	359
124.	Newark Castle, on the Clyde	361
125.	Scotch Castle	362
126.	Old Glasgow University, north side of inner Court	363
127.	,, ,, south and west sides of inner Court	366
128.	,, ,, Stair to Fore Hall	369
129.	,, ,, the Fore Hall	372
130.	Part of House in the High Street, Edinburgh	374
131.	Ordinary Classic House	376

HOUSE ARCHITECTURE.

CHAPTER I.

INTRODUCTORY.

To build a house for oneself is an excellent education in architecture. By the time it is finished, and the owner has lived in it, he feels how much better a house he could build with the experience he has acquired, if he had to do it over again. While the work is going on his attention is called to questions he had never thought of before, which are now of the greatest interest to him. He examines the houses of his friends, and discovers features in them which he wishes, when too late, he had introduced in his own plans. The designs are altered and the cost increased. His taste in architecture, and his ideas about planning are changed by his new experience; the building is too far advanced to adopt the improvements, and the house which he had hoped would be perfect, is a source of trouble and disappointment.

He could build another house to his mind, but to go through the experience once in a lifetime is enough for most people.

To have, before commencing the building of a new house, the knowledge which the experience of building gives in some imperfect and fragmentary way at the end of the process, would save the owner trouble, expense, and after-regret. To attempt to supply this is the object of this book.

I do not imagine that any information I can give can supersede the services of an architect. It can no more do this than a treatise on medicine enables us to do without a doctor. Book knowledge is useless in practice without the tact, gained only by experience, when and how to apply it. But architects have frequently told me that they wished they had such a book as this which they could put into the hands of their employers; as one of their great difficulties is, that those for whom they are working do not understand what is meant by the plans, and after they are executed find out that the result is not what they wanted. If the employer could have understood what was proposed, and the results which were possible, misunderstanding and disappointment would frequently have been avoided.

I shall try to treat of all matters connected with the building of a house, so that any one may understand them and have grounds for forming his own opinion. This will involve the discussion of questions interesting to numbers who have no intention of ever building a house. It will necessitate, as one important branch of investigation, an account of Architecture; some inquiry as to its meaning and aims, the principles on which its rules are founded, and its uses. To attempt to discuss these questions would be useless without some brief statement of the effects which Architecture has aimed at, and has succeeded in producing in various countries.

We must inquire into the conditions, social and intellectual, under which Architecture produced its triumphs, and whether we may hope for satisfactory results, under the conditions under which we work at the present time.

A question which must be settled before commencing a house, is the style of architecture it is to be built in. Till about fifty years ago, this question did not arise; there was only one style in which people could build, that prevalent at the time. Since the modern Gothic revival, architects and all who care for Architecture have been divided as to whether we should adopt Gothic for our houses, or the Classic style, which before that revival had been universally used. Possibly neither of them may be quite suitable for us. The question cannot be satisfactorily decided without examining all the styles which we might reasonably employ with a view to our modern wants and necessities.

Apart from its practical use, such a discussion is interesting, on its own account, to all who care for Architecture; and even those who think the subject technical and dull may find that it is of genuine human interest. The old styles of Architecture were the natural outcome of the character and history of the nations who invented them, and are among the most reliable and interesting records of their social condition and modes of thought. Each of them was formed by a gradual process of development, which it is most interesting to trace. Architecture has of late years become a subject of interest, and every one feels he should know something of it. Truer and more practical knowledge of it, more widely diffused, might give us again houses characterised by good taste and beauty, like those of former times, in place of the dulness and vulgar pretentiousness which disfigure our streets and landscapes.

The second volume treats of the planning and arrangement of houses, building materials, and the conveniences and mechanical contrivances which our modern notions of comfort demand. To get a perfectly satisfactory plan is of all matters the most important in building a house. House-planning is an art derived through long tradition, and, to understand it, we must trace its history, which is full of interest, for it is the history of home life and social habits.

To plan rightly we must know what experience has shown to be requisite in modern house-planning.

Before we can combine the various rooms and offices together into one house, we must understand the purpose of each, and the best form and size for that purpose. The family living-rooms, the servants' offices, and the passages and stairs connecting them, will each form the subject of a chapter, before treating of the best ways of arranging and combining these together.

There is a short chapter on the number of stories and height of houses in different circumstances, and another on the usual plan of town houses.

To attempt a technical treatise on building materials and construction would be impossible in our space, and useless for our purpose; but some information is necessary on the kind of materials we can have at our command, and the right way of using them, so as to produce a good architectural effect in form and colour.

When the house is built it must be warmed and ventilated, supplied with water, a system of drainage, and various mechanical contrivances, such as bells, speaking tubes, and lifts, for convenience or to save servants' labour. These matters will form the subject of a chapter.

As a house is not complete internally without decoration and furniture, nor externally, without its surrounding terraces, gardens and pleasure grounds, a complete treatise on house architecture ought to include chapters on these subjects. They were in part written, but the preparation of proper illustrations would have still farther postponed this publication, already too long delayed.

These questions will be better discussed with reference to a house in the country, where there is some space and freedom of arrangement, than if we are bound by the stereotyped arrangements of town houses.

Every one of them has of late years been a subject of interest and discussion; and information is to be got with regard to all of them in magazine articles, and in books large and small. The literature of the subject is too extensive for easy acquirement or handy reference, and to be of practical use to any one building a house, it requires to be digested, and the conflicting views which abound on every point stated and compared. For any one without practical experience of building operations this process would be difficult, and the results probably wrong. Some notice of the more important works on these subjects will indicate the gap which this book is intended to fill.

Mr. Ruskin, in his 'Seven Lamps of Architecture,' and in his 'Stones of Venice,' has discussed with eloquence and insight the fundamental principles of Architecture, the value of the art to us, and the style we ought to adopt for modern use. By these and other writings he has inspired his generation with enthusiasm for art, and for nobleness and beauty in architecture. I do not know how far he holds to the views expressed in these works, as since their publication he has modified some of his opinions. In them the subject is treated too often from the point of view of Italy to be practically useful or true of England. I think some of his views on architecture are open to question, and that their practical influence on modern architecture has to some extent been mischievous.

Mr. Fergusson, in his 'History of Architecture,' gives a clear and interesting account of all the great styles of architecture which have existed in the world. His three volumes form a complete text-book of great value. He describes the historical buildings of each style, especially those which are landmarks in the history of art, and criticises them with ability and knowledge, and with the confidence which springs from the consciousness of their possession; pointing out faults, and suggesting how the architect should have made his design so as to avoid them.

I do not think he is always successful, but the task he sets himself is difficult. We do not require a critic when he finds fault with a poem to put it right by composing passages to replace those he objects to.

It is, perhaps, a task beyond human ability to re-design the great buildings of the different styles of architecture, for it implies greater insight and architectural invention than their architects possessed. Trying to work out in several instances the results of Mr. Fergusson's proposed improvements on historical buildings, I have found either that they altered the intention of the design, or introduced some new difficulty which it is not unreasonable to suppose the designer had appreciated and avoided. In criticism it is at least safer, and perhaps more instructive, instead of suggesting alterations, to take the buildings as they are, and try to realise their meaning and the impression they were intended to produce.

Throughout the work, Mr. Fergusson contrasts the conditions under which these old styles grew up with our modern method of producing architecture, which he insists we must abandon and return to the old, if the art is to flourish. This question is of interest to all who care for architecture, and especially to architects, as it involves their existence.

About twenty years ago, Sir Gilbert Scott published a little book on 'Secular and Domestic Architecture, Present and Future,' to show how suitable the Gothic style of architecture is for our houses and public buildings. Since then the principles he advocated have largely influenced our architecture, and have been adopted even by our ordinary builders, but the result has not been all that could be wished.

Difficulties not anticipated have shown themselves in adapting the style to modern use, and there is a feeling that the question whether Gothic is the most suitable style of architecture for modern domestic use needs reconsideration.

Since Sir Gilbert Scott's lamented death his lectures to the students of the Royal Academy, which he had previously prepared for publication, have been published in two volumes full of admirable illustrations of English mediæval ecclesiastical architecture. The lectures, which were delivered at intervals during fourteen years, are not a consecutive treatise. They give the results of the author's life-long enthusiastic study of mediæval church architecture, especially in England. His knowledge of buildings, from cathedrals to village churches, was unsurpassed, and it is used in discussing the interesting questions of the development and principles of Gothic architecture. These form a small part of the subject of this book, which would be incomplete without a reference to Sir Gilbert Scott's views.

In his pleasant book, 'Hints on Household Taste,' Mr. Eastlake expresses his conviction that the "Gothic Renaissance" is a reformation slowly but surely taking place in this country, and urges the adoption of Gothic for our houses and for our furniture, even in ordinary Classic houses. His own designs in the book for decoration and furniture are in the Gothic style, but in the illustrations from old work, he shows an incipient liking for the more picturesque forms of the Classic style, which, I have reason to believe time has not diminished.

For the history of domestic architecture in England in the Middle Ages, the work commenced by Mr. Hudson Turner, and continued by Mr. Parker, is exhaustive. I have availed myself largely of it in giving the history of house-planning, and by Mr. J. Parker's kindness I have been allowed the use of several of the woodcuts for these volumes.

There are three systems of arrangement of the matter of the book—by subjects, by centuries, and by counties, so that parts of the same subject turn up at wide intervals—it is difficult to remember where. It is really a collection of valuable notes of interesting facts of mediæval life in all its phases, and a copious index gets over the difficulty of arrangement.

On the subject of the planning of houses, 'The English Gentleman's House' by Professor Kerr, contains about all that need be known. The book is large and would bear condensation. In the chapters on planning I have endeavoured to go over the same ground. I shall have occasion sometimes to refer to it, as I cannot always agree with the statements and recommendations contained in it. Mr. Kerr devotes a small portion of it to the subject of architectural style. He suggests as the answer of the English gentleman, when his architect asks him in what style he wishes his house built? "In no style at all, except the comfortable style if there be one," and, "Take me as I am, and build my house in my own style." He gives, however, as samples for the gentleman to choose from, the same plan done up in ten different styles—Elizabethan, and revived Elizabethan, Palladian, rural Italian, Palatial Italian, and French Italian, the English Renaissance style, the Mediæval or Gothic style, the Cottage style, and the Scotch Baronial style.

The feat is a difficult one; something like translating

a piece of poetry into ten different languages. Mr. Kerr's designs fail in giving the nicer characteristics of the various styles, but this would have been too much to expect from one author. They have all a family likeness, due no doubt to their common parentage. They remind me of a fish dinner at which, cod, skate, and haddock all tasted the same, having been all cooked with the same lard.

Sir Edmund Beckett has given the public the benefit of some of his extensive experience as a builder and amateur architect, in a little book which he calls, 'A Book on Building,' in which his aim is to give practical information to those intending to build, how to avoid legal and structural mistakes. The subject of house-building occupies a considerable part of it, not treated in a systematic way, but by instances of the mistakes which, in his experience, builders and architects are liable to commit. The book does not profess to be a systematic treatise, and assumes the necessity of architects. The arrangement is somewhat heterogeneous; such diverse subjects as kitchen grates, skylights, oak graining (which the author approves of), and windows all being treated of together. It goes into minute detail on some points, but I doubt if the information and directions are sufficient to enable an employer, who had not the practical experience of the author, to keep from error an architect who did not know his business. It leaves a strong impression of the risk which any one runs in building, unless he superintends his architect not only in making the plans, but in carrying out the work.

The first chapter treats of agreements with architects and builders, giving model forms of contract, to prevent the employer surrendering his authority over the work, and controverts the doctrine which, it seems, is held by some architects that, "after the plans are settled and the work commenced, the 'client' must yield himself absolutely to his professional adviser." It is reasonable rather that as he pays his money he should have his choice. Employers may sometimes insist on things in a building which an architect could not carry out consistently with his own credit. But it is seldom that the employer's wishes, though they may not be what the architect thinks best, cannot be worked into the design.

One plan of a house is given, which Sir Edmund Beckett designed for himself. It has a central hall lighted from the ceiling and contains many of the usual modern arrangements, but the want of facility in getting over difficulties, not uncommon in the work of amateurs, may be detected in parts, and a single instance is in any case insufficient to give an adequate idea of house-planning.

The views expressed by the author are always decided, and many of them are the same as my own experience had led me to form. In judging of the architectural merit of buildings he takes, as we must all do, his own taste as the standard, with too little appreciation, perhaps, of the possibility of a different opinion in others.

The book also contains chapters on the theory of domes and on the great pyramid.

The late M. Viollet-le-Duc, the author of the admirable 'Dictionary of French Mediæval Architecture,' recently published a charming little book, which has been translated into English, under the title of 'How to Build a House.' The title is somewhat deceptive; the French title, 'L'Histoire d'une Maison,' describes the contents more accurately.

It would not help any one in building an English house. The conditions of building are those of French country parts, where the materials and modes of work differ from ours in England. The plan is eminently French; no isolation of the public rooms, but all opening one into another, the bedrooms sufficient only for the limited size of French families; the whole nursery accommodation in a house which costs £6000 being a small bedroom over the kitchen.

The book, in plan a novelette, is a pleasantly told lesson on the principles of common-sense architecture. A lad, idle at home during the German war, is set, under the guidance of his cousin, an architect, to build a house as a surprise for his sister on her return from her marriage jaunt. Knowing architecture only from the treatises on the five orders in his father's library, he had thought it a dreary subject, but his interest is awakened by being taught by practical experience how every feature of architecture springs from use and convenience. It is not shown, however, how pointed arches, and some other features introduced into the design of the house, spring from any necessity of construction or use. The book is an excellent one for creating an interest in the subject.

The same author had recently published another book also translated into English, under the title of 'The Habitations of Man in All Ages,' also in form a novelette. Two "beings" with an interest in house building visit, after the manner of the Wandering Jew, the various countries of the world, beginning with the times of the cave men, and taking leave of us at a dinner at a Paris restaurant in the days of the Second Empire. One of the companions is conservative, the other in favour of the successive improvements in the construction of dwellings which they come across in their large experience. Both are rather bores, while the descriptions and pictures of the houses they see are, like the celebrated treatise of the author's countryman on the camel, drawn largely from his own imagination. The addition of the data, if any, on which they are founded, would have made the book of more value. It does not profess to treat of modern houses.

M. Viollet-le-Duc's 'Dictionary of Gothic Architecture' is well known in this country, where the greater favour for this style has made it more popular than in France.

It is a complete encyclopædia of French mediæval architecture, containing admirable treatises on its principles and history, and on the arts connected with it; every detail being explained and illustrated with a wealth of knowledge, which seems to include every example of the style. I have been largely indebted to it for a knowledge of Gothic architecture in its history, its principles, and its forms. The illustrations are very clever, well drawn and well cut on the wood. In their style, clean and sharp and rather thin, they suggest modern Gothic, and they somehow impart an air of modern Gothic to all the buildings, even the Classic ones, which they illustrate. The pointing of the stones is always carefully shown, which gives an air of surface and reality to the drawings.

It is possibly on account of its success in the drawings that M. Viollet-le-Duc has occasionally in his restorations applied the same process to the buildings themselves, by filling in the joints of the stones with black mortar, making the interior a net-work of black lines. This is not what the old builders intended. In the desire to show the construction the architecture is lost. M. Viollet-le-Duc was more successful as an author than as an architect.

Information on all the subjects I purpose to treat can be found in the Cyclopædias and Dictionaries of Architecture, such as Gwilt's 'Encyclopædia,' or Raynaud's 'Traité d'Architecture,' Paris 1863. The former, even in its later editions, is somewhat out of date in its information and its views. The short chapter on house-planning takes as a standard houses about a century old—in its criticism of buildings it judges of their merits according to their Classic purity.

Raynaud's book is more modern and thorough, but it is

based on French practice, and is an unsafe guide for English methods of work. Such books are of more use as books of reference to the profession than for teaching beginners, for which purpose an alphabetical arrangement is unsatisfactory.

On the important subjects of draining, ventilation, heating, &c., many treatises have lately been published, advocating different systems, and inventions are constantly advertised, which it would be tedious to enumerate. I have attempted to explain the principles of systems which have proved successful in practice.

There is justification, I think, for a book which aims to collect together all that need be said on these subjects, for ordinary practical purposes. On each of them books have been written, but what is essential to be known may, I think, be given within a few chapters.

As I do not presume to teach the profession, but only the unlearned, I shall try to avoid technical terms, taking nothing for granted, but deducing everything from common first principles.

In former days, when the old styles of architecture flourished, there was no occasion for such investigation of the principles and practice of these arts, for each age had only one way of working in them; all others being either inconceivable or false. The only difference consisted in doing better or worse the same things in the same way; and the changes of style were so gradual, like those of natural growth, that though obvious when measured over centuries, they were unnoticed as they occurred.

We have cut ourselves loose from tradition. Instead of accepting and trustfully following the ways and customs handed down to us, we claim to be absolute judges of right, and make our individual preferences laws. It would need omniscience not to fail. It may be some explanation of this state of matters with regard to architecture, that since the Middle Ages closed, the same uncertainty has prevailed in other matters. In religion, philosophy, politics, even in morals, as well as in architecture, it seems as if the grounds of our faith had to be settled anew. We cannot, as of old, trust the experts, for they are not themselves agreed. The thread of tradition has been cut, and in these, as in architecture, there are now no authoritative standards or articles of faith to which appeal can be made, and judgment given.

Some may be content in building to accept at haphazard the first advice that turns up; but to form rational decisions, and to have an intelligent interest in the work, a man must understand the principles of the arts which find a place in it, especially of architecture in its double purpose of ministering to convenience and beauty. He must know its aims, and wherein its goodness consists—the causes of present failure, and the conditions necessary for success—and something of the nature and merits of different styles, if he has to decide which is best to choose.

Till the public care more for it, and know more about it, we cannot look for much improvement. Why should they spend money, and put themselves to trouble for mere display or to gratify whims of architects, which they neither appreciate nor understand? Better take the builder's house with its compo-dressings and vulgar ornament. It is sensibly planned and seems cheap at the money. But it has been built to sell. The principle of construction seems to be that it shall be always out of repair, so as to provide constant work for the building trades; and that at the end of the lease it may be worthless to the ground landlord.

The walls are thin and let in the cold and the sound even of conversation from the next house. But for the floor timbers which tie them together, a gust of wind would overturn them; the floors shake with the slightest movement; the plaster is half sand, and is kept on the walls mainly by the paper pasted on it; doors and windows do not fit; the plumber work is bad; the smell and poison of the drains come in, and the water-pipes freeze; the "compo" outside, imitating massive stonework, requires constant painting, and occasionally scales off in masses. Its existence is a constant process of going to pieces; workmen are never out of it, and the tenant finds that to keep it habitable adds a third to his rent. The architecture, however small the house may be, is a union of vulgar pretentiousness and mean shams.

The houses which men build for themselves need not have these faults of bad workmanship, but they are sometimes ill planned and often ugly. The owner may have had every desire to make his house a charming residence, and have spent money ungrudgingly, but too often his hopes are not fulfilled. It is not perfect as he intended. If he had to do it over again, he would make it different. He finds, perhaps, that he has miscalculated his requirements, and the destination of the rooms has to be changed, destroying the cherished arrangements of the plan; or in his desire for light and view, he has made his drawing-room all window—scorching in summer, cold in winter, and without wall space for the furniture; or possibly, notwithstanding every care, the damp comes through the walls, some of the chimneys smoke, or the water-pipes freeze. Frequently he finds that while it was being built his taste has changed. With better knowledge, from the attention he has given to the matter since he became practically interested in building, he now sees how much better his house might have been; that what he thought would be beautiful and grand is fantastic, or vulgar and pretentious; or, if he does not see it, it may be none the less true. From whatever cause it arises, it is generally admitted that a large proportion of modern houses are architectural failures.

The art in them, such as it is, usually stops at the outside. Here they may have some resemblance to a mediæval castle or an Italian palace, but we know that on entering we shall find neither the bold stone carving—the construction everywhere apparent—the tapestry, and stained glass of the one, nor the marbles and frescoes of the other. Whether Classic or Gothic, the lobby will be painted in imitation of marble or granite; the dining-room with a plain tint of light green, and a whitewashed ceiling; the drawing-room paper of the last fashionable pattern; the bedrooms as commonplace as those of an hotel; the carpets attempting to look an uneven surface of holes we would stumble in, and bunches of flowers we would crush in walking over; the furniture a mass of unmeaning curves; the pictures mere furniture, and no part of the architecture. In both there are the same gigantic mirrors, and great plate-glass windows with muslin curtains, occasionally, perhaps, a few old buffets or carved chairs from Wardour Street—reminiscences of the time when the same art and style governed not only the outside architecture of the house, but its internal decorations and everything it contained.

In old times it was not so. A man was certain in building to get his money's worth in art. Every old house is interesting, not because it is old, but because it is good. The style of one age may be better than another, but all are good in their way. The houses of Pompeii were all works of art; so are the few remains of Romanesque domestic architecture, at Cluny and elsewhere. Old Gothic houses of every period of the style are beautiful. Our streets are not to be compared in beauty with those of Venice, even in their decay, with all their colour gone, or in picturesqueness with those of Nuremberg (frontispiece), which was no better than many another city of its day, but has had the good fortune to have been preserved till now from modern alterations. For the charm of homeliness nothing can surpass the houses of the Tudor age, with their mullioned windows and oak-carving; and we can only feebly imitate the sumptuousness and elegance of those of the Renaissance of Francis I., or of our own Jacobean. Some may be better than others, but there are no failures such as we now constantly see produced. All are good architecture of their kind, not great mansions only, but farmhouses and cottages in village streets. And these results were accomplished, not by a specially educated profession, like the architects of the present day, directing the tradesmen by means of drawings and instructions, but by common tradesmen themselves, without any superintendence. Every village mason could build houses and churches such as for excellence and accuracy in architectural style we vainly now, with all our knowledge, attempt to imitate. Every village carpenter could make furniture more beautiful and in truer taste than the best town-made nowadays—solid in construction, graceful in line, and rich in carving.

As for house-painting, we have ceased, justly enough, perhaps, to consider it an art. We do not look on those painters as artists who work on the walls of our rooms. Every London builder thinks himself competent to design and execute decoration. Some call themselves plumbers and decorators, and one large London upholstering firm advertises that it includes decoration in its house agency department. Cheesemonger and decorator would be about as congruous. We prefer to give artistic work to "practical men," as they are called, that is, to those who know nothing about the subject.

In old time people thought great artists were the proper men to do the work—Michael Angelo and Raphael were proud to be wall-decorators. If our houses are to be works of art, they must possess not only outside beauty, architectural proportions, and good colour, the artistic expression of their purpose and of modern life, not of uses and habits long extinct, but they must have the same qualities, the same art, inside, in all their decorations and furnishing. We copy only one part, and that the least important in the general effect of former systems of architecture—the stone mouldings and ornaments which time happens to have left to us—omitting the decoration, and making the furniture discordant, because in the buildings we copy from the one happens to have perished and the other to be removed.

To be really a high work of art, a house must not only be beautiful outside, and all its surroundings in harmony, but inside there must be not only no shams and meannesses, but good art throughout; the walls and ceilings rich in colour and in art expression; paintings as good as art can make them, their decoration—a part of them—not hung on them by strings; the sculpture only the decoration of the architecture, the crowning points of its ornament or the enrichment of its surface, and in thus aiding it, acquiring an interest it never has when thinking only of itself; the furniture good in construction, graceful in its lines, and in harmony with the architecture; all the resources of art and manufacture, carpets, rich hangings, stained glass, gilding, carving, painting, good as art, and ministering to one harmonious effect.

The thing has been. The houses of Pompeii were second-rate performances in their age, but for wealth of art throughout them, and unity of design down to the smallest details, our richest mansions cannot compare with them.

A few battered buildings pulled about and altered, their furniture removed long since, when their old owners left them, a scrap of colour here and there on the walls, telling that they once glowed with it, are all that remains to us of the houses of the Middle Ages.

But in their churches we can still trace the evidence of

what architecture then meant. Their windows here and there, as at York, or Bourges, or Chartres, still show us a splendour of colour in their stained glass which, but for them, we should never have dreamt of; the marble pillars remain; in places the floor, after the treading of forty generations, still glows with rich patterns of coloured tiles, and, under accumulated coats of whitewash, every now and then we discover traces of the painting which once covered their walls, was concentrated in brightness on the tombs and altars, and culminated on the ceiling; great crowns suspended from the roofs, studded with jewels and sparkling with lights; vestments, hangings, and furniture, admirable in colour and design, all uniting in producing an effect of rich, glowing splendour, of which these churches now are but the grey, white skeletons. The tiled floors and stained glass remain, for the colour in them was in imperishable material; but they are only isolated scraps of a system of decoration which pervaded the whole building. Floors and windows are the last parts of a room we should think of colouring. The object in using encaustic tiles and stained glass was merely to carry out over windows and floors the colouring of the other parts of the building; and we think we are reviving mediæval art when we copy these only, and leave the walls and ceiling cold stone, or raw, grey plaster.

It is of some interest to investigate the reasons why art in our houses is so hopeless and helpless, so often mere failure, and its greatest successes only bad imitations of the art which nations and periods inferior to us in wealth and resources produced constantly and naturally, and without apparent effort.

It may be that the present degraded state of house-building is inevitable; that we must submit to see the country covered with miles of dismal, uninteresting streets, and spotted over with villas which violate good taste and destroy its beauty, and be content with houses which make our lives in them a succession of annoyances; but if a remedy is to be found, the first step must be to know the causes which have produced our failure.

There are indications of a prevalent desire for a better state of things; and a knowledge of the objects to be aimed at, and the results attainable, in convenience and beauty, in a house and its belongings, may prevent a waste of effort in wrong directions, along paths by which advancement is impossible—may give higher and truer aims to those who are building for themselves, and, in time, might even improve the houses built on speculation by diffusing better taste, and creating a preference for houses sounder in construction and less vulgar in style.

It is not because we are too poor that our buildings now cannot attempt to rival, in completeness and splendour of art, those of Greece or Rome, or of the Middle Ages. Nor is it even from our unwillingness to spend money. I suppose no age ever supported a greater number of artists, not in comfort merely, but in wealth. I certainly do not grudge it them, for none know better how to spend it. Besides those artists whom we know, who furnish the walls of the principal exhibitions, there is an innumerable company whose names we never hear, who turn out moonlights, or mills, or mountain scenery with the regularity of manufacture, and somehow find a continuous sale. There are miles on miles of new pictures exhibited each year, which must get sold somehow, or the supply would cease. Sculpture, perhaps, is more a drug in the market; though the number of British Philistines and others who each year have their features immortalised in imperishable marble is considerable—much greater than those we see ranged close in rows like gallipots on shelves in exhibitions. And of expenditure on architecture there is certainly no stint. Old churches are pulled down for the mere pleasure of building new ones (more's the pity); new town halls, law courts, country houses, town mansions, clubs, churches, colleges, are rising everywhere—in many cases the building motive being the desire of increased magnificence, and the pleasure of building, rather than the necessity; and to this expenditure I object, of course, still less than to that on easel pictures. But are the results satisfactory? are the churches as good as old ones? Do the mansions in town or country approach in beauty, in completeness of art, those of the times of the Tudors or Stuarts? Does the result in the club-houses justify the money spent on them? It is not sufficient answer to point to one or two perfect houses or churches among the thousands built. In the old times there were none bad. They may not show originality, or genius, or cleverness; but from palace to cottage they are natural and harmonious throughout, and yet they were no doubt built by common builders, for architects were not thought of, except for the most important works.

There was a sense of art in the people, which did not need grand buildings or great expenditure for its manifestation, but showed itself in the cheapest and commonest structures. Here is a mere shed for holding ladders at a small German village (fig. 1, next page), which shows the old instinct, which we seem to have lost, to make the commonest things interesting and pleasing.

Nowadays, except in rare and special instances, our buildings are bad and inartistic. And these special buildings are all imitations, more or less perfect, of old work.

It is of little use asking who is to blame. The most obvious answer is, that it is the architects themselves, and the most obvious remedy, to hang a few of them; but the answer, though simple, is only half true, and the remedy, though severe, would be inadequate. The evil is not so much ignorance of architecture on the part either of its professors or the public, for every one with any pretensions to taste knows something about it, has read Ruskin, and considers himself (or herself) a judge; and never in the world's history were there so many styles understood and practised, more or less correctly. It may be that we know too much about architectural styles—that the variety of our knowledge confuses us, and prevents us doing what would be natural—that our restlessness prevents us sticking to any one of them till we have perfected it, and made it our own. Or our wealth, instead of helping us, may be the

Fig. 1.   SHED FOR LADDERS AT HOCHBERG, NEAR WÜRZBURG.

cause of our failure. We may be so devoted to its acquisition that we have no time left to learn how to spend it; for money alone can no more give us art than it can give us learning. Or we may not really care for art—paying for it, not that we like it, but because we think our position in society requires a certain amount of display, which bad art will satisfy as well as good. Or the character of our buildings, as in all architectural styles, may merely express the character of the people who produce them; the display of magnificence in coarse form and cheap material be the natural outcome of our vulgarity; the attempts to make things look, not what they are, but like something else which is thought grander—as a row of little houses clubbing together with the help of stucco ornaments so as to look like a palace, or a dwelling-house with a quarter of an acre of ground from which the owner goes up to business every morning, and where the newspaper is delivered before breakfast, frowning with battlements, and making believe as if it held the country round in serfdom—may be the reflex of our pretentiousness and falsity, and signs that in our hearts we are ashamed of ourselves.

No doubt all this is partly true, but not, I believe, to the extent which the universality almost of such qualities in the architecture would indicate; for I think it can be shown that the conditions under which architecture works at present in this country give a facility and amount of expresssion to such qualities altogether disproportionate to their prevalence among the people.

The subject has really a greater than mere dilettante interest. Though we may not be conscious of it, it is no slight evil that the houses in which the greatest portion of the people live are built independently of art at all, or in defiance of it. Within the last twenty or thirty years whole towns have come into existence, which exhibit what seems a new characteristic in the human race—namely, utter disregard to the beauty of their dwellings. Never, so far as I know, have there been collections of human habitations so dismal, so completely without one artistic quality, or consequently so inhuman, as the miles on miles of uniform streets in our new manufacturing towns. The hut of the savage is at least picturesque; for love for the beautiful—a desire to ornament and turn into objects of art the things they use—has hitherto been a characteristic of all men, even the most degraded.

If a town is old, however poor, it is sure to have some beauty or interest; if new, we look for neither, but get out of it as soon as we can.

Those who live among this ugliness possibly feel it no hardship. If so, it only means that it has entered their souls, and that they are losing one of the characteristics of humanity; and it is a question, whether the intense restlessness of modern life is not aggravated by the places we live in, even where art is attempted, being so devoid of any beauty which can give lasting satisfaction.

CHAPTER II.

WHAT CONSTITUTES GOOD ARCHITECTURE?

THIS question has of late years, in this country, been obscured and rendered almost impossible of answer by the rivalry of competing styles. One party would almost say that good Architecture is Gothic architecture, the other that it is Classic. But some specimens so bad in both styles have been perpetrated, that even their own friends cannot acknowledge them.

Not only may architecture be good or bad in any style, but it is essentially the same qualities that render it so in every style.

Architecture is simply the useful art of building elevated to a fine art, following the tendency which all human beings have to make articles of use beautiful as well. Out of the same instinct, in all ages, the necessity of clothing has developed the art of dress. On the oldest pottery there is ornament, and carvings on bone utensils have been found coeval with the elk and the reindeer in France. No amount of decoration was thought too great in any tribe for their weapons, axes, clubs, and swords: what was always beside them they wished to be beautiful; and when they became settled, they ornamented their houses from the same motive. But they also built houses for their gods; and Architecture, with religion as a motive-power, has had a higher and more poetic development than it could have had in merely ministering to human wants.

As the art to begin with is a useful one, that a building should be good architecturally, the first condition is that it should serve its purpose—houses must be suited to the wants and habits of their inhabitants; castles must be strong; churches and temples adapted to the worship or the rites celebrated in them.

Again, as it is a structural art, consisting in putting materials together for a certain purpose, the second essential of good architecture is good construction—disposing the materials in the best form for strength and stability.

Thus far we have merely good building; to become architecture, which is a fine art, the element of beauty or of artistic expression must be added. From the first dawn of civilisation all building was architectural. It has been reserved for our age to find out that beauty in our dwellings is not worth striving for, that material wants are all that need be attended to.

Various means have been used for arranging and treating buildings so as to add to them the element of art, and so make them architectural. Some nations covered them with ornament wherever they could put it. But, though this practice is not without advocates and examples in our day, it is unthinking and savage art.

An illustration in Mr. Owen Jones's 'Grammar of Ornament,' of the tattooed face of a New Zealander, shows how hideous may be the results, even of ornament in itself beautiful, when used in the wrong place; and the same effect would be produced in architecture, though not perhaps so strikingly, if a Doric column were covered with ornament instead of the flutings which mark its purpose.

Architecture, to attain its highest development, must have something more than mere ornament — the intellectual qualities of proportion and expression. This is true of all arts: music is proportion in sounds; painting is proportion in colour and forms; and architecture, proportion of masses, of solids and voids. But to constitute true art there must be something more, the expression of human feeling or character.

That music and painting can express these, we know; but that with stones and bricks, and wood and plaster, and while pursuing the vulgar human need of shelter, an architect should not only express human feelings and character—such as power or tenderness, refinement or coarseness, grandeur or meanness—but his own character, seems strange,—stranger rather that he cannot help doing it. But to do this a power of architectural expression must be presupposed, just as a man must have the faculty of musical expression, to be a composer. So that to get good architecture, what is wanted is a good architect, one who has the power to construct and arrange the masses and forms of a building, and by means of them to express nobleness or beauty.

There are various ways of disposing building materials so as to produce artistic results. Mere height has been an object of architectural effort since the builders at Babel commenced their tower to reach to heaven, while more imposing even is the effect of length in endless ranges of columns and arcades.

Mere mass of perpendicular windowless wall, even where there has been no conscious aim at architectural effect, is a most powerful one. It is mainly from this cause that old Scotch castles are so grand, while their modern imitations, riddled with windows, are so weak and feeble.

Fig. 2.   TILQUHILLIE CASTLE, ABERDEENSHIRE.

But perhaps the more powerful means of producing grandeur is by shadow—from great projecting cornices, or under deep porticoes, or in the dark recesses of great arches.

To the most impressive architecture, mystery is essential—the feeling that there is something more than we see. Glory half hid is double in effect. The half, as the Greeks knew, is often greater than the whole. The plays of 'Medea' and 'Macbeth' prove that this is equally true in dramatic art.

TRUTH is essential in good architecture, as it is in all art, though in architecture, as in other spheres, it may be impossible satisfactorily to answer the old question, "What is Truth?" "Truth" generally means the correspondence of a representation with the facts; and architecture, to be true, must be the expression of building necessities. Convenience must not be sacrificed to appearance; materials must show themselves to be what they really are, and not something different; the construction which appears must be that which actually supports the building. But, in architecture, as in other arts, the representation must be artistic; not a dull, unarranged, unmodified statement of facts as they happen to turn up. It is tiresome to tell everything, as an old woman tells her story, wearisomely relating whether a thing happened on a Wednesday or a Friday, giving genealogies and dates of marriage of all the persons mentioned, though these have no bearing on the point. The object in a work of art is to convey an impression. To this all the parts must tend, and what is irrelevant must be suppressed or modified. A photograph is true (except that the relation of light and shadow is destroyed by green or red and yellow all being turned to black), but even if it represented Nature's colour, or her relations of light and shade, it would not be a work of art: it is not the impression on the mind of an artist expressed by him in such a way as to impress others; it tells a great many things which no one is interested to know. So in architecture there is no need for painfully making every constructive expedient apparent, and bringing into prominence those meaner accessories of a dwelling-house, which, however essential, one does not care to refer to, or force on the attention. Language shows us that art is not a merely bare and true representation of facts, in the meanings it gives to "artless" as truthfully simple, and to "artful" as cunningly false. The border-line at which the production of artistic effect becomes falsehood must always be difficult to define. There may be ugly necessities of building construction, which it is right to conceal under beautiful forms or fine colour, as Nature conceals our bones and muscles under the rounded forms and marvellous flesh-colour of our bodies. As in these, so in architecture, the fundamental construction, though it need not be offensively obtruded, should be truly indicated; and the greater the amount of truth in materials and construction that can be expressed without losing sight of the artistic idea at which the architecture aims, the nobler is the architecture. That of the Romans is not satisfactory. They ornamented buildings, in which the main construction was arched, with pillars and lintels borrowed from Greek architecture; and although great magnificence resulted, it was never satisfactory, because it was at bottom untrue. Gothic architecture, on the other hand, was truth itself. Happily for it, no other better architecture was known which they might have been tempted to copy for the sake of its beauty, and whatever the materials or construction employed, they were allowed to tell their own tale.

Fig. 3.   ROCK-HEWN ARCHITECTURE, PETRA.

In the course of their growth many of the older architectures imitated forms in stone, which had been developed in older wooden construction, or hewed out an architecture in solid rock, which had grown in constructions of built stone (fig. 3).

Such things are interesting to trace, as illustrating the continuous but inconceivably slow progress of human ideas, but no architecture can be perfect which retains them. Nowadays, with the beauties of all known architectures available for imitation, which can seldom be natural or truthful modes of expression for us, the temptations to this form of falsity are almost irresistible.

Perhaps no age has ever indulged more than our own in the shabbier and more vulgar form of untruthfulness, of attempting to make cheap, mean materials look as if they were rare and valuable,—painting and sanding deal boards so that they may pass for solid stone, or graining them to look like oak or rare marble; or copying in stucco the architecture of Italian palaces, and plastering it on common houses. Some people seem to think that tricks and deceptions are legitimate means of producing artistic effects, such as making a range of small houses look as if it were one palace, or filling in the pillared recess at the end of a room with a single mirror without a frame, in the hope of making the room look twice as large. The deception is soon found out and becomes ridiculous. One house gets painted which includes half of some architectural ornament shared with the next, while the rest remain dingy; or some stranger breaks his nose on the mirror by attempting to walk into the supposed extension of the room. The people who like these little tricks are often honourable and truthful. Their morality does not lie in the sphere of art. One of the honestest men I know was charmed at my mistaking a wooden oriel window in his house which had been skilfully sanded over for a stone one. His honesty lay in a different sphere. Just as, some artists who have a zeal for their art as earnest as ever burnt for religion—who pursue it for the love of it, independent altogether of profit—are often careless about getting into debt, and regard money obligations as altogether secondary to doing their work honestly and well.

In the sphere of art, truth and honesty are as essential to excellence as to morality; and our only hope of freshness and originality in our architecture must lie in allowing it to express our actual necessities, with perfect naturalness and truth.

BEAUTY, though there may be good and noble architecture without it, is essential to the highest forms of the art. It would be too great a digression in a book on domestic architecture to attempt to discuss the question why certain lines are more beautiful than others. One theory is, that beauty in objects depends on their power of suggesting pleasing associations. And it is true that these may so warp our judgment as to give such objects a beauty in our eyes which they do not in themselves possess. But it will not account for new objects, with which we have no such associations, appearing beautiful.

The theory is rather that objects are beautiful because they suggest pleasing associations from some sort of resemblance to them—that a colour, for instance, is beautiful because it recalls tenderness or purity, or a line because it suggests strength or grace.

Association of this kind affects our perception of beauty more subtly and powerfully than accidental contiguity, sometimes by making us think things beautiful, but still oftener by suggesting something unpleasing or ludicrous, and so preventing us seeing beauty where it exists. Beauty is something distinct from pleasing associations, and we seem to have as good evidence of its independent existence as of those pleasing associations which are supposed to account for it, namely, our perception of it. Its essence may perhaps lie in the fact, that as we are a part of the harmonious system of nature, those objects are beautiful to us which are in harmony with our material and spiritual being. This would account for the variety of opinions as to beauty held by different nations, and for the basis of essential agreement among them all, which is shown by the fact that, by entering into the feelings of their producers, we may come to understand and admire various and apparently opposite productions in art.[1] It is not a valid objection that some men cannot see beauty in things undoubtedly beautiful. That is a defect of their nature, like the want of a musical ear. The poet and painter, by their sympathy with it, perceive beauty in nature which others do not, and become its interpreters to these by means of human sympathy.

No theory of beauty, however, can assist us in deciding what things are or are not beautiful. For this we must have "taste," an organisation which is affected by beauty or ugliness, as the palate is by sweetness or bitterness.

To produce beautiful things something more is needed —that creative faculty to which new combinations, new ideas of grandeur and beauty come unsought, which in old times was believed to be the inspiration of the Deity.

To the greatest architecture the idea of SIZE is essential. Its glory is, that it creates its forms on the scale of Nature's grandeur. To draw a line of three or four hundred feet against the sky, exquisitely modelled along its whole length, is an achievement which raises our opinion of humanity. Cities are always proud of their spires. St. Paul's, or one of the great French cathedrals, makes the same impression on the mind as a great mountain.

A characteristic of the best architecture, and one which art of every kind must have in some form or other, is DELICACY—not the mere avoidance of all coarseness and vulgarity, but the presence of some kind of refinement—in form, in colour, or in modulation of shadow. It is for this

[1] Mr. Darwin is of opinion that the taste of animals in regard to beauty is substantially the same as in mankind.

reason that those who have a little knowledge of an art are such bad judges of it. Coarse, obvious effects strike them: they do not see the highest, which are always hidden, like the violet, and have to be sought.

The main element, however, of architectal excellence is PROPORTION. It is difficult to say wherein it consists—as difficult as to say what beauty is, of which, indeed, it is one of the elements. No rule can be laid down for it, for it is of many kinds—tall or low, sturdy or delicate. People have sometimes amused themselves calculating proportions by mathematics, which undoubtedly has the power of expressing them, but only after the proportion has been invented, just as mathematics can express musical harmonies. But it would be as possible to design architecture by mathematics as to compose tunes. A musical ear in the one case, an eye for proportion in the other, are the only tests of right. The faculty of expressing ideas by notes harmoniously arranged, of throwing words into harmonious verse, or grouping the parts of a building in order and proportion, is the only means of production in music or poetry or architecture.

The chief sphere in which proportion finds expression in architecture is in the relation of solids to voids—of the supported parts to their supports. It does not look at the problem involved merely from a constructive or engineering point of view, asking, Will the building stand? but, Does it stand with ease and grace? The building must not only be secure, it must look secure. To attain this result, a strength beyond mere constructive exigencies is often required. A massive stone building should not stand on a glass case, even when there are thin iron pillars behind the glass, concealed by haberdashery, quite sufficient to support it. The strength should be visibly ample. But neither ought the supports to be too strong for their work: a Doric column carrying only a statue, instead of

Fig. 4. HOUSES AT MÜNSTER, SHOWING VERTICAL AND HORIZONTAL DIVISION OF THEIR SURFACES.

its mass of entablature, is a disproportionate waste of energy.

But although resistance to gravitation is the chief motive of proportion in architecture, it should equally govern every space and form of a building—the size and shapes of the windows, and of the window-panes; the amount of light and shadow; the ornaments and enrichments, not only in their quantity, but in the mutual relations of their parts. A common means of attaining it is by lines or mouldings dividing the surface of a building into spaces, and giving emphasis where it is wanted.

Such lines when drawn horizontally are called *string courses*. They originally were flat beds of solid stone going through the whole thickness of a wall composed of rough irregular materials, so as to strengthen the wall at intervals, usually at each floor, a level bed for the floor to rest on. The projecting edge was naturally ornamented with moulding or carving, and later on became a pure ornament of the architecture, seldom now going farther into the wall than the few inches necessary to fix it in its place, and I think it is legitimately used to give to the design the effect of horizontal division, though it does not necessarily indicate the precise position of the floors. Similar effects of proportion may be obtained by piers or pilasters dividing the building perpendicularly.

Two houses at Münster (fig. 4) show this mode of producing architectural effect. In the farther house, to the left of the picture, which is late Gothic in style, the idea of height is more dwelt on; the upright lines, which take the form of pinnacles, are kept as a fringe on the outside of the gable; in the other it is rather the horizontal lines that are enforced. Instead of the front running up into the gable, it is stopped by a strong cornice. The upright lines take the form of Classic pilasters.

Mr. Fergusson disapproves of the use of pilasters, and, if

he were Chancellor of the Exchequer, would put a prohibitory tax on them. But in every style of architecture effects of proportion have been obtained by enforcing the perpendicular or horizontal lines. The Greeks enforced the upright lines by fluting the columns. These bear the mass of entablature—the frieze and cornice, the horizontal effect of which is heightened by the deep projection of the cornice, while the sense of weight in the mass is aided by

Fig. 5.   Fig. 6.

the triglyphs of the frieze, which, even if they represent the beam-ends of old wood construction, are now purely ornamental features (see fig. 20, p. 56).

In our ordinary town houses, where we have only a front to deal with in which the position of the windows is fixed by necessity, such expedients are almost our only means of obtaining architectural effect. Figs. 5 to 8 illustrate some modes of doing this common in Classic architecture. Fig. 5 is the most naked form of building. In fig. 6 an appearance

WHAT CONSTITUTES GOOD ARCHITECTURE? 39

of strength is given to the angles by building them of larger stones. The angles of the windows are also protected and enriched by a framework round them, and dignity and shadow is given by ornamenting the cornice and increasing its size and projection. But if we repeat this process through the five or six stories of our London houses it becomes monotonous.

Gothic delighted in height, but the tendency of Classic architecture was to dwell on the horizontal line, and various

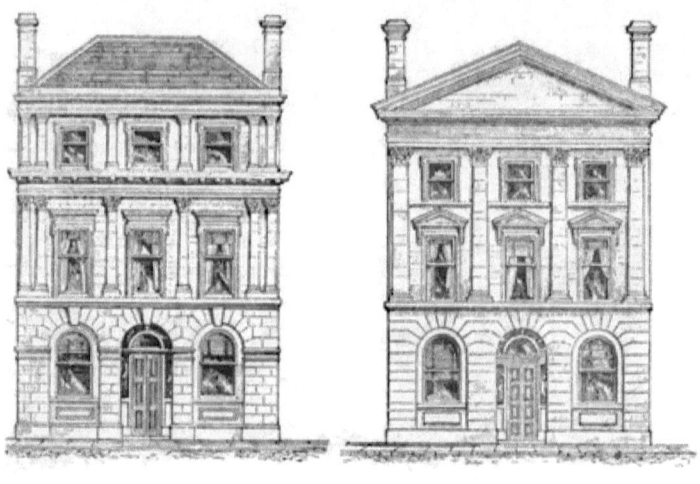

Fig. 7.   Fig. 8.

expedients were resorted to to reduce the apparent height of the building. One was to bring down the strong line of the cornice, as in fig. 7, to the top of the main floor of the building, as if marking its importance and giving it dignity, and treating the rooms above as if they were only bedrooms, as '*an attic*,' as it is called. In the old Italian palaces, where the great entertaining rooms were at the top of the house, it was fitting that the great cornice should be immediately over them.

Fig. 8 shows the common Classic mode of producing architectural effect. The only architecture being in the orders derived from temples, the house is treated as a temple. The windows are accidents or necessary evils in the design. The ground floor is merely a base for a correct superstructure of columns and entablature. That it comprises two stories of the house is a regrettable accident which we must not dwell on. Yet noble effects have been gained by these means, and dignity and grace given to buildings otherwise dull.

Fig. 9. HOUSE OPPOSITE THE CATHEDRAL AT AUGSBURG.

SYMMETRY, which may be considered a species of proportion, is almost essential to the noblest buildings—at least when it is absent, whatever the other merits of the building, the highest dignity is unattainable. In every style, Greek, Gothic, and Renaissance, symmetry controlled the designs of temples and churches.

In dwelling-houses, though often ruling the design as in this instance (fig. 9), it frequently gave way to the necessities of domestic convenience. It means that the parts on either side should be balanced and similar, not necessarily identical, like the two spires at the end of a modern church, both executed from the same drawing; but similar, like those of an old cathedral, each retaining its own individuality. Of late years symmetry has not been much in favour. In the last century it was a universally acknowledged principle. That the door should not be in the centre was inconceivable. If the kitchens formed one wing the stables had exactly to match them in the other. The summer-house at one side of the garden had its duplicate on the other, even if it was half a mile off. Perhaps the Scotch gardener carried the principle too far, who shut up his son in one summer-house to balance a boy whom he had locked up in the other for stealing apples. Nowadays, we carry the opposite principle to an extreme. We put a spire at the side of a church rather than in the centre; and where a door comes naturally in the middle of the house, we run up a gable on one side only to destroy the symmetry, under the delusion that we are carrying out Gothic principles.

Fig. 10. OLD HOUSE IN GLASGOW HIGH STREET.

It appears from this catalogue of the artistic effects which architecture is capable of producing, that they are widely various in kind, and that many of them are incompatible with others. Now, for the perfection of any work of art, HARMONY is essential. All its various parts should suit one another. Nothing should be out of keeping. Ladies appreciate this principle in dress; it would be absurd to wear a brilliant bonnet with a rough stuff gown. It is so much the essence of music that the word is used as a name for it, and it is the chief essential in good colouring. And so in architecture it forbids discord; there must be no jarring, no part too rich or refined, or out of keeping with the rest. To strive after irregularity for its own sake is affectation, but when it arises naturally from the conditions of building, as in the little Scotch house (fig. 10, p. 41), it may be very pleasing. It is not the result of hap-hazard, but comes through a sense of art and grace in the builders, of which they may have been quite unconscious.

In the design of this house at Nuremberg, (fig. 11) the architectural effect is obtained without any ornament, solely by means of proportion, exercised in a skilful disposition of the windows and roof. By simply lowering the wall in the centre, we get the effect of a mass of roof flanked by two towers. If the wall were built up between these towers to the level of their cornices, as a London builder would have done, the design would be commonplace. It is irregular, but there is method in the irregularity. The necessities of internal arrangement make the towers different in size, but the centre of each is carried down and a feeling

Fig. 11. HOUSE NEAR THE TOWN HALL, NUREMBERG.

of height given by the line of windows one above another. But for this, the horizontal line would have predominated, and there would have been no effect of towers in the design.

Harmony is a universal law of Nature. In a few years she tones down the harshness of a new building, the rawness of rough scaur or broken rock with moss and lichens, into harmony and keeping with everything about it; and in architecture, even when the forms are bad and the style feeble, mere harmony will sometimes produce the effect of beauty.

We dispense with it in our modern architecture to a wonderful extent; more than any time or nation hitherto has done. We think nothing of putting rich stained glass in a bare, white plastered interior, like a jewel in a swine's snout, or spotting the dingiest of cement house-fronts with flower-boxes made of the gaudiest coloured tiles, and making abortive attempts at art by furnishing our houses of commonplace builders' Classic with fiercely Gothic furniture.

On the other hand, so intent are we sometimes to obtain harmony, that we compel all the houses in a street to be made from the same design so that a man cannot tell his own except from the number on the door. In our restorations of old buildings it has been carried so far that immense quantities of valuable art have been removed from our churches and destroyed as not of the same date as the rest of the building, in forgetfulness of the fact that these are historical monuments—that their interest lies in each generation having left its mark on them—that the impression of wealth and magnificence, and contrast also, produced by the rich Jacobean carvings so ruthlessly removed, are valuable effects in architecture, as well as harmony. Harmony consists rather in identity of feeling than of form or style. The quaint old Classic screens and tombs, the grace of Inigo Jones, and the elaborate richness of Grinling Gibbons, are in better keeping with the old buildings than the modern Gothic which, alas, has so often supplanted them!

Still harmony must be our rule, as it is Nature's—a rule not to be broken without cause—to express some higher meaning, or to preserve some work our fathers have left us.

CONTRAST is also a means of obtaining artistic effect, more telling than harmony, though not capable of producing such perfect results. An exquisitely carved and moulded window in a great field of plain wall looks more delicate itself, and makes the wall look grander. In Perpendicular Gothic, on the other hand, the tracery of the windows is carried over the walls, making the whole surface harmonious. This system was thoroughly carried out by Barry in the Houses of Parliament. But if the building has gained thereby in harmony and richness, it has lost in power.

Who shall decide where and how far either principle shall be carried out? what rules can we lay down? Only the same as for composing poetry or music—the insight and invention of the musician and the poet—of one who has the power of composition, of so combining words or notes or colours as to express human feelings or ideas; or, in architecture, of one who can so use his materials as to produce a building possessing any of the artistic merits we have enumerated.

In painting and architecture, the laws of composition are essentially the same: the same kind of considerations regulate the lines and masses of a picture and of a building. Its chief aim must be to produce unity, so that, however various the ideas it is concerned with, they shall unite in producing one idea, one work of art.

ORNAMENT.—Architecture can produce artistic effects of this kind without the aid of sculpture or painting or ornament of any kind, by the mere arrangement of masses of building. Not even such an amount of ornament as a cable moulding is needed, without which Mr. Ruskin thinks a mere utilitarian building, like a fortress, cannot be considered architecture. There is no ornament, not even the simplest chamfer, on these towers from the walls of Nuremberg (fig. 12); yet they are examples not of building only, but of architecture, and not unworthy of the designer, Albert Dürer. Are not grandeur and impressiveness artistic qualities? and when old fortresses possess these by their

Fig. 12.   TOWERS ON THE WALLS AT NUREMBERG.

mass and strength, and the skill with which they are fitted to the rocks they crown and give dignity to, although they may be the most utilitarian of buildings, without a single ornament or moulding, they may possess the noblest qualities of architecture. The parapets in old castles projected on corbels, as in Borthwick Castle (fig. 13, p. 46), are not designed for ornament, but for the practical purpose of dropping down stones on assailants.

But though architecture is possible without ornament, it cannot without it reach its most perfect manifestations. In the great ages of art, sculpture and painting had almost no existence except as its decorations. The Elgin Marbles are the decoration of a frieze: the Theseus, a piece of architectural sculpture. In the Middle Ages sculpture was almost unknown, except as adorning doorways and other parts of

Fig. 13. BORTHWICK CASTLE.

buildings; while the paintings of that time, and even of the great ages of Venetian and Roman art, were generally decorations of the walls or altars, and essential parts of the buildings.

It may be questioned whether painting and sculpture

have gained by their present independence. Architecture certainly has lost one of the most powerful means of giving it interest.

Ornament, when employed in architecture merely for its own sake, and because it is pretty, is weakness. It is valuable only when it assists the meaning of the design, enforcing certain lines or points and giving it richness or softness. For this purpose such an ornament as a Greek fret (figs. 14, 15) or a chevron (fig. 16), or lines and dots (fig. 17), may be not less suitable than the direct imitation of natural objects, such as leaves or animals, probably more so; for, as a building is necessarily largely composed of straight lines, straight-line ornament may harmonise with it better than the free and irregular curves of nature.

Fig. 14. Fret.

Fig. 15. Fret.

As, in weaving, even a pattern on a table-cloth so simple as squares like a backgammon board may be perfectly satisfactory and ornamental because it is suitable to the material, and arises naturally from the processes of weaving. To follow the spirit of Nature, not to imitate her forms, should be the aim of art.

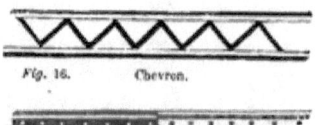

Fig. 16. Chevron.

Fig. 17.

I do not know whether even Mr. Ruskin himself now holds the theory, stated in 'Seven Lamps of Architecture,' "that all beautiful lines are adaptations of those which are commonest in the external creation"—that in the Doric temple the cornice and triglyphs are not beautiful "because unimitative"—that the fluting of the column derives what low beauty it possesses from its feeble resemblance to "canaliculated organic structures." "The Romanesque arch," he continues, "is beautiful as an abstract line.

Its type is always before us in that of the apparent vault of heaven, and the horizon of the earth. The cylindrical pillar is always beautiful, for God has so moulded the stem of every tree that is pleasant to the eye. The pointed arch is beautiful; it is the termination of every leaf that shakes in summer wind, and its most fortunate associations are directly borrowed from the trefoiled grass of the fields, or from the stars of its flowers. Farther than this man's invention could not reach without frank imitation. His next step was to gather the flowers themselves, and wreath them in his capitals." And again, " I believe that we may reason from Frequency to Beauty, and *vice versâ*; that knowing a thing to be frequent (*visibly* frequent), we may assume it to be beautiful, and assume that which is most frequent to be most beautiful "—" that forms which are not taken from natural objects must be ugly."

On this ground Mr. Ruskin "convicts" the Greek fret of "ugliness," because it has no precedent for its arrangement but the forms of crystals of bismuth, an artificial condition of a rare metal. The theory is a total misconception of the whole meaning and use of ornament in architecture. It is a certain sign of weakness and decay when architectural ornament is a profuse imitation of natural forms. The beauty of the Doric column does not consist in its resemblance to some forms of reeds—some Egyptian ones are much like reeds, but are coarse and clumsy in comparison—but on its form being so perfectly contrived for supporting the weight, and on its flutings and the line of its capital so delicately marking this purpose; just as the triglyphs have a meaning (whatever their origin), and therefore beauty, because they mark the downward pressure of this weight, and the cornice as giving protection and shadow. The beauty of Greek Doric does not consist in ornament, which would ruin it, but in its perfect proportion and delicacy of line. The Corinthian order, which is a close imitation of natural forms, is vulgar in comparison, and it was consequently a favourite with the more inartistic Romans. Columns half the thickness would be liker reeds; triglyphs carved with natural leaves would not improve the temple. Without its sculpture, the Parthenon is still beautiful. No doubt it has lost the last finishing touch, but the loss is far less than that of its painting and colour. Alter the relations of the weight of entablature to the supporting columns, or of the masses of light and shadow, and its beauty would be gone at once, and all its sculpture and painting would not restore it.

That Mr. Ruskin's theory convicts the Greek fret of ugliness is of itself sufficient to prove it false. If the old test, "quod semper, ubique, et ab omnibus," is any test of truth, the Greek fret can show a higher antiquity and a wider catholicity than any opinion or religion. In Asia, whence the Greeks probably got it, in India, in China, in Japan, it is a favourite ornament. It occurs frequently on the "sculptured stones of Scotland," and in caves once tenanted; it is found in the New World on the pottery of Indian tribes in South America. Even Mr. Ruskin himself, though calling it a "horrible design," admits that it may be employed with advantage as an ornament on coins "when it is small," as it must be when so used, though it need not be small in proportion to the size of the coin.

Accepting the fact that mankind regards it as an ornament, let us ask what there is in its form to make it so. May it not be because it is a succession of spirals *architecturalised*—reduced to straight lines, and brought into harmony with the lines which, from its essential nature, are dominant in architecture; just as the chevron, or the simplest form of Greek fret, would be a wave architecturalised? Ornament composed of straight lines was no doubt first adopted in barbarous times because it was easily executed, but it continued to be used in the most refined Greek buildings because it was felt to harmonise with the architecture. The fret is not a Gothic ornament, though something very like it is occasionally found among the scarce examples left of painted decorations in that style, which in those parts of the building not governed by curved lines of construction, abounded in ornament equally composed of straight lines, and equally unlike anything in nature; such as, for example, the lines of "stoning" found on old Gothic buildings (fig. 18).

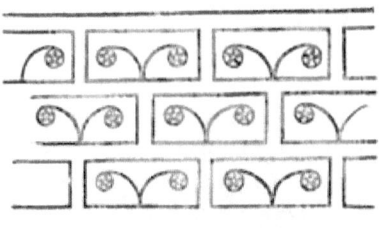

Fig. 18. DECORATIONS ON CHAPTER HOUSE, BURNHAM ABBEY.

The lines of architecture and its ornament must of course be natural—that is, they must be according to *its* nature and constitution; for the imitation of animal or vegetable forms may, for it, be unnatural. It has an organism of its own—a life which, like all life, evidences itself in resistance to gravitation, a character which is noble and beautiful when it fulfils the purposes of its being, and only that ornament is valuable which aids in expressing this. "The leaves which shake in the summer wind" are beautiful in their own place and way, but their forms may be utterly unnatural in architecture, and therefore ugly. Gothic arches are beautiful, not because they are like leaf points—an accurate imitation of leaf points might make very ugly arches—but because they are a true, excellent, and vigorous mode of construction.

Mr. Ruskin's theory of architectural ornament is opposed by the practical evidence of every style of architecture. Even when architectural ornament represents natural forms, it cannot do so by imitating them; indeed, it is generally good in proportion as the resemblance is distant. Very little of the full beauty of a plant can be imitated in stone or wood-carving. The softness and colour and delicacy of

Fig. 19.   TEMPLE OF KARNAC IN UPPER EGYPT.

nature are unattainable even in marble. The feeling of growth may be represented; but this is often best done by not attempting accurately to imitate the form, which must be forced and stiffened, so as to have the nature of stone or wood put into it, and governed by the lines of the architecture, before it can become a harmonious part of wood or stone constructions. It may then be coloured simply, without any attempt at the gradations of Nature's colouring, with red, or white, or gold. The forms of honeysuckle, or of the rose or lily, are scarcely recognisable in the Greek honeysuckle ornament, in the Tudor rose, or the French fleur-de-lis, though these are much better ornaments in architecture or heraldry than a more exact imitation of the several plants.

The term "conventional" has been applied to this treatment of ornament, as if it were only by a common agreement or understanding that it could stand for the natural objects it is supposed to represent.

The aim of all architectural ornament, whether sculpture or painting or carving, is to give richness or expression to buildings; and its excellence must be judged of, not by the accuracy with which it imitates nature, but by the extent to which it accomplishes its objects in harmony with the architecture.

These modes of giving expression to buildings have been employed in different degrees by various nations, in their several styles of architecture.

Mass and stability—the sense of eternal duration—seem to have been what the Egyptians aimed at in their buildings. They used stones of enormous size, and of the hardest kind, and long ranges of monolithic columns and figures. They built their walls sloping inwards, as being the most stable form of construction; carrying this so far in the pyramids as to sacrifice to it every other kind of architectural expression. Their ornament, grand, simple, and restrained in its lines, aided the general effect. They sometimes covered their walls with hieroglyphics, but the cutting was so shallow that it never destroyed the sense of mass.

The engraving of the Temple of Karnac in Upper Egypt (fig. 19) gives some inadequate notion of the gigantic size of the masses of the architecture.

The Greeks worshipped beauty, and of all nations had the greatest success in realising it in its highest form of perfect proportion and exquisite purity and delicacy of line.

In the architecture of their temples the construction was of the simplest and most primitive kind. In those of the Doric order, the purest and most characteristic expression of Greek art, the building is placed on a platform formed of great stones, in the finer temples of white marble, spreading out in steps so as to give the idea of perfect solidity. On this solid base the columns were placed. The Greek temple (see fig. 20) was not an enclosed building, but a portico built round the shrine of the god, giving shelter to the crowds who came to worship, from rain and sun, not from the cold.

The Doric column is without a base, or that widening at its foot used in the columns of other styles of architecture to obviate the impression that the weight it carries might sink it into the ground; because the platform looks solid enough to prevent any such impression arising. The column widens from top to bottom in a gentle entasis or curve, which counteracts the disagreeable appearance a simple cylinder would have had, of looking thinner at the bottom than in the middle and top. It is marked along its length with flutings, a series of slight hollows and edges, producing delicate gradated lines, which carry the eye along it and suggest its function of supporting weight.

Fig. 27.

TEMPLE AT PÆSTUM, MAGNA GRECIA.

WHAT CONSTITUTES GOOD ARCHITECTURE? 57

To receive the weight it spreads out in the capital, on which is placed the *abacus*, a simple slab of stone. On these, stetching from column to column, rests the *architrave*, a series of solid square stone blocks.

Above this is the *frieze*, which occupies the place of the roof beams of older wooden construction, the traces of which still remain in the *triglyphs*, representing notched beam ends. In the perfected architecture these fulfil the purpose of marking the downward pressure of the weight. On them rests the roof, which projects in the cornice, so as to throw the rain off the building, and which crowns it along its length with a mass of dark shadow. The roof is flat pitched, for the idea of length, rather than of height, rules the disposition of the architecture, and forms at the ends of the building low gables or pediments.

Of architectural ornament there is none; there is no carving of the parts into flowers, or cable mouldings, such as Mr. Ruskin says makes the difference between architecture and building. The Greeks did not use sculpture like the Gothic architects, marking the construction and forming a part of it. Many temples, like this one of the group at Pæstum, in the Greek colony of Magna Grecia, were without it. Where the Greeks used sculpture they set it in the pediments, grouping it so as to fit their triangular form, or filling up with it the spaces between the triglyphs; but they never applied it or any representation of natural forms either to the base or architraves, or to the columns, which are the working members of the architecture. In these it would have tended to destroy the idea of Greek architecture, the expression of weight supported with perfect stability and perfect grace, which gives an impression of strength, repose, and beauty the highest attainable in architecture.

Mr. Ruskin says it is not much to have done, to rest a lintel on the top of posts. There is nothing clever in it; any infant can do it. The arch was a much cleverer thing to invent. The Greeks knew the arch and used it in drains underground, but they never showed it in their buildings. It would have destroyed their god-like repose; they felt, as the Hindoos say, that "an arch never sleeps."

The form of the perfect Greek temple was, doubtless, that of the earliest, which, with the persistency of religious traditions, has never been departed from. To the simple forms of Doric architecture the Greeks with their artistic instincts gave such exquisite proportion as to make it, while the race lasts, the standard of perfect beauty in architecture.

The Romans were a practical people—builders and engineers rather than architects. In the time of the Republic they seem to have had very little art, and scarcely a single building remains which was erected then.

When, under the Empire, they commanded the wealth of the world, they were the greatest builders the world has seen.

Every country they conquered still retains the traces of their occupation in the paved roads which led from Rome to the farthest station among the barbarians, permanent camps defended by towers and enclosed in a great square of massive walls, so admirably built that they have defied the weather and the continuous attempt to use them as quarries ever since,—of aqueducts carried for miles over plains and bridging great rivers, baths with magnificent halls, basilicas or covered porticos for administering justice, temples, villas, theatres, and amphitheatres, where the fights would have lost their interest without the death of the conquered. The Flavian Amphitheatre, even in its ruins, fitly expresses this wealth and universal mastery. (Fig. 21.)

In its system their architecture was that of rulers rather than of artists. It made admirable use of the means at its command. The Romans used the unskilled slave labour which they had in abundance in raising the masses

Fig. 71. THE COLOSEUM AT ROME.

Fig. 72.   GOTHIC ARCHITECTURE. WESTMINSTER ABBEY.

of rough concrete and the great stones of their buildings. They covered these with slabs of rich marble, or adorned them with ranges of arcades, rich vaulted ceilings, floors of mosaic, monolithic columns of marble and precious stones, and paintings and sculptures by Greek artists.

Their buildings were the expression of themselves—powerful and practical rulers, with an outside coating of Greek culture, which had not become part of their own being, and which indeed they did not rightly understand. The splendour is all gone; but wherever the Romans planted themselves, the solid masses of their buildings show the power which in Roman law and literature and art still rules our spirits from their urns.

Gothic architecture also had its own expression, characteristic of the races who invented it. It used to be thought that the idea of a cathedral was derived from an avenue of trees—the pillars representing the great trunks, the crossing vaulting ribs copied from the intermingling branches. The Gothic builders certainly never intended any such imitation; their aims were much more practical. From copying, as well as they could, the remains of Roman architecture beside them, they were led, as we shall see, in the development of a mode of fireproof construction, to a new and characteristic style, which has in it the spirit of the forest and of the growth of vegetable life, just as Greek architecture has in it the spirit of the beauty of animal and human form. Their buildings express strength and vigour, sometimes almost savage, and high aspirations and striving, rather than repose,—characteristic of the race that raised them and of the faith they held.

In the same way every natural architecture expresses the mental characteristics of the people among whom it has grown up. We understand most Eastern peoples too little to judge how far the same is true in their case. The Hindoos have expressed in their architecture, their love of subtilty and intricacy and minute refinement, their patient laboriousness and their want of grandeur of character.

At the time of the Renaissance, or Revival of the fifteenth and sixteenth centuries, the whole social system, the philosophy and the art of the Middle Ages, which had served their time, and the religious faith also in great measure, were broken up.

The rediscovered literature of the Greeks and Romans flooded men's minds with a new light which made the previous ages seem dark. Beside the massive grandeur and simplicity of the old Roman architecture, the worn-out Gothic seemed everywhere trifling. Ancient literature and art were deemed *Classical*, the standards of perfection.

The forms of classic art were universally accepted, but the Gothic spirit, still vigorous among the northern nations, worked them out into a new architecture, thoroughly Gothic in spirit, with a character which for want of a better name we call picturesqueness. Its effect seems due to happy accidents, and is rather marred by the regularity and symmetry which ruled every previous style of architecture, including Gothic.

For the irregularity which we find in many old Gothic buildings was not part of their original design. The Strassburgers at first intended that their cathedral should have two western towers, but, when they determined to have a higher spire than any other city, they felt that the symmetry became absurd and abandoned the building of the second spire. A similar feeling probably influenced the builders at Cologne, and when its two western towers are finished, I believe the result will show that in finishing only one tower the Gothic builder was right.

The sense of freedom and emancipation which the Revival

VOL. I.

Fig. 23.   ST. ÉTIENNE DU MONT, PARIS.

brought, mingling with older mediæval ideas, showed itself in the architecture of which the Church of St. Étienne du Mont, beside the Panthéon at Paris, seems to me a typical example. There is a richness and sumptuousness in the building which express the increase of physical well-being and the joy in physical life of the times. In features and ornament the design is mainly Classic, but there is nothing of Classic repose or correctness. The pediments are broken and twisted into curves, and the Classic mouldings and ornaments are altered with a freedom which horrifies Classic purists. The old Gothic spirit shows itself in the general form, in the high-peaked roof, and in the movement and energy of the design. The general effect of the design is rich picturesque confusion, which fitly expressed the spirit of the times which produced it; perhaps also of our own.

Such are the characteristics of the styles of architecture which we know best, but they do not exhaust the effects which architecture can produce; for if it expresses human feelings and ideas, it must be infinite in its manifestations; and every original building will have some new form of expression.

It is impossible to lay down any laws by which good architecture can be produced or tested. It would be a great comfort if we could have fixed tests in art criticism to decide what is beautiful; but no law was ever laid down which a great artist could not break, and yet at the same time produce good art. Sir Joshua Reynolds said that no picture could be harmonious in which blue preponderated, and Gainsborough painted his 'Blue Boy.' It is a law of composition in painting, that a principal figure should not be placed in the centre of a picture; yet artists have put it there, and the picture has looked all right.

Such laws only mean that the harmony they forbid is difficult; when it is achieved, the success is all the greater.

Blue and green are supposed not to go together; yet, in other instances besides trees against the sky, it is the most exquisite of harmonies. As well say that the music of a fiddle is harsh; yes, as we hear it in steamboats. Yet some people would prefer a popular air so played to a sonata of Beethoven performed by Joachim.

Who is to decide? In architecture, as in music, the test of excellence is the approval of those who combine a technical knowledge of the art with an inborn power of appreciating it. Art criticism consists in some one who possesses this power telling how an art production affects him, its value depending on the truth and delicacy of his judgment; or else in his giving the public such information that they can see from the same point of view as himself.

When a subject is of national interest, the sense of the community itself perceives a certain way, and, when doubtful of its own opinions, knows whose it ought to trust, so that it comes to have settled and well-grounded judgments; while those who know nothing of the subject are made aware, by the general sentiment, that they are not entitled to have opinions of their own.

When the nation generally does not care for an art (as is our own case at present with regard to architecture), and has little knowledge of it, it appreciates its coarse and vulgar manifestations (which, like popular airs, appeal to lower but more widely-spread sympathies) better than its most exquisite refinements. In art criticism the public do not know whom to trust. The mere accident of the critic being in a good position in society, or being an eloquent writer, or knowing a little of the subject and being very rich, if he is an amateur; or, if he is an architect, being a good business manager,—are common reasons with us for recognising a man's authority on architectural subjects; and, the art not being generally understood, we seldom meet any one who does not consider himself a perfectly competent judge of the merits of a building. The ultimate object of architecture is no doubt, to please the public, not the architects; but if, at first, it pleases only an ignorant public, it will soon be distasteful even to them. Its flashy crudities will pall, like popular airs, but unfortunately its permanence forbids us forgetting it as we do these.

Of the artistic effects of architecture enumerated in this chapter, many, such especially as grandeur or sublimity, would be out of place in ordinary houses. They are attainable in palaces; some of which, notably those of Florence, are as impressive in their architecture as great religious buildings.

Nowadays palaces generally are only larger houses to accommodate a large establishment. State and grandeur have become irksome to us, and are even despised, no doubt because so frequently the sign of power which has departed; and the sense of power consequently seems more exquisite to us when unencumbered by its trappings. Comfort and convenience are all that are insisted on.

This change is not advantageous to the development of the highest type of domestic architecture; but there is still room for better art in modern houses than is usually attained. To express our domestic life, it should be more pleasing than impressive, more beautiful than grand, characterised by refinement rather than by state.

CHAPTER III.

THE CONDITIONS NECESSARY FOR PRODUCING GOOD ARCHITECTURE.

WHY is it, that with all our mechanical skill and appliances, with a power of construction, and a knowledge of the art of all times which the world never before possessed, our own productions in architecture are inferior, in art and in grandeur, to those of our ancestors in the Middle Ages, who had not a tithe of our wealth or knowledge—that the churches we build are only imitations (often far enough off) of theirs, while our best houses are far inferior to those of Elizabeth's time? Not only are we incapable of rivalling the granite structures of Egypt, or the marble ones of Greece, but in truth and perfection of architecture we have been distanced even by poor and half-savage nations.

The causes of this are an interesting subject of investigation, even apart from the chance that a knowledge of them may help us to do better.

It may perhaps be said, to account for our undoubted inferiority, that we are not a building race like the

Egyptians, or an artistic people like the Greeks. But our cathedrals and our old mansions show that, in our own way, we were once both great builders and great artists.

It might be urged that this is not a building age—that our life is too hurried, our minds too unsettled, for works of permanence. A man seldom now looks forward to living in the same house all his life; he regards it with no love, and does not care what it is like, if it is water-tight and large enough. But with a population rapidly increasing in numbers and wealth, and in the desire for greater comfort and magnificence, we must go on building houses, and in fact the ground was never more rapidly covered—not with mere tents for shelter, but with houses often absorbing much of the new-made wealth. We build even for the pleasure of it, pulling down our cities to re-construct them with wider streets and handsomer buildings. The country has been studded with new churches; and public bodies, from the Government to small town corporations, engage eagerly in erecting all sorts of buildings, almost all with some attempt at architectural magnificence. It is not, then, want of wealth, nor of desire for art and grandeur, nor that the necessary talent is not born among us, nor a want of constructive skill, which makes our architecture a failure, as compared to the old, very much in proportion as it departs from the old forms. Nor is it ignorance, for we have a knowledge of the styles and buildings of the world such as no age ever had before, not by description merely, but in drawings, measured so accurately that we might reproduce the buildings.

The cause is not far to seek: it lay in the method or system under which the old styles were practised, by means of which success in what they aimed at was universally achieved.

These old styles were traditional. They each contained the accumulated experience of the time and country, which had grown up gradually during centuries, each age having its own methods, being confident that they were the best, and incapable of even conceiving of any other. For all men under the same influences of climate, race, and religion, there was one style of architecture as there was one language. As the people changed, their style changed with them. Rude and barbarous at first, it was gradually refined and improved; and it decayed with the decay of the nation, or of the social arrangements within the nation with which it had arisen. Changes were not made in it for the sake of change, any more than new words are invented without cause; but it was not stereotyped—each tried to improve on what had been done before. Constructive and artistic problems were gradually solved; imperfections, crudeness and errors corrected; till, having arrived at its highest perfection, the necessity of change in all living things gave it some new aim, generally lower, less simple and true.

The same system is followed in painting and in all the arts, and it is the only one by which constant success has been attained. Though each sees but a little way, he has the advantage of the thought, the discoveries, and the failures of his predecessors; his work is cut out for him—to make use of, and improve on them. If it is essential to success in painting, where the picture is the work of a single man, it is a hundred times more so in architecture, where the labours of many men and of a dozen different trades and arts must be united in the construction of a building.

An art conducted in this way must always be right, for it is natural and true; always interesting and worthy of study, as reflecting the thoughts and feelings of the people, their character and history, how they influenced surrounding nations, or were influenced by them. Its laws and development are as regular as those of nature. We can almost reconstruct an old building, and tell its date from a scrap of its mouldings, as Professor Owen could an extinct animal from one of its bones.

Architecture with us at present works under very different conditions. Instead of one settled style, which every one understands, and in which all workmen and artists are trained, we try Gothic one day, in all its modifications, from Norman to Perpendicular, and the next, every possible variety of Italian Classic, with an occasional change to Greek, Chinese, or Hindoo. In regard to each of them, we are in the position of a schoolboy making Latin verses. By the help of dictionaries, and a knowledge of the best originals, he may correctly and elegantly express even modern thoughts and feelings; but his work is not living art, and can have no human interest except in determining his place at an examination, by showing how closely he can copy.

This system of copying arose in the fifteenth century with that enthusiasm for everything Classic, which tried to reproduce, not merely the language and architecture, but even the dress and mode of life, of ancient Rome. But there are earlier instances in England of copying before the Classic mania commenced. In the western part of the nave of Westminster Abbey, built in Henry VII.'s time, the style of the older work is copied so closely that few but architects notice the difference. The arches have the same form as in the earlier work, but the mouldings are perpendicular in character. In so doing, the builders were no doubt artistically right, but it would have been impossible for them if they had thoroughly believed in their own style.

The vitality of the native style was spent. It was to succumb to the first invader, and the revived Roman art being received as the outward expression of the new intellectual life, spread resistlessly throughout Europe, irrespective of creed, among Catholics, Protestants, and

Jews, and has since been carried over the world with modern civilisation. Spanish, Dutch, and English settlers took it with them to America. Later emigrations have localised it in our new colonies. The Hindoos are copying their masters in this as in other things; and the Turks are now adopting it as a sign of their capacity for Western civilisation.

This system of copying, which pronounces architecture good and correct, the more closely it resembles some style long since obsolete, produces results very different from the old, natural method. Instead of changing and advancing with the life of the nation, it has a tendency to go back to its starting-point. At first the old model is not understood, and modern elements are mingled with it; just as a boy, writing Latin verses, will at first destroy their purity with English idioms and constructions, all traces of which he may succeed in removing, when he becomes better acquainted with the originals. The style is subject to continual aberrations, making its course not progress, but see-saw; for it is dependent not on the accumulated labours of generations, but on the knowledge and caprice of individuals.

The earliest Classic in France and England, and wherever else, as in Venice, the old style was vigorous, was half Gothic, but gradually it became more classically correct and uninteresting. Our earliest revived Gothic at Strawberry Hill is really the ordinary builders' Classic of the period, with some pointed windows in it, and ridiculous imitations of Gothic mouldings. The Perpendicular churches of thirty years ago are better, but no one could mistake them, like some we build now, for old ones. Since that time, the Gothic style, especially in its earlier and more perfect development, has been thoroughly studied and illustrated; some of the churches built in it being nearly as good as old ones, showing here and there modern developments, while a very few are accurate to the minutest particulars. Gothic architects, however, do not acknowledge that absolute obligation of old authority, which ultimately deprived the revived Classic of spontaneous life. Those who have known the style so well as to be imbued with its spirit, have produced works both original and true; but Gothic freedom has oftener merely meant liberty to go wrong.

One of the worst effects of this system of copying is, that the striving after correctness and perfect imitation of the dead standard leads to the adoption of features unsuited to modern wants. Great porticoes block up the windows of English country houses; "the orders," with their proportions immutably fixed, trammel and spoil the designs; great pillars block up chapels built for preaching in, and windows in houses are made pointed, rendering their woodwork inconvenient and window-blinds impossible.

The evils of copying are multiplied and aggravated when, as at present, we attempt a number of styles at the same time. When only one style was practised, there was some chance of its being understood, at least by experts and by the learned; and of its being correct, though to the public uninteresting and unintelligible. How can any one master the principles and details of half-a-dozen styles, so as not only to know them correctly, but to enter into their spirit so thoroughly as to be able to compose in them? Some one told Wordsworth of a friend of his who knew seven languages. "Indeed," he replied; "there are few people who know their own." Ordinary architects have about as much knowledge of the different styles they practise in succession, as couriers have of the half-dozen languages they profess to speak.

Half-a-dozen different sets of laws being in vogue—some opposed in principle, and some, those of Gothic especially, proclaiming the right of variety and individual freedom—

ignorant architects, instead of following old work, perfected by the continuous labour of ages, dignify their own crude conceptions with the name of originality.

While we confined ourselves to Classic there was a standard which, though a dead one, recognised as essential an adherence to laws of proportion and harmony, which experience had gradually perfected. Correct dulness was often the result, but we were at least saved from the utter defiance of these laws, which make some late specimens of modern Gothic the most impudent and offensive erections which the depravity and ignorance of man has perpetrated.

When a profession is established on fixed principles, like medicine or law, those who need its assistance may go to a village doctor or attorney, confident that they will be well advised, according to the best light of the age; just as in old times, when there was only one style, village masons built good Gothic churches or Classic houses. If we practised indiscriminately French and English law, with their variations through five centuries, and a man could elect to have his case decided by the law as it existed at any period in either country, only the most extensive reading and knowledge could fit a lawyer for his profession, and those who understood their work would be very few. The actual state of architecture is nearly as absurd as this wild imagination.

If this is true of those whose business it is to know it (and that it is so is shrieked through the land by music-halls and cemetery chapels), what hope can the public, who have no training in it, have of understanding its principles? To the unlearned and ignorant all its styles must be unknown tongues.

Similar views as to the advantage of the system under which old architecture was produced, have been expressed by Mr. Fergusson in his able and interesting 'History of Architecture' and throughout his works. But, as to the remedy for the present state of things, opinions differ.

"The great change which was introduced at the Reformation," Mr. Fergusson says, "was this. A Technic art came to be cultivated on principles which belong only to one of the Phonetic class;" that is to say, architecture, which is only the useful art of building elevated to a *fine* art, as "cooking may be refined into gastronomy and tailoring into an important art without a name," came to be treated as if it were like poetry, painting, or sculpture, one of the phonetic arts, "merely different modes in which men's thoughts can be communicated to other men, or perpetuated for the use of posterity." In the technic or useful arts, those, for instance, connected with food, clothing, or shelter, progress has been slow and gradual. Each worker is heir of an accumulated experience, so that any mechanic can now make a better steam-engine than Watt: "as in India, at this hour, local masons, who can neither read, write, nor draw, can design as beautiful buildings as ever graced that land." But in the phonetic arts, poetry, painting, sculpture, "the individual stamps the value." "We do not now find men writing better epics than Homer, or better dramas than Shakespeare. We do not see finer sculptures than those of Phidias, or more beautiful paintings than those of Raphael." "No one dreams," therefore, "of altering a poem or of improving a statue or picture, though they may be the production of inferior artists. But in the Middle Ages no one ever hesitated to rebuild the nave of a cathedral, or to add towers or chapels in the newest fashion to the oldest churches," just as "no Comptroller of the Navy ever hesitated to cut one of Sir W. Symond's ships in two, if by lengthening her he could improve her qualities." "No one has cared to record the names of the designers of the mediæval cathedrals; probably nobody knew who the architects were. The art was a true art; it was more difficult to do wrong then than to do right now. No genius, however great, could then enable an individual to get much ahead of his compeers, while the most ordinary ability enabled any one to do as well as the rest." But "the individual is now everything in architectural art, while the age is of as little importance as in a poem or a picture." And so "it would be considered sacrilege to meddle with or attempt to improve St. Paul's Cathedral, out of respect for Wren" (I only wish it were so considered), "and Blenheim must remain the most uncomfortable of palaces, because it was so left by Vanbrugh." "The new system subjects art to the caprices and vagaries of individuals." "What a man learns in his lifetime dies with him;" "his successor has to begin at the beginning;" "their careers probably cross each other." "An architect in practice can never afford many hours to the artistic elaboration of his design," and hence "the remarkably small amount of thought that a modern building ever displays. The evil has been aggravated in modern times by architecture being handed over too exclusively to professional men who live by it, and generally succeed more from their businesslike habits than their artistic powers." In conclusion, Mr. Fergusson says that, " without a reorganization of the whole system, we must be content to allow copying to the fullest extent, and must be satisfied with shams, either Classical or Mediæval, until at least the public are better instructed, and demand or initiate a recurrence to the principles that guided the architects of those ages when true and real buildings were produced."

I do not think it is a straining of Mr. Fergusson's opinions to say that his view is that, under the present system in which architects direct the construction of buildings, by means of drawings, good architecture cannot be produced, and that we should return to the system of the "true styles," when there were no architects, in the modern sense, but the employer communicated directly with the workman who executed the work; in fact, that architects should be dispensed with.

These opinions of Mr. Fergusson were restated in three articles in the 'Quarterly Review,' entitled "The State of English Architecture" (April 1872); "The Completion of St. Paul's" (December 1872); and the "Hope of English Architecture" (December 1874). In these articles the writer argues that in Greece, Rome, and mediæval England (which last, with more patriotism than accuracy, he says, was "for six centuries the finest scene of architectural display that the world ever saw"), as well as on the Continent, architecture was produced not by architects directing workmen by means of drawings, but by men who, while working with their own hands, had charge of their fellows as foremen or master-workmen. He quotes numerous cases in proof of this from Mr. Street's book on Spanish Architecture, in a tone which seems to imply that he convicts Mr. Street of inconsistency in relating them and yet continuing to practise as an architect on the system now prevalent. His latest article concludes as follows:— "Such was the master workman of the past, whose free imaginative power has ever been the life of art; and in like manner the emancipated workman, gloriously 'impelled,' must always be, and is, the only real hope of English architecture." He expresses his hostility to architects unrestrainedly. "These eminent persons," he says, "have been the bane of art for the last three hundred years." Again, he calls them, "A spurious, we had almost said a quack profession;" and again, he says, "There will then be no need of the 'profession,' and architects will subside into their proper places as bookmakers, artists, business men, students of symbolism and archæology, and, in fact, pupils and illustrators of those very workmen whom they now profess to direct and to control."

The opinions above recited assert or imply not only that in the best times of the art architecture was produced without architects, but that this is the only right way of producing it. If they have any practical meaning, and are to influence the conduct of any one in the present day who is thinking of building, they amount to an advice to him not to go to an architect for his plans, but to work them out himself with some intelligent foreman or builder.

The subject is of importance, not only to architects, but to the public, who, I believe, would get worse architecture than they get even at present, if they attempted to put the advice into practice.

Mr. Fergusson believes that our modern architecture is bad, because since the Reformation the art has been conducted on a false method; that whereas it is a "technic" art, it has been treated as if it were a "phonetic" art, like sculpture or poetry; and that instead of developing by a natural process of evolution, it has been under the control of individuals.

This distinction has not, I think, any existence in reality. The arts which Mr. Fergusson calls "phonetic" do not arise out of the gift of speech, as Mr. Fergusson asserts, but are rather substitutes for speech. He seems to have classified the arts as technic and phonetic, putting aside the familiar distinction of the arts as useful and fine, in order to avoid classing architecture as a fine art with painting and poetry. But in truth the distinction between these arts does not lie in the subject-matter of the art, but in the *manner* of treatment. Any useful art may become a fine art by having added to it the element of *fineness*—of beauty of colour or form, or of expression, that is, any element making it the vehicle of human feeling or emotion, such as tenderness, gladness, solemnity, or even, perhaps, mere refinement and perfection in work. "Every useful art,"

Mr. Fergusson admits, "is capable of being refined into a *fine* art."

Architecture is not only a fine art, but it is included in Mr. Fergusson's definition of the "phonetic" arts, being one of the noblest and most lasting "modes by which men's thoughts can be communicated to other men, or perpetuated for the use of posterity."

Now, one of the results of an art developing into a fine art is that, the art expressing the personal emotions and feelings of the artist, we come to have an interest in his personality. We resent the alteration and interference of others, as destroying the value of the work—the art becomes individual.

This, at least, is the case in our present state of society and civilisation. But in certain states of society we find arts flourishing in what we may call a traditional manner. Their origin is lost in the past. They are handed down from father to son. They are understood by the whole community, and seem the expression of the national character. Their progress is slow and gradual, and we can measure it only by comparing the productions of the art at long intervals. This is what Mr. Fergusson means by a "true" style of architecture. But he is in error in saying that architecture differs in this from poetry and other arts; for, in primitive states of society, we cannot recognise the individual inventors in poetry and sculpture any more than in architecture. They are lost in the community, or in a school of poets or sculptors handing down a tradition. In them as in architecture the age seems everything, the individual little or nothing. Mr. Fergusson ranks Homer with Shakespeare, as both equally historical personages. But few now hold that the poems of Homer are the work of any one man. They and other early Greek poems come to us as the collected traditions of the schools of professional singers and rhapsodists, who recited them at the public festivals. In the early history of every race literature and all the arts exhibit the same characteristic. The folk's lore and national tales, characteristic of the genius of each people, even when traceable to some source common to them with other races, and the national proverbs are all authorless, so far as we know, and with as much truth as a style of architecture or ornament might be said to be the result of slow accretions of tradition. But no one would think of calling only such national poetry and literature true, and what has been written by poets whose names we know false, or of lamenting that under our modern system literature had lost its ethnological value.

The art of sculpture was practised in the same anonymous traditional manner. It was a useful art to begin with—to supply idols for worship, of the rudest kind, as we see from those lately found at Hissarlik (claimed as the site of Troy). The growing refinement of the Greek race, which tingled with art to the finger tips, in time made these statues of the gods the highest expression of art which the world has seen. Early Greek coins show a slowly developing tradition. The later coins of Syracuse are signed by their engravers.

It is the same in the art of music; each nation has its national airs, breathing the spirit and sentiment of the race, handed down by tradition, and doubtless changing and growing as each musician passed them on. But since the time of Palestrina, composers, like architects, have asserted their individuality, and the history of music, like that of architecture, as Mr. Fergusson complains, has become an account of the lives of inventors.

In other departments the same thing is seen. Any ship carpenter used to be able to build a ship about as well as any other. Now we have individual inventors; and though this takes from us the safety of slow progress, and renders us liable to a fiasco like the *Great Eastern*, no one thinks of urging that the designing of ships should be relegated back to the working carpenters.

In like manner the so-called phonetic art of painting has passed through a stage similar to that of the " true " styles of architecture—the state in which it was in Italy when Cimabue gave it life, in which it still exists, in the supply of pictures for Greek churches—a fine art in a sense, not without a sort of beauty, under its conditions—a tradition transmitted by common workmen, gradually changing with the advancement or decline of the race.

The state of society in which the arts are traditional, is a state of stagnation. There is a very small stock of ideas common to all the tribe; every man thinks exactly as his neighbour and as his fathers did before him. All wisdom comes from them, and the old men as nearest the source are the sole repositories of truth. New ideas are regarded as blasphemy, and if they spring up are crushed out by the common sense of the people. The thoughts and ways of other nations are regarded with hatred as things the earth should be purged of; or, if with tolerance, as strange and inconceivable. Customs are often circumscribed in the narrowest districts: each village has its own peculiar dress, each district its own type of building.

The period during which a nation may remain in such a state is absolutely indefinite. Many savage tribes appear never to have changed since the stone age. The East is still much as it was in the time of Moses, and from its daily life supplies illustrations of Biblical customs. The breaking up of such a state of things is always an epoch in a nation's history, filling it with the gladness of new birth.

It came to the Florentines, in the art of painting, when Cimabue for the first time painted a Madonna with some touch of human feeling—when he made the art phonetic, as Mr. Fergusson would say; and, however feeble the flicker of life in the picture, as it hangs gaunt on the wall in Santa

Maria Novella, may seem to us who know what the life grew to of which it was the germ, it filled the people with such joy that they carried it with shouting and triumph through the streets; so that to this day the suburb through which it passed is called the Borgo Leto.

In our own day a new birth has come to the Japanese, affecting not their art only, but their social state and all their customs. Their art, which to us was a new sensation, seems now crude and barbarous to themselves. They are delighted with the new idea of perspective and distance. Marching in the ranks of European civilisation, they glory in black trousers and tail coats, as the outward and sensible sign of their new inward life. One who was present in Japan during the change told me that though the command of the Mikado, believed to be divine, was needed to start the nation on its new road, even that would be powerless now to arrest it.

The same sort of thing is happening everywhere. Travel is losing its interest, for every place is getting like every other. The beautiful national costumes of Norway are disappearing. All our own old ways are dying out. The Great Exhibition of 1851, it has been not untruly said, destroyed the last remnants of art in England. Everywhere, the old traditional arts are perishing. New Turkey carpets are harsh and bad in colour. We only know what their colour once was when we see an old one in some country house where the furniture has been unchanged for a century. Every year, in India, carpets with the exquisite old colour have to be sought for farther up the country. If Mr. Fergusson went back there, I fear now he might not find his village mason building the traditional tombs. In Persia the art of carpet weaving has perished, by the destruction of the old weavers in the famine, and the country has taken to European ways. All over the East the art which has lived there since the days when the mother of Sisera looked for her son returning from battle with "a prey of divers colours of needlework," is disappearing. Our age of steam and universal inter-communication is witnessing the destruction everywhere of arts which have their roots in the earliest traditions of the race. Their continued transmission depended on a stagnant social condition. When that is broken up they perish with it. It is sad, but it is inevitable; for, once a man has known individual freedom, he can never again be a mere transmitter of tradition.

And this is the age in which Mr. Fergusson tells us to return to those old ways in architecture, which he says we gave up three centuries ago. He might as well tell the dead to rise. His 'History of Architecture of all Countries from the Earliest Times to the Present Day,' is of itself a proof that we have emerged from the state which conceives its traditional ways the only possible ones—that we can appreciate new and foreign ideas. If they seem better to us, we are sure to follow them under the guidance of their originators, not of common workmen who do not understand them.

There is thus no ground, in fact, for Mr. Fergusson's division of arts into phonetic and technic; the first produced by individuals, whose names we know; the latter anonymous, transmitted by tradition, and, advancing by the slow improvements of ordinary and unknown men; anonymity and transmission by tradition have been at certain times a condition of all other arts as well as of architecture.

Equally erroneous is the assertion, on which depends Mr. Fergusson's division of the history of architecture into two markedly different periods, that, till the Reformation, the so-called true system everywhere prevailed; and that, since then, the so-called false system has prevailed throughout Europe.

It is no doubt true that most of the old styles of architecture, especially those which continue, as in India, to the present day, were practised by common workmen during long periods as traditional styles, and continued gradually progressing without any such change as to be marked by the names of the architects. But I think it can be shown that this is not true as regards the rise of Gothic architecture. It arose in France in the building of the great cathedrals, during a period of remarkable social and mental activity, when the towns threw off the fetters of the feudal system, and gained their liberties and the right of having walls. It was an outcome of that Renaissance within the Middle Ages, which produced the free thought of Abelard, the love poetry of Provence, the new music of rhyme. The rise of the new architecture was rapid, the whole of the French cathedrals having been built and left almost as we find them within a period of eighty years.

It was not a slow improvement of traditional ideas by unknown workmen. On the contrary, we find in it one of Mr. Fergusson's characteristics of a "false" style; we know the names of the architects.[1] They seem in many cases to have been laymen, judging from their names and the layman's dress in which some of them are represented on their tombs.

In the centre of a labyrinth marked in lines on the pavement of Amiens Cathedral, lately destroyed, were engraved the names of the "masters," who in succession directed the works in the beginning of the thirteenth century—Robert de Luzarches, Thomas de Cormont, and his son Regnault. Peter of Montereau, in 1240, was commissioned by St. Louis to build the Sainte Chapelle at Paris. With his wife he was buried in the choir of the Lady Chapel of St. Germain des Prés, now destroyed, which also he designed.

[1] The Cistercian Abbeys in Yorkshire, which are the earliest pure Gothic works in this country, seem to have been the works of the monks themselves. William of Sens and William "the Englishman," were both Benedictine monks.

Libergier was the architect of the very perfect Church of St. Nicaise, at Rheims, as his tombstone, removed on the destruction of the church to the cathedral, tells us. Peter de Corbie built several churches in Picardy, and probably—Viollet-le-Duc thought—the chapels of the apse of Rheims. John de Chelles constructed, in 1257, the gables of the transept, and the first chapels of the choir of the Cathedral of Paris. In 1277, Erwin of Steinbach commenced the great doorway of the Cathedral of Strassburg.

The names of the masters who directed the work at Rheims, Noyon, Laon, and built the façade of Paris, are lost; as, they well might be, from the lapse of centuries and the destruction of records in France. But the instances given, collected by Viollet-le-Duc, show that Mr. Fergusson is wrong in stating that no one seems to have cared to preserve the names of the designers of the Mediæval cathedrals. The preservation of Villars de Honnecourt's sketch-book shows that the small respect in which the Reviewer holds architects and their drawings was not the feeling of the thirteenth century.[1]

The Reviewer and Mr. Fergusson may, perhaps, answer that these men were not architects, but master-workmen. But while the sketch-book proves that Villars designed and directed work by means of drawings, there is nothing to show that he worked with his own hands at the buildings; while the plan which he gives us of a church, designed by himself and his friend, Peter de Corbie, seems as much individual work as any produced under the "false" system.

These men, it is true, may have been engaged on only one cathedral at a time. But a cathedral, as then conceived, with its wealth of design, furnished ample work for the lifetime of any man. It might, perhaps, be an improvement

[1] Britton gives in his 'Christian Architecture' a list of over 150 architects employed in England during the Middle Ages, together with the churches which they erected.

on our practice if we had a greater number of competent men among whom our great works might be distributed, so that one architect might give his whole time and thoughts to each. But this does not prove that architects should be superseded by workmen. Our difficulty is the system of building contracts, which compels the planning of the building to its minutest details, usually in haste, before it is commenced, and which makes after-revision and improvement difficult. And when we see the enormous number of buildings, sometimes designed by modern architects—as, for example, the brothers Adam—all over the three kingdoms,—all full of invention, elegant, finished, and correct according to their own style, we are bound to admit that the fact of an architect designing a great number of buildings, does not prevent his doing good and original work, full of variety. The result, however, is harder to attain now than formerly, when all workmen were trained in the same style as the architect himself.

The instance of the Cathedral of Gerona, in Spain, where, in 1320, an agreement was made with a French architect, Jacques de Favariis, to superintend the works, and to visit them six times a year, seems very like our modern practice. We have documentary evidence that the design of these buildings was in each case the production—or, at least, under the control—of an architect superintending every part of the work from the foundation to the furnishing. The structure of the buildings themselves proves it, from their unity of design, and from the admirable adjustment of the various parts—a result which, in a new art rapidly developing, and before its principles were settled, could not have been attained by any mere understanding among hosts of workmen. It might perhaps be possible in a fully-developed art, with established principles and traditional modes of work, as in fact happened in late Gothic art, the various trades, without an architect to direct them, working harmoniously enough together at the sort of buildings to which they were accustomed. But this system might fail, as Viollet-le-Duc shows it did, in the restoration of Rheims Cathedral after the fire in the reign of Louis XI., when the building and its architecture were strange to the workmen.

I think, therefore, there is ground for believing, that, at the rise of Gothic architecture, buildings were designed by architects having much the same functions as those of the present day.

It can be shown still more easily that the second part of Mr. Fergusson's statement, namely, that the so-called false system has prevailed throughout Europe since the Reformation to the present day, is erroneous; for the evidence of the contrary is everywhere round us.

Architecture took a new start in the fifteenth century in Italy, in the sixteenth in England. Gothic had solved its problems, had reached the limit of height in cathedrals, the limit of twisting stone in tracery windows, and of tracery decoration on the walls; while in England it had stiffened into Perpendicular, and, for reasons, logically good, the pointed arch had been gradually flattened till it became a straight lintel. The art could go no farther. In a stagnant state of society it would have lingered on, degraded like modern Chinese pottery, but in the creative age of the Renaissance it had lost its interest and was thrown aside like a sucked orange.

In the state of Gothic at the time, it was impossible that an age which had found a new life in Classical literature and sculpture, could avoid adopting Classic architecture. But the Renaissance architecture was not mere copying, as Mr. Fergusson seems to assert by his nick-name of "copying styles." The great palaces of Rome and Florence are original works, not copies of old Roman remains. The age was fortunate in France, Germany, and England, not

only in the possession of great original architects, but in
the good sense to employ them instead of mere copyists
and bunglers. Thus the new style became established as
the style of Europe and of every country which adopted
European civilisation. It soon came to be worked on
the system of what Mr. Fergusson calls a true style, not
by original architects, but by workmen following a tradition. It mingled with such traditions of the old Gothic as
remained in each country, each of which produced its own
type of the new style; and, notwithstanding the more
frequent employment of architects during the last few years,
it still remained the traditional style everywhere. Every
workman has been apprenticed to it and understands it; and
in it builds without drawings, according to Mr. Fergusson's
"true system," those houses which Englishmen who must
live in them justly abuse. The style has, to borrow a
term applied in ecclesiastical controversy to a true church,
a *note* of a "true style;" it is practised by workmen as
by an instinct; its productions can be reasoned about
with the same certainty as those of the instincts of the
lower animals; and, like them, it sometimes produces
curious results by being followed out in unsuitable circumstances. I remember once seeing a row of houses in a
street where the side wall of the last house overhung a
wooded bank and commanded an extensive view. *Reason*
would have put the windows in this wall, but the builder's
instinct prompted him to make this house exactly like the
others, and to make the wall blank like the other party-
walls, with the chimneys in it.

It would seem then from the history of the Gothic and
Renaissance styles that it is law of progress in architecture
that architects with the gift of originality, and whose
names have consequently been remembered, design original
buildings. The new fashion is imitated by the ordinary

workman, and a traditional, or true style (if Mr. Fergusson prefers so to call it), is established, which continues developing by constant changes, till a new "epoch-making" period of mental activity gives a chance to original minds to make a new start. The same thing happens in other arts. Our original painters, like the old masters, have each their school of followers. When railways were first started, original minds, like George Stephenson's, were needed to lay them out; now any contractor, even any common workmen, can make them. Any fool now can go to America or make an egg stand on its end, though it needed a Columbus to do either for the first time.

The late Gothic revival is an instance of the same thing. Pugin and others started it, and his works, though among the earliest, are still among the best, because they possess the originality of genius. The style has now become traditional, with established forms and modes of work, if not for houses, at least for churches; not among workmen who, though they make abortive attempts in it, being still imbued with the degraded Classic traditions, have never understood it; yet with architects who, except when they unite with bad taste a belief in their own originality, design fairly good Gothic churches.

This is also true of the new fashion of so-called Queen Anne; although those whom accident may have caused to be accounted its leaders may not be those who first started it. The London builder is adopting its features, with more chance of success than in Gothic, since it is the natural outcome of London materials and modes of work; but it is to be feared that both he and the more ignorant architects, in attempting to avoid commonplace may run into vulgarity, to keep clear of which, in this style, requires the constant restraint of good taste and refinement.

We see, then, that in architecture, as in other arts, in

times of which we have any record, we can trace the rise of new inventions and know the names of their authors, while in times of which the records are lost, the names of the poets and sculptors have perished equally with those of the inventors of new styles of architecture. The anonymity of the "true" styles of architecture is an accident of our ignorance, not inherent in the nature of the art, and forms no ground for distinction between it and other arts. Reasoning from what we know to have happened in historical times, we may be certain that the earlier improvements in architecture, great or small, were not made by common workmen or by the general sentiment of the community, but by individual inventors whom then, as now, the multitude copied and followed. If these old works of art express the feelings and genius of the race, it is because the race adopted them as the expression of their own thoughts. National poetry is the creation of individual poets, national music of individual composers, and national architecture of individual architects, and the patterns and colours which we admire in Eastern carpets, are the invention of some long dead and forgotten designer. These, each in his own art, impressed their thoughts on the nation, so that they became the expression of the national sentiment. Everywhere, and in all time, progress has been determined by the individual. Tennyson's soft music has infected all the youth of our age. Before him was Campbell, "blowing trumpets and beating drums." For a time all aspirants to poetry were Byronic. When we go far back in time, we must believe that there was same infection of personal influence and mood.

Now, as in all time, individuals, however remarkable they may be, are, in a sense, the products of their age and country; but there is no reason for thinking they were more so formerly than now.

And architecture is necessarily a product of its time,

and influenced by national movements rather than by individuals, to a greater degree than an art such as poetry, for several reasons. For in the first place, in domestic work, it must suit itself to our life and habits; and these do not readily change, even for the better, at the bidding of any single individual; while, in its application to religious purposes, it is dependent on the prevailing religious sentiment. The romantic revival in architecture was a sequence of the romantic spirit in literature and religion, and it will last as long as these.

In the second place, originality has not the same chance of showing itself in architecture as in poetry. A poet produces his work notwithstanding that his audience is unfavourable; and if, as in the case of Wordsworth and Tennyson, it is received at first with opposition and ridicule, if the work is genuine, time will give it currency and favour. But an architect's work must be approved before he is employed; and in his case, as in the poet's, new ideas being strange, are received with opposition and dislike all the greater the better they are, and the higher they rise above the heads of the people. It is sad to think of the good buildings which have been lost to us from this cause. We wasted our gift of Pugin. We may see in his little church at Ramsgate, where he had his own way, and which seems almost to contain in itself the whole Gothic revival, what a wealth of architectural design he could have given us if we had had eyes to see and hearts to receive it.

A third reason why architecture cannot be so dependent on individual originality as poetry or literature, is that a building cannot, like a poem, be the work of one man. No doubt, by full and careful drawings, one man can direct a work down to its minutest details, and in the present state of workmen's training, this is the only way to get it right. But in such a state of things architecture labours under enormous difficulties. The men who are capable of doing this when, as at present, architecture has no settled rules, and they are left to their own innate taste and sense of right, are necessarily few, and they are the least likely to be employed. The public taste is ignorant and uninformed; debased by a vulgar sensationalism to which the boasted freedom of Gothic has too readily lent itself. It is otherwise when the laws of art are settled, when they are universally diffused, learned as traditions of the trade by apprenticeship, and practised without difficulty by men who could never have invented them. Then the work of architects, sculptors, carvers, painters, furnishers, fits together naturally and without effort. If we ever get back to such a state, it will not be by a fortuitous concourse of common workmen, but by men who can conceive, see clearly, and work out new order and beauty. The hope of our architecture depends on our having men who can do this, and on our giving them the opportunity of doing it. But, as in Pugin's case, there is more chance of our having the men than of their being employed.

We agree with Mr. Fergusson and the writer in the Quarterly, that the present unsettled state of architecture is a misfortune to the art. But the causes lie deeper than architects can control; they cannot change the spirit of an age; they are but straws in the tide of opinion which, in more important matters than architecture, is in a state of flux and movement.

But all the more on this account does it seem to me our duty to preserve, instead of destroying, such building traditions as remain among workmen, to give new vigour and interest to a style still living, though commonplace and degraded, and to give beauty and refinement to forms which, left to uneducated builders for half a century, had become vulgarised, while the talent and refinement of the country were following the new cry after Gothic.

This consideration is, I think, a good justification of

the reaction towards the freer forms of Classic, which is now influencing our architecture, though its cause lies deeper.

When the Reviewer says that the hope of English architecture lies in the working man working without the aid of architects, on the traditional system of the true styles, we answer, that we have had that condition for fifty years, and the result is our dismal suburbs of London builders' houses. It was not in this way, as we have seen, that architecture progressed in the past, and, as Bishop Butler says, there is no reason to believe that it will be otherwise in the future.

There may be virtue in working with our hands. The digging and delving to which Mr. Ruskin has set some Oxford undergraduates may be wholesome moral training. Mr. Gladstone may find benefit in felling trees. Monks, old and modern, have believed in the virtue of manual labour. It might be well for everybody if the old custom of apprenticing every lad, however rich, to some hand-working trade still prevailed. But the discipline has been recommended for its moral rather than its intellectual benefits, and in architecture especially it is brains, not hands, that are wanted for designing; where a workman has them it is waste to keep him to manual labour. That architects, as well as poets, will be born among them is to be expected, and the instances which Mr. Fergusson and others give of common workmen designing great buildings in modern times are merely examples of this, not of a return to his "true" system of architecture. The church at Mousta was a break in the current building tradition of Malta, a bad copy of the Panthéon (including the two modern towers which spoil it), cleverly carried out. That its designer, Anthony Gatt, got only fifteenpence a day is an accident similar to Milton's getting only ten pounds for 'Paradise Lost.' Both ought to have got much more, but the best reward of both, as of every true artist, was their delight in doing the work.

The Reviewer's instance of the Scott Monument at Edinburgh, designed by Kemp, originally a working carpenter, is still more unfortunate for his argument. Not without faults, for the worst of which—the spoiling of its line at the top by the introduction by the Committee, after his death, of a projecting gallery—Kemp is not responsible, it is a true work of genius, striking in design and perfectly truthful in construction. But it is not a production of a true style, but something altogether new to Edinburgh. Neither is it an instance, as the Mousta Church may be, of the designer working at it with his own hands, for it is one of our few buildings which are wholly of mason work. Kemp, its architect, was by trade a carpenter (or wright, as he would call it), who probably never cut a stone in his life, but whose trade gave him the practice of making working drawings. He was, in fact, one of the sketching architects whom the writer condemns. One of his friends, beside whom I worked in the office at Edinburgh where I was apprenticed, told me that Kemp used to disappear for long periods, during which he went abroad, and, working at his trade sufficiently to support himself, employed himself in sketching the old buildings of continental towns.

The talent for designing architecture, like that of making poetry, may be born in any rank. Bishops may have had it, and when the principles and practice of the art were commonly understood (as we may hope to have them again), they may have found no difficulty in carrying out their ideas; though in the instance the Reviewer quotes, where the church tower fell down from having a bad foundation, it might have been better for the bishop if he had had a competent architect to consult. I see no reason why women should not have it. I have known some ladies excellent planners. One of our best artists in furniture and decorations is a lady. Lord Burlington, doubtless, was an architect, though Colin Campbell, in his 'Vitruvius Britannicus,' inserts Burlington House as his own design. Builders may have it, and some large firms supply the want of it by keeping an architect on the establishment, though their designs often fail, not only through commonplaceness and poverty of invention, but in the management of lighting and in planning. It is within my experience that a builder, asked to do some work requiring design, has come to an architect to advise him. I think he showed more wisdom than his employers, and that we would have better architecture if builders oftener did the same.

To say that workmen only can produce good architecture is absurd and contrary to fact, and I do not believe they would thank us for pushing them into this position. I have had occasion to know something of them, and have found them mostly honest and sensible, perhaps with an overveneration for acquirements in others which they did not themselves possess, with an interest and pride in their work and in the design they were helping to carry out, and conscious that, to produce better art than they were used to, they must work under guidance. I have heard a different account of them—that they take no interest in their work, that all they care for is to get as big a wage and to do as little work as possible for it. Doubtless, this is partly true, and the trades' union regulations seem framed to foster these feelings. But who first taught them to give as little and to get as much as they could; that their only value was their market value; that it was all a question of hard bargain, in which considerations of sentiment or honour were out of place? If, in dealing with men, political economy has dropped out humanity as a factor in the problem, it is not the teachers of its dreary gospel who should complain that the workmen have taken them at their word.

Working men would not appreciate being left to make designs themselves, or understand the writer's veneration for them. Hero worship has reason in it, but I can see none, nor would they, in his new worship of the working man.

We have no directions, either from Mr. Fergusson or his supporter, as to the practical steps which the public should take to introduce the "true" system of architecture. On one point I would desire information, namely, which of the numerous trades connected with house building—bricklayer, plasterer, carpenter, plumber, bell-hanger, decorator, &c.— is to have the direction of the work? Old buildings were not so complicated; the other trades were subordinate to the mason; but a mason nowadays would find himself very helpless in adjusting the requirements of a modern house. Our London builders' houses, though each merely a repetition of what has been done a thousand times, do not give hope for the system of leaving workmen to their own devices. It is, indeed, a curious theory that knowledge, education, and refinement should be hurtful to an art, to the proper practice of which, in the present day especially, they are essential. Because architecture, in a wholly different state of society when good art was traditional, was practised successfully by men who could neither read nor write, there is no reason to infer that the right way to advance it now is to leave it in the hands of ignorant men. If our architecture be in the deplorable state which is asserted, it needs to raise it not ignorant men, but men who unite the faculty of original design to education, refinement, and special training for the work.

But, it may be said, have we not precisely such a class in the architectural profession? Why, then, is our architecture a failure? Why are so many bad and uninteresting buildings now erected? Why does our architecture alternate between mean commonplace and forced striving for effect?

Several answers may be given. It may be said that our system has failed, because the architectural profession has not, on the whole, possessed the necessary requirements for their work.

Or it may be said that our system has not failed; that our architecture is in a very satisfactory state; that the recent criticisms are false; and that if the public are dissatisfied with us, as we are told, it only shows their ignorance and unreasonableness. I do not think it would be wise for architects to rest content in such assurance. It would not tend to restore the confidence of the public in them; and, indeed, none of them believe it, for though each may consider his own works excellent, he thinks other new works faulty, and far inferior to old ones. Architects should remember that, unlike painters and authors, they have hitherto almost escaped public criticism. Those who had the necessary knowledge felt they could not with propriety criticise unfavourably the work of professional rivals, and amateur criticism was generally valueless from ignorance.

A great deal of the architecture produced is, it must be confessed, very bad. In Gothic, the plainer buildings look poor and raw; the more expensive are overloaded with ornaments and pillars and tracery not called for by use or construction, or are hacked with wild ugly coarse notchings, as if attempting to look barbarous; while our Classic buildings generally want the finish and refinement which characterised those of the last age when the style was better understood. Nor do I believe that those who come after us will thank us for our restorations, which, conducted apparently on the principle that the memorials of Tudor times and of the Church of England since the Reformation are of no value and are even abominations, have destroyed the interest attaching to so many of our churches as continuous records of successive generations; have altered buildings which have been landmarks for centuries; have substituted for the memories of the past the meddling of an architect; for the grey tone of age, Kent rag with black pointing, bad stained glass, and Minton's tiles. If the few churches still untouched are left alone, and merely kept in repair, they will be the most interesting in England, well worth a pilgrimage. The destruction of historical records, which the restoration mania has achieved, is due, however, less to architects than to the zeal of the clergy, whom architects have often prevented from perpetrating some favourite vandalism.

While maintaining, then, that the views of Mr. Fergusson and the 'Quarterly Review' as to the mode in which architecture should be conducted, are impracticable, I must admit that they are right in declaring the state of English architecture unsatisfactory. What are the causes? By discovering them we shall best know where to look for the remedy.

There is not less zeal or talent, less knowledge or enthusiasm in those who practise architecture now than in old times. Architects do fair work for their pay, quite as much as engineers, surveyors, or stock-brokers, or even painters or sculptors, and they are, I believe, as competent at their work as other artists or authors. Consider, however, the conditions under which architecture is practised. There is probably as large a proportion of bad poetry and bad literature produced as of bad architecture. But the bad books get buried in library shelves, or, reduced again to pulp and made into clean paper, they cease to trouble us. Only the selected books which have stood the test of time remain, and from them our literature is judged. Our painting we judge of by the pictures selected for exhibitions, and happily never see the thousands rejected. But no such selection is possible among buildings; the bad ones, equally with the good, continue to force themselves on our notice, like vulgar tunes on a street grind-organ. And as our taste like our manners is formed by our surroundings, the evil tends to perpetuate itself, and every bad building breeds more by corrupting the public taste. If the art were in the condition it ought to be no bad buildings at all should be produced. But the architect is exposed to the same risk of error as one finding his way through a pathless forest instead of along a beaten track. As we cannot get rid of his productions, the freedom and individualism, which is a characteristic of our modern architecture, is a far greater evil in it than in the other arts and in literature.

Under the old system of architecture, when there was an established style and manner of work, there was not the same risk of individual error; for, living in the age, they could not help learning the style. Just as in social intercourse those who are brought up in refined society acquire, unconsciously, good manners. Some men have a power of forming them for themselves. Carlyle says of Robert Burns, when he came straight from the plough into the society of Edinburgh, that high duchesses were charmed with the manners of the man; and what are good manners, he asks, but the rules and refinements of intercourse, which such men have invented for us. Without such an inheritance of traditional manners, instilled into us from infancy so that it becomes a part of ourselves, most men would have bad manners or no manners at all; but by the training of good society, men who are naturally boors, may acquire and practice a real refinement.

In architecture, as in every profession, there are incompetent men without any natural gift for it. Apprenticed to it young, before they know their own minds, they do not care for it, but are unable to leave it: sometimes they even come to believe in their own powers of design, and measure the merit of their works by the uphill labour it has cost them to produce them. Others have a power of composing bad things and of expressing their own vulgarity in their architecture.

In architecture, under the old system, these men were harmless. The first, instead of the inanities he now perpetrates, reproduced the traditions he had learned, the second was restrained in his vulgarity by the rules of the prevailing style. And when that style, which was characteristic of the time, was understood by every one, architects who did not understand it had little chance of employment.

Employers judge by those things which they understand, not by art considerations, for which they care nothing. The architect makes a design good enough to please them, or, perhaps, commits the matter to some clerk who, from want of connection or lack of business pushing, has failed to get jobs of his own. In the latter case, the result may be satisfactory if the clerk can design, and is not thwarted by the architect's or his employer's bad taste. But it would probably be better for the art if those who could themselves design had the responsibility of carrying out the buildings. They are quite as likely to be honest as the mere business man, and as competent for carrying on the work; for the old notion that poets and artists generally are imbeciles in business matters has not been found to accord with fact. Seeing then that individual talent and power of design is so much more important in the present condition of architecture than in old times, the greatest good which could befall the art would be that those who have such powers should get the opportunity of exercising them.

If architects would advise pupils, who show no capacity or liking for the art, to give up the profession, the number of bad buildings would be sensibly diminished; and the pupils' lives would be happier by their taking to some pursuit they cared for, before it was too late. The thing to be desired is to utilise the designing power that is born in the country. Any mechanical obstructions which hinder this are an injury to an art, the practice of which should be as free as that of literature or painting.

No natural talent for design, however, will be of much practical value without training, and for this there is nothing better than the old system of apprenticeship. We might, however, do something more than we do to secure that those who are to practise the art are taught the principles which the experience of mankind has discovered and established. We cannot give the power of original design to those who do not naturally possess it, but we might help to establish a standard of taste which would keep those who have no natural ability from common blunders.

There is some truth in the Reviewer's assertion that the training of architects is too much at the desk among drawings, and too little among actual buildings. Instead of thinking out his buildings in brick and stone, and using drawings as mere directions to workmen, he comes to look on the making of drawings as the aim of the art, and unconsciously thinks of building materials merely as a means of imitating, as nearly as they are capable of, the effect he has realised in the drawing. Where the design requires a break he puts a half-brick projection, or a rain-water pipe, which make quite a strong line in the drawing, but are nothing in the actual building.

Old buildings appear strange and wrong when drawn out accurately in elevation. Indeed, they must do so if they look right in execution. There is a story of an architect who lately restored an old church, and on being appealed to by a well-known artist in the neighbourhood to spare the quaint old tower, answered that it was true it looked well in the landscape, but that if the artist would glance at an accurate elevation of it he had made at his office he would see what a ridiculous-looking thing it was. So the old tower is now replaced by a very commonplace one, too weak to ring the bells in; which, however, probably looks well in drawing.

An architect sometimes deceives his employers and himself by making pretty effects in his drawings which he cannot build. He is wise in his generation, for it is by the drawing he is judged, and the execution of the work determined on. We wonder often what can be the meaning of curious features in modern buildings, till we perceive that they are abortive attempts to imitate, in unsuitable materials, some effect of cross-hatching. A reflection from some irregular patches of glazed tiles on a wall we discover, on examination, to be the only parts spared by London dirt of an elaborate design of wall decoration, which must have been the most conspicuous feature of the hatched drawing. A dirty bullet sticking out on a wall was doubtless conceived and drawn as a polished marble ball, giving a bright point of light, and a long dark shadow on the wall. Or a church, which in the drawing looked like a cathedral, turns out, when built, like a toy church. There has been a mistake in scale—you can put your hand on the top of the nave piers.

The power of producing clever effects in cross-hatching is therefore sometimes a snare to an architect. All that he wants with drawing is accurately to convey his orders to the workmen. This is all the Middle Age builders seem to have had. Inigo Jones' perspectives are very washed-out and feeble-looking productions. Working drawings may give no more idea of the finished building than a score of music of the tune.

An architect, besides knowing his own profession, may be skilled in painting or cross-hatching, as he may be able to model in clay or play on the German flute. But these are different faculties, and it is as unreasonable to require it as a proof of an architect's competence in his own art, or as a condition in exhibited drawings that they should be done by the architect's own hand—as it was stated the Royal Academy proposed to do—as to judge a sculptor's skill by his capacity for copying his own statues in oil or water-colour drawings. The picture of a building or a statue will be best done by an artist whose natural mode of expression is in drawing, not in stone and lime or clay and marble.

To hope, however, that architects should be judged by their power of producing good architecture, and should get work according to their capacity for doing it, would be to expect too much from ordinary common sense. We might hope for improvement in our architecture if there were more general training in the art, and a better knowledge of it such as a general interest in it would bring. It is becoming a subject of interest to educated men, who are eager to understand it if the confusion and the uncertainty of its principles would admit.

For exciting this interest and inspiring a belief in the reality of art and the duty of following it with truth and earnestness we owe a debt of gratitude to Mr. Ruskin; and if, from the occasional impracticableness of his advice or from ignorant attempts to carry it out, confusion and bad art have been too often the immediate result, investigation and discussion may in time clear away these errors, and give the impetus a true direction.

Without an appreciation of the value of the art for its own sake, and some real knowledge of it in the community, we cannot hope to see much good architecture. Until this comes about, architects will be selected for the qualities which their employers *can* understand—energy and business habits, the faculty of writing good letters, plausibility and pleasing manners, and especially that power of inspiring confidence which makes employers feel themselves safe in following their advice and intrusting their purses in their hands, and skill in getting work to do, which by no means implies the power of doing it. Such faculties would find a more legitimate sphere in an agency for a life insurance company, in pushing some new arcticle of commerce, or in building and contracting rather than in art. In old times the architect had nothing to do with the business arrangements, he simply gave the designs and superintended the work. This was possible, when the work was done not by contract but by day's wages; and the system had the additional advantage of permitting improvements in the design as the building was going on, evidences of which we find in all old work. This is generally impracticable now; but unquestionably we increase the difficulty of getting good art by our system, which compels an architect, besides (or instead of) being an artist, to be a sharp business man, and selects him generally on that account. No doubt it is so in other professions. Skill is presumed in doctors from their having a carriage, or from a judicious manner, but to a great extent the judgment of their own profession tends to keep their reputation at its true level.

In painting, happily for it, the decision as to merit lies with brother artists. A committee of painters decides what pictures the English public shall be allowed to see, and apportions their merits by their places on the walls; but in architecture judgment by the profession of each other's productions is impossible, partly because, since an architect will undertake any amount of work, you may as well give him the job as consult him as to rival architects; but still more, because from the variety of styles the art has no recognised principles or standards of excellence.

It is governed, consequently, by amateur criticism, which too readily recognises surface merits. Every one thinks himself a critic in architecture with as good a right to his opinion as anybody else; especially if he has travelled on the Continent, and knows the meaning of words like "distylar in antis," or "sexparíte vaulting." In music or painting, those who know nothing are modest, and frankly confess that they do not pretend to be judges; for there is a chance they may be set down by some one who is an authority, or by a reference to principles; but in architecture, at present, there are no authorities and no principles, so that a town councillor or vestryman considers himself a judge.

Nor, though the principles of composition in sculpture painting and architecture are essentially the same, is a painter necessarily a judge of architecture unless he knows its technical difficulties; just as a good critic in painting or etching, though he may not have mastered it, should have tried it, to know when difficulties have been overcome, and to appreciate the merit of what may look quite simple. Do these arts, then, exist only for experts? By no means, but no one can form a true judgment on them who cannot see, beneath their surface, truth which lies deeper and will last, and which the ignorant who do not see it at once may in time come to appreciate.

When the public do not resign themselves into the hands of an architect, but judge the productions of his art by their own ideas of merit, as burial boards and chapel committees attempt in competitions, they are sure to select the most striking and flashy design as clever and original, while those which are quiet and unobtrusive, whose beauty has that strangeness which Bacon says all lasting beauty has at first, are passed over. The ignorant prefer paintings crude in colour to those toned into quiet harmony, and popular airs to classical music. Fortunately they soon tire of the popular air and discard it, and they tire also of the building which pleased them so much, but unhappily they cannot pull it down. It must remain corrupting the public taste through generations. Hence no architect who has much self-respect will engage in a competition, unless either he has friends in the committee who believe in him, or the decision is referred to some one who understands the subject. Usually, however, the selection of the architect is made, as in other professions, from his reputation, with the same result as at the bar, of heaping so much work on a few, that even with great ability and hard work they cannot get through it without scamping. To make an architectural reputation, very little art, and that rather of an obvious kind, will suffice; practical qualities and the faculty of getting work are of more avail than the power of doing it. A better knowledge of the art by the public might give us some hope of better architecture. What would give most hope would be for a country to return, if it be possible, to a single style. There would then be some chance of the art being generally understood. The attempts of architects would not, as at present, so far outrun their knowledge, and builders and workmen might possibly again put good art unconsciously into their ordinary work.

During the last half century, since the Gothic revival commenced, the difficulties of architecture have been aggravated, by several different styles being practised at the same time. It is like trying to speak three or four different languages. Some men may express themselves correctly in all, but the chances are in favour of bad grammar and composition, and of a want of that mastery of the refinements of language which makes the charm of good writing. We have it is true in numberless books accurate records of all the styles we practise—at the time when they were universally current and understood—by which to form our taste, but their quantity overpowers us; it is more than we can digest. Our buildings, therefore, are apt to be made up of scraps of design badly put together. We cling slavishly to precedent as our only security from error, instead of the style being a part of ourselves and our natural mode of expression.

Allowing—an enormous admission—that architects could master all the different styles they practise, or supposing that each architect only attempted one, yet the tradesman who comes across a new one at every new job has to acquire fresh habits and modes of work, and, being taught that his last methods in which he has been working are wrong, gets a medley of them all into his head, which makes it impossible for him ever to work correctly by himself in any style again. As most of the ordinary building of the country is done by tradesmen without the direction of architects, the degradation of the art thus caused is serious. The Gothic movement has now spread from the architects to the builders; villas made to sell and streets of small suburban houses are being built everywhere in a style meant to be Gothic, but with none of the characteristics which made old Gothic beautiful, with only some of its features, rendered absurd by the way they are used, like the spurs and swallow-tailed coat which constituted the whole of the King of Tahiti's court dress.

Nor do the evil effects to the workman end here. The characteristics of style must descend to the minutest particulars to obtain work with refinement and harmony in it. Thus the workman has lost the power the old workman had of doing good work without an architect; the architect must furnish drawings for everything. The result is as hurtful to the work as to the workman. No doubt we may obtain harmony and correctness by drawings, but only at the expense of interest and life. We lose what gives the main charm to old Gothic buildings, and to old Greek and Roman ones also—the impression on them of the thought of a number of different minds working to one end. Not that there is always a great variety of ideas in these old buildings—the same ornaments are repeated a hundred times—but, instead of as now being a lifeless copy from a drawing, they are the expression of what had become part of the workman's nature, and have in them something of his life. He understood it so well that he could give it variety and interest without losing its meaning and idea. And if he had originality there was full freedom for the exercise of it. In these old Gothic buildings the portals are crowded with saints, each under a canopy typifying the new Jerusalem. Imagination ran wild in the oak carving of the benches, and in the grotesques into which the gargoyles, or stone water-spouts, were formed (the action suited usually to their purpose in the building of spewing water from their mouths). They were vulgar and coarse no doubt sometimes, but full of human interest; for they expressed the minds and feelings of the carvers. And this variety was obtained without the risk of losing harmony, for only one style was known at the time in which they could express themselves.

In old Greek architecture there is the same individual life, not only in the higher sculpture, but in the repeated ornament; less wild, it is true, more under subjection to law, but as different from the frozen regularity of our imitation of it, as the leaves of a tree are from stamped-leather ornaments. Each egg and dart is different from its neighbour, each leaf has its own individual grace. And so on old Greek vases the painting is as free as in any Gothic work, not the stiff perfect thing we should imagine from our copies of them. This power in the workman of carrying out a design correctly in detail has only been lost in our own day. Till the Gothic revival in the last century he had his one style, which, though it might be dull and unimaginative, he understood and could work in without fear of going wrong. Now working one day at a Classic building, the next at a Gothic one, his ideas are a confused jumble, and he is unable to do anything of himself in the smallest details without guidance. A church in Glasgow of last century is a curious proof of this. It is a copy of St. Martin's-in-the-Fields in London, from Gibbs' published design, by a local carpenter, whose traditional knowledge enabled him to carry out the style creditably in detail.

The result is a correct though somewhat dull piece of architecture. It would have been better if Gibbs had himself carried it out, but as a large proportion of the buildings of the country have been and will continue to be carried out by builders, and as, they are sure, if not as in this case actually to copy an architect's building, at least to follow the fashion set them by architects, it would be an advantage if both the builder and architect worked in the same style so that the builder might copy with understanding.

Another evil resulting from the variety of styles leaving the workman without any of his own is the increased expense of producing work with any artistic character. Formerly he put art into what he did unconsciously, carrying out the traditions in which he had been trained. It was to him the easiest and consequently the cheapest way. But it takes far more time carefully to follow a drawing, and in doing so he is always making mistakes: each new design is like a new training; he never gets his hand in. Hence the simplest and cheapest-looking piece of furniture from an architect's design costs more than an elaborate one in a style the workman is used to, even leaving out of account the remuneration of the architect.

In the mere *architecture* of our houses (in the limited sense in which we usually employ the term as finished with the plaster-work) we manage, by reducing it to its simplest expression, abstracting from it its life and spontaneity and not trusting ourselves except in copying old ideas, to have everything pretty well in keeping in whatever style we work. But it is impossible, without an expenditure of time and money such as few can afford, to carry the same harmony throughout the furniture and decorations, and without this the house does not attempt to be a work of art. For we are dependent on a host of different manufacturers for carpets, paper-hangings, upholstery, chairs, tables, grates, lamps, crockery, and the thousand and one things which make up the furnishing of a house; and it is impossible that these can be produced in variety sufficient to give a reasonable choice in all the different styles we follow, especially as what we can buy in shops is mostly bad in taste.

The only resource is to have everything made from special designs, which is only rarely practicable and does not necessarily guarantee success. Architects' designs may give us something like harmony and a relief from modern upholsterers' work in the last dregs of Louis Quatorze taste with all its absurdity of illogical construction and none of the grace which was its merit; but they often, at least in their first attempts, miss the first requisites of practicalness and comfort. Chairs are so heavy that it takes two people to lift them, or the carving and ornament, which looks simple on paper, takes weeks of work, and does not tell when executed. French architects, who are accustomed to design the furniture for their houses, do not fall into these errors; and I have known British upholsterers get a reputation for taste, and live for years on copying two or three chairs from French architects' designs that they had picked up.

This harmony throughout, essential to a finished work of art, has been attained in the building which, in spite of all that has been said against it, is the most complete specimen of the Gothic revival—the new Houses of Parliament.

Sir Charles Barry's good taste could endure nothing out of harmony, and from the bridge and terrace outside, the architecture, carving, furniture, hangings, and stained glass, down to the knives and spoons in the dining-room, and the ash-holders in the smoking-room, everything is in the same style. But it needed all his learning and correctness and power of designing, with Pugin's marvellous faculty of inventing ornament, working continuously at it for about twenty years, to produce the result. What was done would have been impossible, without practically unlimited draft on the nation's purse. Yet it is not perfect; notwithstanding that a special army of workmen were trained for it, there is a certain correctness and sameness in the carving very different from the living irregularity that gives its charm to old work; the higher decoration of painting and sculpture could not be brought under the influence of the style, and is out of keeping and out of harmony.

If there was failure here, who can hope to succeed? The results of having no style of our own at present in architecture are that, as a general rule, architects cannot understand their art, and builders, who do most of the actual work, can have no hope of doing so, that the public generally are equally ignorant, that the workman is degraded into a machine, that harmony in the furnishing is impossible, and that the work is bad.

"If there be any condition," says Mr. Ruskin, "which in watching the progress of architecture, we see distinct and general, . . . any one conclusion which may be constantly drawn, it is this, that the architecture of a nation is great only when it is as universal and established as its language, and when provincial differences of style are nothing more than so many dialects. . . . Other necessities are matters of doubt. Nations have been alike successful in their architecture in times of poverty and of wealth, in times of barbarism and refinement; . . . but this one condition has been constant, this one requirement clear, in all places and at all times, that the work shall be that of a *school*, that no individual caprice shall dispense with, or materially vary, accepted types and customary decorations; that from the cottage to the palace, and from the chapel to the basilica, . . . every member and feature of the architecture of the nation shall be as commonly current, as frankly accepted, as its language or its coin. . . . We want no new style of architecture. . . . But we must have some style. It is of marvellously little importance, if we have a code of laws, and they be good laws, whether they be new or old, foreign or native, Roman or Saxon, or Norman or English laws; but it is of considerable importance that we should have a code of laws of one kind or another, and that code accepted and enforced from one side of the island to another, and not one law made ground of judgment at York, and another at Exeter."[1] "I think all the arts will languish until architecture takes the lead, and (this I don't think, I proclaim as confidently as I would assert the necessity, for the safety of society, of an understood and strongly administered legal government) our architecture will languish, and that in the very dust, until the first principle of common sense be manfully obeyed, and a universal system of form and workmanship be everywhere adopted and enforced. It may be said that this is impossible. It may be so—I fear it is so: I have nothing to do with the impossibility of it; I simply know and assert the necessity of it. If it be impossible, English art is impossible. Give it up at once. You are wasting time and money and energy on it, and though you exhaust centuries and treasuries, and break hearts for it, you will never raise it above the merest dilettanteism. Think not of it. It is a dangerous vanity, a mere gulf in which genius after genius will be swallowed up, and it will not close. And so it will continue to be unless the one bold and broad step be taken at the beginning. We shall not manufacture art out of pottery and printed stuffs; we shall not reason art out by our philosophy; we shall not stumble upon art by our experiments, nor create it by our fancies: I do not say we can even build it out of brick and stone; but there is a chance for us in these, and there is in none else; and that chance rests on the bare possibility of obtaining the consent, both of architects and of the public, to choose a style, and to use it universally."[2]

[1] Ruskin, 'Lamp of Obedience,' pp. 186, 187.
[2] 'Seven Lamps of Architecture,' pp. 189, 190.

But what style are we to choose? It is now that the real difficulty begins, for it is the difference of opinion on this point, among men whose knowledge gives them a right to have one, which is one main cause of the existing confusion.

"Why not do without a style at all?" is one of the most obvious and most frequently suggested answers; "build simply as our wants demand, and never mind style." This is precisely what we do to a melancholy extent in those new manufacturing towns, utterly devoid of grace or beauty or interest, though even in these dismal heaps of bricks and slates there are still some traces of old style or methods of work. Happily we cannot rest satisfied in this return to barbarism. Then "let us be original, and make a new style for ourselves." It would be about as wise to say, "Let us invent a new language." At the shortest, the process takes a century or two, even when it is only a change or development of an older one.

There is an appearance of reason in imagining that we might add to what we build for practical need some of the qualities of beauty or grandeur enumerated in the last chapter. But the progress of art ideas is inconceivably slow. We have still in daily use forms of ornament invented thousands of years ago; and why not, if they suit our purpose and, are better than we can invent ourselves?

The problems involved in clothing the necessities of house-construction in artistic forms have already been solved for us, with a perfection of art from the accumulated thought of centuries, compared with which any new attempts of ours would be mere crudities. We need no new forms of windows. For spanning spaces we cannot improve on the arch and lintel; and any new form of mouldings we might invent would most likely only be variations for the worse from what we find ready to our hands. If we could divest ourselves of our civilisation, of our power of construction and sense of beauty, we might, like the early Mediæval builders, begin at the beginning again (though their attempts, too, were copies of Roman buildings, but so bad as to be original), and start the art anew on a fresh course. But our knowledge of the purity and refinement of Greek art, the nerve and poetry of Gothic, and the sumptuousness of Roman and Renaissance, gives us ideas which we can satisfy only by appropriating forms already perfected.

Consequently we must continue to copy; our architecture must be founded on some old style.

In this way former architectures have grown. Greece got the first ideas of her art from Egypt and from Asia; Indian architecture is derived from Greek; Romanesque, Gothic, and Byzantine, from Roman. Copying is not necessarily an evil, if only we compel ourselves to vary from the standard when necessity requires. But it is not easy to clothe such new requirements with the same beauty as the old; we are apt either to sacrifice our convenience to the style, or to retain features which are useless, for their beauty. If we can *master* some old style, so that we can use it in spirit rather than in form, and can give artistic expression to our new necessities in harmony with it, we may hope in time to have a style of our own.

We must found on some old style,—which shall we choose? It is now that the real difficulty begins.

Mr. Fergusson, after describing and criticising the new Federal Palace at Berne, a building in a round-arched massive style with something of the character of Florentine palaces, and contrasting it with our Houses of Parliament, concludes: " A few years hence, few probably will dispute that a simpler, a more massive, and more modern style, would have been better suited for our Parliament Houses than the one adopted; whether it ought to be the one the Swiss have employed is a question not so easily answered. It seems, however, clear that they are nearer the truth than ourselves; and with some modifications, their style might be so adapted as to make it approach more nearly to what is really right and truthful than anything we have yet seen in modern times."[1]

On the other hand, Mr. Ruskin says: "I have said that it was immaterial what style was adopted, so far as regards the room for originality which its development would admit. It is not so, however, when we take into consideration the far more important questions of the facility of adaptation to general purposes, and of the sympathy with which this or that style would be popularly regarded. The choice of Classical or Gothic, again using the latter term in its broadest sense, may be questionable when it regards some single and considerable public building; but I cannot conceive it questionable, for an instant, when it regards modern uses in general; I cannot conceive any architect insane enough to project the vulgarisation of Greek architecture. Neither can it be rationally questionable whether we should adopt Early or Late, Original or Derivative Gothic. If the latter were chosen, it must be either some impotent and ugly degradation, like our own Tudor, or else a style whose grammatical laws it would be nearly impossible to limit or arrange, like the French Flamboyant. We are equally precluded from adopting styles essentially infantine or barbarous, however Herculean in their infancy, or majestic in their outlawry, such as our own Norman or the Lombard Romanesque. The choice would lie, I think, between four styles: 1. The Pisan Romanesque. 2. The Early Gothic of the Western Italian Republics, advanced so far and as fast as our art would enable us to the Gothic of Giotto. 3. The Venetian Gothic in its purest development. 4. The English earliest Decorated. The most natural, perhaps the safest choice, would be the last, well fenced from chance of again stiffening into the Perpendicular; and

[1] 'History of Architecture,' vol. iii. p. 367.

perhaps enriched by some mingling of decorative elements from the exquisite decorated Gothic of France, of which in such cases it would be needful to accept some well-known examples, as the north door of Rouen and the Church of St. Urban's at Troyes, for final and limiting authorities on the side of decoration."

These views as to the style we should adopt are sufficiently antagonistic, and counsel and practice might be quoted recommending others. The fact that there should be any question as to the style we ought to adopt is in itself an absurdity, parallel to that of the French Constitution-mongers, who persuaded themselves that the establishment of monarchy or republic was to be determined on the ground of the theoretical excellence and logical symmetry of either system.

Clearly the question cannot be settled in Mr. Ruskin's offhand way, by the mere expression of individual opinion and liking. It is doubtful if any settlement is possible, any more than if we attempted at this moment to fix the views of the age on religion and philosophy. If it be possible, such a settlement will be determined not by intrinsic merit, but by the simple consideration whether any one style has a chance of being generally adopted. The advantages of adopting one and sticking to it would be so great that it is at least worth while making the inquiry.

Fig. 21.

CHAPTER IV.

WHAT STYLE OF ARCHITECTURE IS MOST SUITABLE FOR OUR HOUSES?

IN the last chapter some of the inconveniences were pointed out which arise from practising various styles of architecture at the same time, such as the impossibility of so many styles being understood either by architects or by the public, and their consequent faultiness and imperfection; the waste of time and energy in teaching workmen various ways of doing their work, and the impossibility of their learning any style so thoroughly as to work without the direction of one who has studied old styles, with the consequence of bad and ignorant work when they are left alone (as in the great mass of common building throughout the country must be the case); and of spiritless accuracy, instead of the charm of intelligent spontaneity when they are directed by an architect; and, in domestic architecture especially, the difficulty and great expense of carrying any style consistently throughout the whole decorations and furnishings of a house, consequent on the necessity of getting every article specially made from special designs. So that it is only in the most expensive houses, and but rarely in these, that there is the harmony essential to a work of art.

But is it possible for us to confine ourselves to one style? Certainly no imperial enactment could make us do so, much less any counsels or persuasions in books.

There are probably too many opposing modes of thought at present for one style to be a suitable expression of them all. Neither the social conditions nor the philosophy are yet born which can bring unity into thought and into art. Nor can we delay building our houses and cities till this happens.

All the styles of the world are open for us to choose from. They have all been studied, and we know something about each. We have even built Chinese pagodas. Egyptian has been attempted (in plaster) and Byzantine has its advocates. We must go on building with good architecture or with bad as we can get it, and each one will, as at present, adopt whatever style his inclinations or those of his architect dictate. It is also to be feared that the desire which characterises our time for constant change and new fashions may prevent us from continuing any style long enough to let it fix its roots and grow naturally.

But an approach to unity of opinion and practice may be helped by an examination of the different styles possible for us with the view of determining which of them is, on the whole, the most suitable for our houses. A knowledge of what is possible in our circumstances may at least do something to prevent us spending thought and energy and money uselessly in devious courses on isolated attempts which can have no permanent influence on our general architecture.

There are several practical limits to our freedom of choice.

In the first place, as unity of style in our architecture is the object we are aiming at—that we may have some single one which might be generally adopted, the style we fix on should not be strange and unfamiliar, but should be intelligible to builders and workmen and to ordinary people, otherwise its productions will not be good in point of architecture, or, if they are, their merits will not be understood.

The style we adopt should utilise the traditional habits and modes of work in which workmen of all trades have been trained; it should not compel them to learn new ones, which would require a new apprenticeship.

It should adopt the ordinary modes of construction familiar in the building trades, provided they are not vicious or bad.

It should express our present civilisation, our modern feelings and ways of thinking. This does not necessarily preclude the adoption of some old style of architecture.

Accurate mechanical finish is a characteristic of English work and by many is looked on as fine art. Though it is not so, it has its value and should be a characteristic of our style.

We ought to be able to get furniture and fittings manufactured in the usual way by ordinary workmen, if not exactly of the usual designs, to harmonise with it.

To fulfil these conditions, any style must, Firstly, be one at present generally practised and understood, or some natural outgrowth or modification of it.

Secondly, It must be *free*, with power of change and development; neither so tied up with rules and precedents that it cannot be adapted to the irregularity and multifarious necessities of modern house-building, nor so logical and perfect that any alteration will spoil it. It should be capable of incorporating all sorts of materials, rude and refined, and of adopting any mode of using them in construction.

Thirdly, Regarded from the point of view of art, it should be such that the best art of our sculptors and painters may find it a suitable home. If Architecture is again to have these arts as her handmaids, she must rise to their level and suit herself to their style.

Out of the multitude of the world's styles the first test reduces those possible for us to a very few. The only styles which have been lately, or are at present practised among us to any extent, are GREEK, GOTHIC of several dates, and various forms of the revived ROMAN or CLASSICAL architecture.

I propose to examine in succession each of these styles of architecture with the view of determining, if possible, which of them best complies with these requirements and is therefore best suited for use in our modern houses.

The only satisfactory mode of doing so is by giving an account of each style, of its development and of the circumstances and necessities out of which it grew. We may, then perhaps, judge how far any of them is likely to satisfy our modern requirements in house building.

Independently of this more practical purpose, these styles are so important in themselves, as they constitute a considerable part of the mental development and history of our race, that an investigation of them should be of interest to all who care for art.

CHAPTER V.

GOTHIC ARCHITECTURE.

OF the styles which I have enumerated as practised among us, Gothic, especially in its highest and most perfect development in the reigns of Henry III. and Edward I., has had in late years the full tide of enthusiasm, eloquence, and fashion in its favour.

In church-building it has had the field to itself, reproducing and finding perfectly appropriate the forms and arrangements of the thirteenth century; and it is also now generally adopted for those places of worship in which preaching occupies a more prominent place, and in which consequently a modification of the ancient form is necessary.

It does not follow, however, that because Gothic may be, for several reasons, the most common style for our churches, it is the most suitable for our houses. The wants to be satisfied as well as our traditions in each case are very different. But in some respects a stronger claim can be made for Gothic houses than even for churches. In churches a Classic regularity and restraint is proper and fitting, while the freedom and pliability of Gothic make it specially suitable for buildings like dwelling-houses, which must have apartments of all sizes, and in which it is often convenient to have various levels of floor and various sizes of windows, and not to be tied down to the regularity of Classical arrangement.

Gothic, too, was the natural growth of the country, and suited to the climate. It was the art language of our ancestors, always familiar to us in the village churches; so that when the Classic was worn out, men returned to it as to an old friend absent only for a time. The romantic revival, of which Sir Walter Scott was the prophet, and the religious revival, which strove to bring the Church into sympathy with a larger unity and a higher antiquity than had been thought of since the Reformation, may have helped to revive it; but its principles once studied, it was found more practical for our use than Italian porticoes, which were no protection in a rainy climate and blocked out the window-light of a dark one. So that men of common sense and without enthusiasm adopted it.

So far as artistic merit was concerned, the dregs of the Classic had no power to oppose it. It has an interest and beauty of a kind that appeals to common men—the beauties of tracery and carving, of stained glass and coloured tiles—which do not need perpetually to lean on buildings in Italy as the standards of excellence. The causes which produced it gave rise also to a school of painting perfectly in harmony with it, which absorbed much of the enthusiasm and talent of the younger artists, and which, moreover, understood and carried into practice the idea that painting is worthily engaged in adorning the walls of buildings.

By the energy of Pugin mainly, in the first instance, a class of workmen were trained capable of carrying out Gothic designs, and of providing suitable decorations and furniture —not masons and joiners merely, but carvers who could work out their own ideas. The forgotten arts of hammered brass and iron, of encaustic tiles and stained glass, were revived, and have now become flourishing trades.

To the Gothic revival is due the credit of giving a new impetus to all the arts, and of letting men feel that art was a subject not merely for a dilettante few, but in which every one could take an interest. Although it has not conquered the country, its influence has been everywhere felt. This, however, has brought out prominently a weakness in it, which was not developed while it was opposed. The style is attempted now by architects who understand little about it, and by common builders who understand nothing, who, to buildings formed on the old Classic traditions, which still rule the mass of the building trades, add stopt chamfers or quatrefoils or pointed windows, producing a form of Gothic without its spirit or its power. It is becoming vulgarised, and, as a fashion of dress, when it finds its way down to the lower strata of society, disgusts those who first adopted it, by its travesty of the original form; so, many of those who were the most enthusiastic admirers and students of Gothic, who understood its principles and practised it successfully, are giving it up for domestic buildings

But the style is still largely employed, not only in churches, but in civil and domestic buildings. The new Law Courts in the Strand, one of the most important buildings of this generation, are being built in it. Its influence on modern architecture has been so great that, without a knowledge of the style, we should be ignorant of one of the most important movements of our day in the province of art. I shall therefore give an account of its rise and development, of the circumstances out of which it sprung, and the principles which determined its forms. Such an account must be to a large extent theoretical, and its truth must be determined by its being an adequate explanation of the facts. Any views on such a well worn subject cannot be altogether original; if they were I should have a strong suspicion of their truth; but I have ventured to give some theories and explanations which, so far as I am aware, have not been previously advanced.

England and France each developed their own forms of Gothic architecture, similar advances being made independently in both countries about the same time, as is the case at present in astronomy and other sciences. The style was imported into England, already somewhat advanced, from France, and there, from the more logical character of the people, less tolerant of compromise than ourselves, its development can best be traced. It sprang from an imitation of the buildings which the Romans during several centuries of occupation, with their faculty of giving their conquered provinces not only their language but their manners, had left everywhere throughout Gaul, in their own round-arched style, palaces, baths, aqueducts, bridges, basilicas, and villas or country houses like villages, consisting of straggling agglomerations of buildings one story high connected by covered colonnades for country residence and the cultivation of the soil. After a century or two of pillaging excursions, the German barbarians settled in the land. By the middle of the sixth century the Franks had occupied the whole country except part of Languedoc held by the Visigoths, the east held by the Burgundians, and Brittany, which was not conquered. By these conquests they lost the social organisation they had brought with them. Ceasing to be a conquering army under a single head, the habit which Cæsar and Tacitus had observed in their ancestors arose again among them, each tribe dwelling apart, isolated from its neighbours by tracts of waste land. Military chiefs became landed proprietors—heads of little independent sovereignties uncontrolled by the central power. Their companions in arms, almost their equals before, were now their dependents. With their love of plunder and fighting, when there were no more villages and towns to pillage, they took to fighting among themselves, and it was some centuries before even the rude national unity of feudalism became a fact as well as an idea.

In this anarchy the monasteries were the only refuge of civilisation, preserving some traditions of Roman art and order, and organising needful trades into guilds, a system afterwards adopted in the towns when, in the beginning of the tenth century, they began to recover their freedom.

When, with rising civilisation, churches or monasteries and towns began to be built, architecture had to begin at the beginning again. Roman buildings remained everywhere, but no one knew how they had been constructed. The people copied them in their new buildings as well as they could, making up for miserable construction by lining them inside with marble and gaudy painting.

When they began to build churches they attempted a reproduction of the old basilicas, or halls for the administration of justice, the form already adopted for churches and which they still retain—a large central nave or vessel, with an aisle or passage along each side, about half the width and height of the nave, opening into it through a range of pillars supporting round arches, above which was a range of windows called a clerestory, lighting the central nave.[1] At first, as they were unable from poverty and want of skill to reproduce the Roman vaulting, the roofs were wooden. But churches in those days, like theatres now, were always being burnt, and attempts were made to make the roofs as well as walls of incombustible material. In the south of France this was attempted—without the use of wood —by a plain waggon vault, as it is called, from being like the cover of a long waggon stretched on half hoops. This

[1] Basilica is a shortened form of στοιὰ βασιλική, *porticus regia*, or royal portico. Originally an open court surrounded by arched colonnades. Trajan's Column stood in the centre of such a portico. In later times the court was roofed in, and became the nave, the side colonnades the aisles.

vault they covered with solid masonry in the ordinary form of a roof (fig. 25). But for this a round arch was very unsuitable; a pointed one saved weight on the apex and had less thrust (figs. 26 and 30). Wherever they got the idea, whether out of their own heads, which is not impossible, or through Venice from the East, where the pointed arch seems

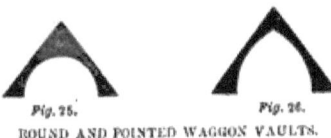

Fig. 25. Fig. 26.
ROUND AND POINTED WAGGON VAULTS.

to have been used continually since the time of the Pyramids and Nineveh, it was almost immediately adopted for vaulting. The arches opening between nave and aisles and those of the windows were still round.

In another way the pointed arch was found advantageous. Attempts, again from a desire for fire-proof construction, were made to build domes. Gothic had once a chance of becoming a domical style of architecture. If a square is supported on four arches, and carries a dome (fig. 27, plan), the bottom of the dome being quite inside the angle pillars, must be supported from them by four spherical triangles (*a a*, figs. 27, 28, and 29) whose points rest each on one of the pillars, and whose upper edges form together the lowest ring of the dome. These triangles resting on their points, their tops a quarter of a circle, their sides each half

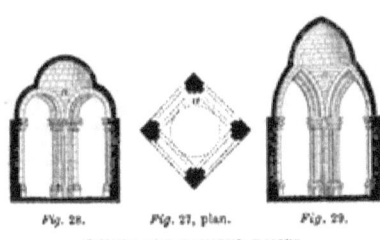

Fig. 28. Fig. 27, plan. Fig. 29.
ROUND AND POINTED DOMES.

of one of the supporting arches, are called pendentives, from their hanging as it were in the air. Now if the arches whose curves their sides follow are pointed (fig. 29), the pendentive will be longer than if the arches were round, and the projection being the same, will not slope so steeply forward; while, if the arches are round, the top part of these pendentives must project actually level. Consequently a dome is more easily placed on pointed arches than on round.

Neither of these styles of Gothic was ever developed. In them the windows and openings always remained round. The domical style with the means at the command of the builders was suited only for small churches, and could not serve the needs of the great towns of the north. The style with waggon vaults was suited only for the south, for churches so constructed were difficult to light. To form an abutment for the massive central vault the lower side aisles had to be carried up to its springing, thus abolishing the clerestory and preventing any light getting into the central nave except from the side aisles, leaving the central vaults dark caverns (fig. 30). Then the roofs all of stone did not do. Water got through their upper surface, as will happen, and filtered through the solid roof in devious courses, the place where it appeared on the inside giving no indication of the position of the leak outside; so that it was found necessary, especially when the vaulting became more intricate in form, to make it merely an inner ceiling, protected outside by a simple wooden-framed roof.[1]

Fig. 30. CHURCH ROOFED WITH POINTED WAGGON VAULT.

Gothic, as we know it, developed in the north of France, in what was called the Royal Domain, comprising Paris, Rheims, Amiens, &c.[2] At first, their churches being

[1] In Spain the roof over the vaulting continued to be made of stone.
[2] Viollet-le-Duc, 'Dictionnaire de l'Architecture Française du XIe au XVIe siècle,' Paris, 1854, which gives an ingenious account of the history and meaning of Gothic architecture.

large, the builders confined their fireproof constructions to the side-aisles, for they were unable to vault over the wider central portion, nor could they afford to lose the range of windows, or clerestory, as it is called, which lighted this central part, by raising the side-aisles so as to make them

Fig. 31.   GROINED VAULTING.

abutments to a waggon vault. For this difficulty they found in Roman work a solution which enabled them to vault the central nave and yet preserve the clerestory. By dividing the continuous waggon vault of the nave into square compartments, and running another vault across each compartment, so that the two vaults intersected, as the Romans had done, they concentrated the thrust on the four angles of the compartment, where it was abutted, at first ineffectually by tall buttresses, but with larger experience completely, being carried down to the ground by half an arch above the aisle roofs, to which is given the name of flying buttress. At the same time an arched space was left clear in each compartment of the nave above the aisle roof in which windows could be opened. These improvements are shown in fig. 31. This form of vaulting is called groining, in contradistinction to the continuous waggon vault, as the masses of the vault are divided and joined at a point like the limbs to the trunk in the human groin.

This system of vaulting it was easy to apply either to the nave, leaving the aisles with wooden roofs, or to the aisles only with wooden roofed nave; but to vault both at the same time, using only the Roman round arch, was a problem of some difficulty. For, if the width of the nave was taken as the size of the square of vaulting, the vaults of the narrower aisles, springing from the piers of the wider nave, become oblong in plan, the arches across the aisles being only half the size of those into the nave (fig. 31), and the vaults rising from these lower arches to the higher ones having an awkward domical appearance.

If, again, the aisle vaults, as well as those of the nave, were made square in plan, each square of the nave corresponding with two squares of the aisles on each side (fig. 32), the thrust of the nave vault was brought on every second pier only.

When semicircular arches only are used, those across the diagonals of the square of vaulting being larger and higher than those of the sides of the square, the windows under them cannot be as high as the centre of the vault.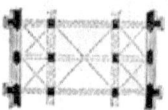

Fig. 32. VAULTING SQUARE IN PLAN.

Light is thus lost, and a mass of dead wall is needed over the clerestory windows to form a level bearing for the beams of the roof above the central vault. In other positions, also, the round arch was found awkward. Where the piers were close together, as round the apse of a church, the arches resting on them, had to be "stilted," as it is called, in order that their crowns might be on the same line as those of the wider arches down the sides of the church; that is, they were perched on the top of straight piers, down which their mouldings were continued to the line of the capitals.

By the use of the pointed arch, all these difficulties were got over. By means of it arches of different spans could be made all the same height. By breaking the round arch into two parts, attached by a point at the top, the arch could be widened or narrowed like a pair of compasses, and by adding to the length of the legs in the longer stretches, it could be kept the same height as in the narrower stretches.

In this way the determination to render churches fireproof by means of vaulting produced the pointed style of architecture which we call Gothic. In consequence of being so constructed, our old cathedrals have been preserved to us. Canterbury and Chartres, in our own time, Rheims in the sixteenth century, have had their wooden roofs which covered the vaulting destroyed by fire, without injuring the buildings under them.

Fig 33. VAULTS OF NAVE OBLONG IN PLAN.

For some time after the discovery of the pointed arch the width of the nave, as in fig. 32, continued to be taken as the size of the square of vaulting, the aisles also being vaulted in square compartments, two to each square of the nave on each side. The defect of the thrust of the nave vault coming on each second pier only was partially obviated by springing a subsidiary rib from the intermediate pier, thus dividing the vault into six parts, instead of four, whence this method is called sexpartite vaulting (fig. 32). Taking the width of the aisles as the size of the square of vaulting, which the use of the pointed arch rendered possible, obviated all difficulties (figs. 33 and 34). The central nave vault became thereby oblong, its length the width of the nave, its breadth the

Fig. 34. VAULTS OF NAVE OBLONG IN PLAN.

width of the aisles, and the arches across the nave twice the span of those against the clerestory walls, which, springing from the same piers as the nave arcade, were of the same span. (Fig. 33.) The clerestory windows were raised to the full height of the apex of the central vault, sometimes even higher, and the thrust of the vault was equal on each pier. Thus, by the use of the pointed arch the problems of making both nave and aisles fireproof by vaulting, of bringing the thrust of the vault equally on every pier, and of making the vaults at the side walls and across the church as high as the diagonal vaults, were completely solved.

Fig. 35.   ROUND-HEADED WINDOW UNDER POINTED VAULT.

Even after the vaults became pointed, the windows under them continued round-headed in form. (Fig. 35.) But a round arch under a pointed one leaves a space something like an arrow-head in shape between them, which it was soon seen could be made available as window. The shapes of the windows were therefore made the same as that of the vaults, and the same form was, from the principles of harmony, carried out everywhere throughout the building.

The development of the style was doubtless influenced not only by the mechanical requirements of which we have traced the development, but by the sense of beauty in the mind of its inventors, and by the environment in which they found themselves placed. If, in the problem which they had to solve, they had been guided purely by mathematical principles, they would have found a more perfect solution, not in the pointed but in the elliptical arch. By means of it arches of different spans could have been made to intersect with perfect mathematical accuracy without recourse to the expedient which, in the light of mathematics, is a clumsier one, of vaulting ribs. But in the light of art the result would have been far less beautiful, and even if they had possessed mathematical knowledge sufficient for working out their problem by the use of the elliptical arch, their instinct as artists would have prevented them from adopting it. Besides this, opportunity had made them acquainted with the pointed arch. The Crusades had carried them to the East, which was its birthplace, and where they would see it still in use.

Sir Gilbert Scott, in his lectures on Mediæval Architecture to the Students of the Royal Academy, opposes the theory I have attempted to state, that the introduction of the pointed arch was due to the necessities of vaulting. Describing the difficulty of groining oblong bays, he says,[1] "The mathematical solution of the problem would have been to make the section of the narrower vault an upright *semi-ellipse*; but this does not appear to have been at any period adopted, or, if at all, in exceptional cases only. The pointed arch would have been an approximate expedient, and its introduction has been very ingeniously attributed to this difficulty—a theory to which I shall have again to allude." The architects of the south of France, he states (page 58, vol. i.), adopted the pointed vault in their barrel

[1] Vol. i. p. 57.

vaults as having less outward thrust, "the same expedient was now had recourse to for groined vaulting, the main arches of which were, towards the middle of the twelfth century, changed from the semi-circle to the pointed arch." "It will be seen from the above" (he continues in page 61) "that the pointed arch was not introduced into Mediæval structure from mere caprice—merely from seeing it elsewhere, and taking a fancy to its form—but from the necessities of construction; from its increased strength and diminished thrust. It was used at first for the main arch only of the greater vault. The same reason soon led to its introduction wherever great weight was to be carried, as under towers, etc.; but for all small arches the semi-circle was long retained. I have alluded to the very beautiful theory that it was introduced for the side arches of oblong groins, simply as a means of obtaining arches of equal height, with only half the span of those of the main vault. True it is that, at a later date, it became most useful for this purpose. But a careful study of the monuments, in which it is first systematically used, clearly shows that its introduction was from *statical*, and neither geometrical nor merely æsthetical motives; for in the face of that theory we find the narrower arch or wall-rib remaining round, long after the wider arch had become pointed. Such is the case in nearly all the earlier French transitional churches, as at Noyon and at St. Germain des Prés, and we see the same at Canterbury. In most of these buildings the narrow arch is semi-circular and stilted, and the crown of the cross vault raised, as before described, thus losing a part of the clerestory wall, a disadvantage obviated when the pointed arch became more frankly acknowledged."

But the theory of the adoption of the pointed arch in vaulting, as I understand it and have attempted to state it, is not as Sir Gilbert Scott here implies, that it was in order to make the narrow side arch of an oblong vault as high as the wider cross arch. Where the pointed arch was demanded, in vaults whether square or oblong in plan, was where it was first used, in the *cross* arches; so that their crown might be as high as that of the *diagonal* arches, and the height of the church continuous along its length. As the windows in the clerestory wall were small, there was no need of increasing the height of the vault over them, and the accustomed round form was continued, till a growing sense of harmony made the wall vault also pointed. I therefore think that though in vaults oblong in plan, the smaller arch at the wall continued round after the cross vault became pointed, this does not disprove the theory that the use of the pointed arch was due to the constructive necessities of vaulting. It solved the problem of making the arches across the church as high as the diagonal arches of the vault. Sir Gilbert Scott considers that the pointed arch was adopted " from *statical*, and neither geometrical nor merely æsthetical motives" (p. 61, vol. i.), as having less outward thrust, the first situations in which it was used being the wide spanning arches of vaulting, and the arches carrying central towers and gables, and afterwards in the wide arches of nave arcades (pp. 235-6, vol. i.). But, as a matter of fact, geometrical reasons are stronger than statical, for its adoption in the arches across the nave. Round arches could be made to stand in this position, and did stand, even with the rude building and imperfect buttressing of the early architects, and they also carried securely towers and gables. But only a pointed arch across the church could have its crown as high as that of the diagonal arch of the vault; and, as the arches carrying towers and gables were continuations of these cross arches, they were naturally made of the same pointed form. The pointed arch, therefore, was not necessary for statical reasons, but it made the development of vaulting possible, and we may therefore conclude that its introduction was due to this cause.

A new impulse was given to the art of vaulting by the invention of VAULTING-RIBS. In Roman groining the angle of the groin consists merely of a line formed by the intersection of the two vaults, and the same system is followed in the earlier Romanesque buildings (see figs. 31 and 36). This line looks poor and weak, the vault seems to spring from a mere point. In St. Mark's, at Venice, the intersecting angles of the vaults are rounded to allow the coating of mosaic to be carried over them. The Romanesque builders disliked the harshness of square angles, and, in their desire to obtain effect by ornament, worked round moulding on the angles of their buttresses, and they did the same on the angles of intersection of the vaults (fig. 35) projecting them from the surface in the form of ribs, which gave the reality as well as the appearance of strength to the angles.

Fig. 36. GROINING WITHOUT RIBS.

The use of these ribs did not at first alter the principle of construction; each layer of stones in the vault was supported as before by the layer below it. But it gave facilities in construction unknown in Roman vaulting. In it the forms of the angles of the groins are determined by the junction of the *surfaces* of the crossing vaults. Where vaults of different sizes cross each other, the line produced by their meeting at the angle is curved, making a weak and unpleasant-looking line. In Gothic vaulting the *ribs* determine the lines of construction, they are the prominent parts which give the appearance and effect to the architecture; the surfaces are comparatively unobserved, they may meet each other at any angle without detriment to the appearance, the junction being concealed by the rib; and are sometimes twisted into forms like a ploughshare. By the use of ribs vaults of irregular plan with arches of different widths could be easily constructed, and be made to look satisfactory.

As the style advanced, these ribs were increased in number; instead of appearing merely on the cross arches, and the angles of the diagonal, the broad surfaces of the vault were broken up first by one then by more ribs (see B and C, fig. 45, p. 160). These additional ribs strengthened the vault, the surfaces, or filling in between the ribs, could be made thinner and the vault lighter, and consequently have less thrust. Æsthetical considerations may also have had some influence. The change was in harmony with others in the architecture; the surfaces of the windows also were broken up by the bars of tracery.

As the style progressed, the introduction of vaulting ribs changed the principle of construction in the vaulting. Instead of the vault being a broad arch surface, the ribs became its bearing lines, a skeleton of curved beams, supporting the surface of the vault, as iron beams support a concrete floor. This surface or filling in was formed of long stones or of flat arches, resting from rib to rib. In Roman vaulting the surface is the vault. In Gothic vaulting we might remove the surface and the vault would stand.

These ribs were made to spring each from a separate slender column, one of a cluster. As the style developed the columns and the vaulting ribs in late Gothic sometimes coalesced, the capitals dividing them became absorbed, the ribs rising without break from the base of the building to the crown of the arch. The feeling of ascent and growth thus given, with the branching groining ribs meeting overhead, gave rise to the popular theory that Gothic architecture sprang from an imitation of a forest with its spreading branches. The history of the style proves the theory erroneous; yet it is true that Gothic has in it something of the spirit and growth of forest life, as Greek architecture has sympathy with the higher forms of animal life.

The windows at first were small, leaving large surfaces of wall to be decorated with colour and painting, and the decoration was carried out over the windows also, by the use of stained glass. This latter mode of decoration, once introduced, was felt to be so brilliant and charming, that henceforth it ruled the development of the style. The object of every change was to reduce the surface of masonry, and give more space for stained glass. The small windows were put closer together, and the masonry between them reduced to single upright bars of stone, called mullions, narrow on the face but deep across the plane of the window, so as to give as much opening as possible for glass, while retaining strength. Openings shaped like flowers of three or four, or more leaves, were placed above them; the corners left between were pierced; the stone between these openings was reduced to bars bending round the foliated forms (to which the name of TRACERY is given); and thus at last one great window was formed, which filled the whole space under the vault (fig. 35).

These mullioned and traceried windows are one of the most charming features of Gothic architecture, so beautiful in themselves that, like Greek porticos, they have been used even when the causes which led to their adoption do not exist. In large windows, however—especially when these are used in the same building along with smaller ones—a division of their surface by some such means must always remain one of the simplest and most admirable means of producing architectural effect. Windows of all sizes can thus be brought into harmony with each other, an immense advantage in domestic architecture. The architecture of the walls is, as it were, carried over the windows by bars of stone, giving them greater strength and solidity and interest, than if they remained mere great holes in the wall.

The form of these stone bars will naturally partake of the constructive lines of the architecture. Under vaultings they will be curved, but when the architectural construction is altogether in perpendicular and horizontal straight lines, as in our ordinary domestic architecture, the straight form which bars of stone naturally take will be simpler and more suitable.

Gothic architecture had a magnificent opportunity of development in the construction of the great cathedrals, which, in France, were all built at the end of the twelfth and beginning of the thirteenth centuries.

These were civil as well as ecclesiastical buildings; in fact, the distinction between the two provinces was a thing unknown at the time, and is wholly a modern idea, which we never probably would have had, except for the differences in religious belief which arose among us at the Reformation. The State is merely the community acting in combination for those purposes in which combined is more convenient than individual action. With us its action is now almost confined to justice, police, war, and possibly education.[1] When religious belief was uniform, as in the Middle Ages, State action included religion. The bishops and abbots were feudal barons, with civil jurisdiction; and all State action had some religious character and sanction. The cathedrals were the great meeting-places of the city, used for secular purposes, such as the administration of justice, and even for histrionic performances[2] (which, again were religious in character), as well as for mass.

They sprung up just after the towns, along with the right to have walls, had attained freedom and privileges, of which

[1] This was written before the Elementary Education Act was passed.
[2] Viollet-le-Duc, 'Dictionnaire de l'Architecture.'

they remain the monuments; and as rivals to the great castles of the lay, and the monasteries of the religious barons. The bishops and secular clergy went heartily with the movement, which asserted for them the power and importance which had been largely absorbed by the monasteries. All the important towns seemed seized with a mania to rebuild their cathedrals with a magnificence previously unknown. The new architecture, taking nothing for granted, governed only by logical necessities of construction, is an expression of the rationalism of which Abelard sowed the seed in modern thought, though devoted, like him, to the service of the Church. The architects were laymen, for the most part, as in several instances given by Viollet-le-Duc we know from their names, and the representations which occur of some of them in the lay dress. He states that the regular clergy—those living under a rule, or monks, who had hitherto been the sole depositaries of art and culture—disliked the movement. It was natural that they should, for it meant that their use, and consequently their importance, was gone; and, after pointed architecture was invented, they still continued to practise their own old round-arched style.

This is the reason why the architecture of the French cathedrals is in almost every instance pointed, while in England it is generally round-arched. In France the cathedrals were rebuilt in the new style. They were the churches generally of the secular clergy, not of the religious orders. In England, in accordance with our spirit of compromise, our cathedrals were generally monasteries or minsters also, and were built while the round-arched style prevailed.

The main characteristics of Gothic are its system of pointed vaulting and its traceried windows, filled with stained glass. The former, in the course of development, led to other peculiar features, such as the clusters of slender columns, each carrying a vaulting rib, by which the lines of the ceiling were carried down to the floor, giving the feeling of height and ascending growth; to harmonise with which, and not from any necessities of structure or of climate,[1] the roofs were made steep and sharply pointed. The style possessed also a beautiful and vigorous style of carving, founded on natural foliage, and truthful and admirable modes of metal work.

The change to copying natural foliage for architectural ornament, instead of the carving of wild grotesques of the earlier round-arched style, which the Benedictines of Cluny carried to its greatest excess, is due not only to the decay of barbarism, and the growth of civilisation and refinement, but to the denunciations of St. Bernard. Preaching at Vezelay, where we can still see them,[2] "what business," he asked, "had these devils and monstrosities in Christian churches, taking off the attention of the monks from their prayers?" In the churches of the Cistercian order which he founded, his puritanism forbad ornament altogether, which does not, however, divest them of their art, but produces the manliest and severest type of Gothic. When the artistic genius of the people was untrammelled, it produced the exuberance of decoration inspired by the appreciation of the beauty of foliage, which usually characterises the style.

This cathedral-building mania (which was really analogous to the railway mania of our own day) lasted in France just about eighty years, the cities then ceasing to find that their privileges and the importance of the clergy (even of the secular clergy) were identical. Strifes arose, the clergy forbad the use of the cathedral bells for town meetings; the building impetus stopped before a single cathedral was

[1] The climate of Switzerland is as severe as ours, yet the roofs of Swiss chalets have a very flat pitch.
[2] These old sculptures at Vezelay have lately been almost completely destroyed by restoration.

finished, and though parts have since been built, most of them are unfinished, and not one has been completed according to the original design.

The style thus developed was, of course, used for other purposes than churches. The possibility of building in any other style than the prevalent one, or even the existence of any other, was inconceivable in times when Roman emperors were represented sitting under pointed arches; and scenes of the New Testament were conceived of as transacted in mediæval cities, by people dressed in mediæval costume.[1]

Castles and houses were therefore built in Gothic, and the mouldings and minor ornaments were the same as in churches. Pointed windows and tracery, however, it was found necessary from the first to modify; while between vaulted floors, when height was valuable, flat arches segments of a circle, were adopted.

Very few specimens of Gothic houses remain anywhere. During the Middle Ages the style of living was poor and even miserable, as is proved by the general prevalence of leprosy, testified to by the necessity everywhere felt of establishing lazar houses. The disease has ceased in every European country except Norway, in parts of which the people are miserably fed.

The houses—except in the rich cities of Italy, one of which, such as Venice, had the wealth and power of a State like England—were generally poor and small. Many of them were built of wood, and in the course of centuries got out of repair; and almost everywhere the more comfortable style of living in every class of society, which the Revival brought with it, caused them to be rebuilt. In

---

[1] One of the most curious instances of this dormancy of the historical faculty occurs in a picture at Antwerp, of our Lord bearing His cross, in which the "stations" are marked by the usual crosses. A Calvary without the "stations" was inconceivable.

144   HOUSE ARCHITECTURE.

Nuremberg, though it possesses two noble Gothic churches, there few of the houses are older than the sixteenth century. Here and there in places whose prosperity had departed,

Fig. 37.   ROMANESQUE HOUSE AT BOPPART ON THE RHINE.

and the people were too poor to rebuild, Gothic houses still exist. One of the most important is the Goliath House, at Ratisbon (shown in fig. 38); so called from the gigantic

Fig. 38. GOLIATH HOUSE, RATISBON.

Fig. 39.   STREET IN RATISBON.

representation of David and Goliath which remains on its wall.[1]

The drawing of a street at Ratisbon (fig. 39) gives an idea of what a northern middle age city must have looked like. Every important house had its tower to defend it and to retire to in case of attack. In these houses there is no attempt at symmetry or regularity; the windows are of any size required, and are placed wherever convenience dictates. The pointed arch is used consistently throughout, the larger square windows being probably later insertions.

But in the application of Gothic to house building from the earliest period, the window openings were made square-headed. Numerous instances occur, where under a pointed arch the window openings are square. Sometimes the pointed arch is purely ornamental, and carved on a simple straight lintel.

The pointed windows in the old house at Boppart on the Rhine (fig. 37, page 144), which appear to be a later alteration of the original design, illustrate this. They probably once had mullions.

The glass in houses was usually set in wooden frames so as to open like shutters, and the architects were too sensible to make these in a form so awkward for wood construction as a pointed arch. These frames of glass were moveable, and in royal progresses were sometimes removed with the furniture from one residence to another.

Even when, in great halls built for civil and domestic purposes, pointed vaults and pointed windows were used, the lower lights, being arranged to open for air and view, were always square-headed. The glass in the upper lights was fixed, being let into grooves in the stone as in church windows. In a house at Rheims, of which I give

[1] Since this illustration was drawn the painting on the house has been restored, and altered not only in colour but in form.

a sketch (fig. 40), called the House of the Musicians (from the statues in pointed arches between the windows, each with a musical instrument), which was built between the years 1240 and 1250, during the highest development of the pointed style; while the pointed arch is used for all the decorative features—such as the niches and the range of

Fig. 40. HOUSE OF THE MUSICIANS AT RHEIMS.

little arches supporting the cornice—it is frankly abandoned in the windows, where the form would not have been practical. The same tendency to abandon the pointed arch in domestic windows is found in England also, as may be seen in the illustration of Markenfield Hall, near Ripon, in Yorkshire (fig. 41), from Parker's 'English Domestic Architecture of the Middle Ages,' for the use of which I am indebted to the kindness of Mr. James Parker.

It is situated in Yorkshire, about two miles west of Ripon, and seems to me a charming example of an English Gothic house. The licence to crenellate it was obtained in 1310, and it was probably commenced about that time. The large traceried window in the view is the eastern window of the chapel, which, as well as the great hall, is on the upper story, in accordance with the custom of the

Fig. 41.   MARKENFIELD HALL, YORKSHIRE.

fourteenth century. The windows to the right are those of the Solar behind the dais of the hall. These are square-headed, evidently made so from necessity, the floor above or the ceiling not allowing space for an arch. Where there is space, the windows are arched.[1]

It may be urged against the statement that vaulting is an essential of Gothic architecture, that Gothic churches,

[1] Parker, quoting Mr. Twopenny. Vol. ii, p. 232.

as well as domestic buildings, in England especially, frequently had wooden ceilings, and this not always from economy, but, even where, as in St. Stephen's chapel at Westminster, the wealth of English art was lavished.

This, however, does not disprove the fact that the pointed style arose from necessities of vaulting; and, indeed, to the use of wooden roofs in England may, I think, be traced the abandonment of the pointed arch, and the adoption of the flattened perpendicular form : while in France, where the use of the vaulting was continued, the pointed arch also was retained to the last. The wooden ceiling left the walls divided into square-headed spaces (instead of the arched

Fig. 42. DECORATED WINDOW.   Fig. 43. PERPENDICULAR WINDOW UNDER LEVEL CORNICE.

ones under the vaulting), which a pointed window could not fill (fig. 42). The window arch formed, with the straight level cornice, awkward corner spaces, called spandrils, which there was always a difficulty to know what to do with. So the haunches of the arch were raised, making the window nearly square-headed, and adding the space occupied by the spandril to the amount of stained glass (fig. 43).

The lines of the flattened arch were drawn in various ways, usually from four centres. Sometimes the upper lines which meet at the apex are quite straight, and in some cases the spandrils disappear altogether. So by gradual change the pointed arched window becomes a simple square-headed window filled with tracery.

Fig. 44.   HOUSE OF JACQUES CŒUR AT BOURGES.

In every instance, in fact, in the history of the style in which the use of pointed vaulting was given up, the abandonment of the pointed arch followed sooner or later.

I have stated that it was not from any necessities of climate or construction that the roofs were made steep pitched, but to harmonise with the tendency to height and upward growth which was characteristic of the rest of Gothic architecture. When in English Gothic the horizontal cornice became predominant, and the arches became flattened, the roofs, as we shall see, became flattened in sympathy. In France the arches remained pointed, and the roofs continued steep pitched. The tendency in the later French Gothic was rather to increase their height. These tall steep roofs became a feature of French architecture, and continued to characterise it when the Gothic styles had passed away, and had been superseded by the Classic.

The house of Jacques Cœur, at Bourges, illustrates this. It was commenced in the middle of the fifteenth century (he purchased the site in 1443), and is one of the most splendid specimens which exist of Gothic domestic architecture. I have given plans of the ground-floor and first-floor in the sketch of the history of planning in Chapter I. vol. ii. p. 28, figs. 139, 140. Fig. 44 shows part of the front, comprising the main entrance, with the chapel over it, and the turret which contains the stair leading to the chapel, carried up into a tall stone roof like a spire. The chapel is vaulted and its window is pointed. The other windows throughout the building are square-headed.

Till the end of the thirteenth century the development of Gothic architecture, as I have described it, was similar in France, England, and Germany.

There are some slight national differences, but every advance of the art was common to the civilisation of these countries. It was even carried as far as Norway, where the Cathedral of Drontheim, built in the thirteenth century, is in the ordinary style of the period. It is built of stone, not in the national wooden construction which the Norwegians did not abandon for ordinary churches. But the style of their carving in wood, which has always been a national art—prosecuted during the six months of continual night in winter—became, and still continues, thirteenth century Gothic in character.

This similarity of style in the different countries of Europe was largely due to the organisation of the great monastic orders, who sent missionaries to found new houses and establish religion and civilisation in outlying districts, as well as to the unity of the Church under the Pope. The new inventions of architecture were carried everywhere, as those of engineering are at the present day.

During the fourteenth century, when the style was established, each country took it into its own hands and developed it into a national style of its own. It is absurd to call these later styles degraded, as has been the fashion of late. Each of them, if studied without prejudice, will be seen to have developed characteristic and interesting, and often noble qualities of architecture.

One common quality they had, as compared with the earlier style—greater lightness and elegance in construction, more window in proportion to wall, giving that effect of space, and height, and light, in the interior, which is the glory of Gothic.

This was attained by more scientific construction and greater mechanical skill, which enabled the builders to dispense with the masses of material necessary in the earlier style. The interior of the church of St. Étienne du Mont in Paris—a last expiring effort of Gothic—commenced in 1537, when Classic influence had begun to affect the forms and details—exhibits the lightness and aspiration which are characteristic of the style more perfectly than purer examples.

The same lightness and excellent construction is characteristic of German Gothic, and especially of our English Perpendicular.

So far as practical convenience is concerned, one of these great Perpendicular churches, unencumbered by massive columns, with its feeling of space, is more suitable for our congregational purposes, than those built in what is considered the more perfect periods of Gothic.

The skill in mechanical construction made wonderful feats of masonry a characteristic of these later styles. Great pendants are suspended in a mysterious way from the roofs. The stone is twisted about like willow wands. The mouldings interpenetrate, the design disappearing as if into the stone and coming out again. Great spires are made of open lace work.

These later styles of France, England, and Germany, were also characterised by a completeness in carrying out the design which was sometimes lacking in the earlier style, even, for instance, in the noble south porch of Chartres Cathedral. But by continual slight improvements and refinements roughnesses were toned down, and hitches where parts did not fit perfectly together were removed, not without some loss of the earlier strength and vigour.

In the tracery of the later styles there was also a common character. As has been explained, tracery arose from combining into one large window the narrow windows and the trefoils and quatrefoils over them in the thin wall which closed the space below the pointed vault. The effect of the window depended on the disposition of these flower-shaped piercings, which seen from the inside showed as forms of light, from the outside as dark forms; leaving between them paces in the stone plate in which they were pierced, of any shape that happened to turn out. The irregular shape of these stone interstices was felt to be an imperfection. The development of tracery consisted in giving form and beauty of line to them as well as to the openings. In the windows of St. Stephen's Chapel, Westminster (fig. 42, page 152), this attained equally for both. In the art of this period tracery reached its highest perfection. But the process could not stop, for growth is the condition of life, sometimes, as in this case, of a life that had passed its prime and was drawing on to decrepitude and death.

Attention was more and more given to the solids, instead of the openings of the tracery. The stone was reduced to regular bars, and the forms and dispositions of these became the objects of design, producing what is called bar tracery, as distinguished from the early form, which is called plate tracery, from the openings being pierced in a plate of stone.

But with these fundamental points of character in common the later Gothic styles were strikingly different in outward form and appearance. In French Gothic, as has been stated, pointed vaults were retained, and the form of the great windows, filling the wall space under these, continued pointed.

In harmony with the curved forms of the arch, and in the desire for increased softness and refinement of line, the bars of the tracery were bent into curved flowing lines, like the form of the flame of a torch, whence this kind of tracery is called Flamboyant. The chapel of Jacques Cœur's house, at Bourges (fig. 44), illustrates these flowing lines of tracery which are playfully formed at the top into a fleur-de-lis.

In the church of St. Eustache, in Paris, commenced in 1532, in the last stage of Gothic, when the Classic influence had begun to prevail, the tracery of the windows is bent into the shape of hearts and ovals. The softness and sweetness of the flowing lines had begun to pall. In spasmodic efforts to avoid this, by producing new sensations, the forms of the tracery became sometimes uncouth and ugly.

But in the glory of the stained glass, with which the windows were filled, this was not marked. The buildings were light and splendid, rich in delicate carving, relieved by intervals of plain simple masonry which gave massiveness and strength.

In English Gothic also, in the later decorated style while it still retained the pointed arch, the forms of the tracery were flowing, and the design often beautiful. They never sunk to the degeneracy of the later French and German. The latest Gothic of England took a different direction. The explanation I have ventured to suggest, that the arches became flattened as a consequence of the adoption of wooden ceilings, is not disproved by the fact that vaulted churches were built in which the vaults were of the same flattened form. The vaults were flattened to suit the windows. The architecture gave up the tendency to curvature of line which marked the earlier styles; its masses and its lines were characterised throughout by a squareness of form in sympathy with the shape to which the windows were tending.

A peculiar character of the latest English Gothic is the singular system of vaulting, found I believe, in no other country, called from its resemblance to an open fan, *fan vaulting*.

It is found usually in conjunction with the flattened arch, and it has sometimes been imagined that the one feature was dependent on the other, that the flat arch was the cause of the fan vaulting, or the fan vaulting of the flat arch. The former cannot be the case, for instances of fan vaulting are found with sharp pointed arches, and we have seen that the flat arch arose from a different cause. The principle and origin of each are wholly independent.

I venture to give an explanation of the principle and origin of fan vaulting, which is so simple that it looks as if it were true. My only doubt is that, so far as I am aware, it is new.

I have already explained (page 138) how the broad surfaces, or filling in of the vault (A, fig. 45), were divided by intermediary ribs, first by a single one in each space as at B, then by several as at C.

It will be seen on the plan (B and C) that these ribs are all

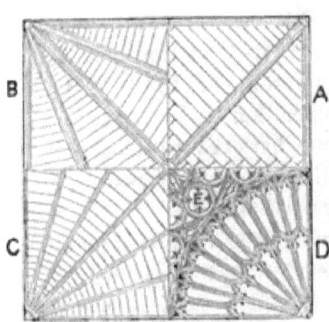

Fig. 45. PLANS OF VAULTING SHOWING DEVELOPMENT.

of different lengths, that they are like a badly shaped fan. The angle rib looks too prominent and awkward; the arrangement has an incomplete and unfinished appearance. This is got over by making all the ribs of the same length, by cutting off their points within the line of a quadrant as at D, thus making a perfectly-shaped fan.

But this breaks the continuity of the diagonal arches These fans or quadrants must tumble together unless the diagonal arch is completed by a keystone or its equivalent. For this purpose a ring is dropt in at E, formed of stones with radiated joints, which thus resist the inward thrust.

This ring we might fill in with a flat stone, or we might drop a pendant from it, like a stalactite from the roof of a cave. The construction seems to suggest this—and it did suggest it, as we know by innumerable examples.

The vaulting of the crossing of St. George's Chapel at Windsor (fig. 46) is a splendid example of fan vaulting. The nearer bay shows another mode of breaking up the

Fig. 46. VAULTING OF THE CROSSING, ST. GEORGE'S CHAPEL, WINDSOR.

surface of the vault, the ribs branching out as the spaces between them widen with carved bosses at the junction.

I have said that fan vaulting was not caused by the low Perpendicular arch, for it is found with sharp-pointed arches. But it is clear that its adoption must have made it more easy to vault with low flat arches, when the crown of the vault was a flat stone or a descending pendant, instead of an ascending point.

In the latest style of English Gothic the tracery of the window heads ceased to flow, and became straightened into upright bars, whence the style derives its name of Perpendicular. But, as expressing the true character of the style, the name (like Gothic itself, 'Queen Anne,' and so many others in architecture) is a misnomer. The main lines of the style, as compared with those of any other style of Gothic in England or elsewhere, and the disposition of masses which give it its character, are *horizontal*, in sympathy with the level cornice which, I think, determined its origin. Perpendicular architecture loses the tendency which every other form of Gothic had to increase the height of the building by high peaked roofs, which specially characterises the contemporary styles in France, where the roofs (as we have seen) became steeper than ever. The roofs are flattened to a lower pitch than that of a Greek temple; among the lines of the tracery straight horizontal bars are introduced, the horizontality of which is strengthened by treating them as cornices with miniature battlements (fig. 43, p. 152). The pointed windows in a tier one above the other, in each bay, no longer lead the eye upward ;. but, square in form, they are massed close together in long horizontal lines of light. The belfries cease to be drawn up into spires, and become square towers, finished at the top with a level cornice and parapet. In domestic architecture the sweet low level lines of the Tudor house, in which the roof is often so low as to be concealed by the parapet, are in direct contrast to the tall peaked roofs of the French château of the same period, which still inherited the Gothic principle of height. In Morton Hall (fig. 47), the low-pitched roofs and long ranges of low lights exhibit this tendency. If the name of the style is to be descriptive of its character, it should be called the Horizontal variety of Gothic, instead of 'Perpendicular.'

It has been the fashion to abuse our English Perpendicular churches, and much beautiful work in the style has in the last few years been destroyed, though it had three centuries of antiquity to boast of, because the clergyman or architect disliked it, and preferred a modern imitation of the earlier style.[1]

The dislike to Perpendicular architecture in which we have all been trained has arisen, I believe, from our judging it through the modern imitations of the last generation. For a like reason it is perhaps possible the earlier styles may find little favour with the coming generation. But if we look at the Perpendicular style only in its genuine productions we can appreciate its high artistic qualities.

[1] It is dismal to think of the destruction of historical monuments of the last three centuries, which the demon of "Restoration" has perpetrated in this generation. Perpendicular windows everywhere have been destroyed, as in the great church at Yarmouth, where some which contained old stained glass have been replaced by modern ones. The outlines of churches which have been landmarks for centuries (e.g., Durham Cathedral, and Jarrow Church) have almost everywhere been altered; the towers often swamped by tall new roofs of bright tiles with ornamental ridging, replacing the old flat lead roofs, which, by the contrast, gave them *presence* and dignity. Thus, every now and then some ignorant person, making the obvious discovery that the beautiful Perpendicular porch in the centre arch of the front of Peterborough Cathedral is not part of the original design, proposes to remove it. This porch is an instance, among many, of the skill of the Perpendicular architects in the disposition of the masses of their buildings so as to produce architectural effect. Without it the look of size in the three great arches would be gone; and it has been most skilfully designed so as to hide the disagreeable effect of the middle arch being the narrowest. At St. Albans the flat roof of oak and tiles, though the architect has declared it can be made sound, is to be covered by a tall one of deal; the object apparently being to produce a steep gable at the west end, and so give an excuse for a new front and the destruction of the great perpendicular west window.

Fig. 17.

MORTON HALL, CHESHIRE.

By its common sense and severity it saved English Gothic from the looseness and degradation in striving after new sensations into which Gothic fell in other countries.

So long, for instance, as the piercings were the guiding features of the tracery, it was right that the form should be foliated; but when the bars of stone became predominant, it was more in accordance with common sense that these should be straight, than twisted and contorted into curves.

In few styles of architecture has there been a truer sense of proportion, or greater skill in the disposition of the masses. In the grandeur of its towers it is unsurpassed, and the appearance of height in these is increased by the low roofs and the prevalence of the horizontal line, for which there is the authority of Greek architecture.

GERMAN GOTHIC.—One marked characteristic of the latest German Gothic is skill in performing wonderful feats in masonry. The art was in the hands of the masonic guilds, whose members, clever and highly-trained workmen rather than artists, thought the highest result attainable in architecture was to produce curiosities of workmanship, in forms that seemed impossible in the material.

Great spires, as that of Freiburg, were constructed wholly of open tracery. The plans of spires are sometimes altered at each stage, so as to make difficulties, which skill in construction might overcome. Wonderful double corkscrew staircases, each twisting round the other, were made in some spires; and such feats were thought more of than the outline. Mouldings were made to interpenetrate; as for instance, an octagon moulding on the base of a column being made to look as if disappearing in a circular one, and then show itself again. Some of the shrines in which the Sacrament was kept are marvellous examples of this laborious playfulness. They run up in tall pinnacles, composed wholly of the most elaborate open work; sometimes they are made as if they had grown too tall for the church, but the top, just before it strikes the ceiling, bends and turns round into a crook.

In Germany, as in other countries, the tracery abandoned geometric forms and became flowing in character like the French flamboyant. A favourite form for filling the circle at the head was one which may be made out in one of the chapel windows of the Gothic house at Boppart (fig. 49, page 176) in which the flowing lines form a figure like tadpoles chasing one another.

The over sweetness and softness of the forms of flowing tracery, which began after a time to be felt everywhere, was counteracted in Germany, and a foil given by simply breaking off the lines of the tracery and letting them end in a broken stump, whence the variety is called Stump Tracery.

In the fine *Eckfenster*, or corner-oriel, at Augsburg, fig. 48, this kind of tracery is used as panel decoration, and also to support the base of the window, where it takes the form of intertwining branches. It looks almost as if its designers had believed in the theory that this was the origin of Gothic, and wished to illustrate it. The introduction of such forms shows that no farther advances were to be made in the style by legitimate methods—that it was becoming worked out. It was a sign of old age, and showed that its end was near. The term " degraded," which is applied to the style which produces them, is in a sense true. It has not the simple and direct beauties of the earlier styles which found a legitimate architectural effect in the necessities of construction; but its results are picturesque and interesting, and often beautiful, and it produced noble buildings, of which the nation is justly proud.

Such an explanation of the development of Gothic architecture as we have attempted to give, showing its principles, and the purposes which it was created to serve, enables us

Fig. 48.   CORNER-ORIEL AT AUGSBURG.

to form an opinion as to its suitableness for our domestic architecture.

It disposes at once of several arguments against our using Gothic. It has been asserted that the style is gloomy and dark, and does not give sufficient light. Now, one of its chief characteristics, as has been shown, is that it is all window—that the main aim in its development was to reduce the surface of the wall, and increase the space for stained glass. No doubt old Gothic castles had little window light, and this characteristic, adopted for purposes of defence, has been sometimes foolishly copied in modern Gothic houses; but it was no essential of the style.

It is called a barbarous product of the dark ages, when the people were serfs; and one of the means by which a rich and powerful clergy kept them in ignorance and darkness. On the contrary, it was the product of the revived intelligence of the people, the outcome and sign of their civil freedom; and it gives evidence of a development of art, of skill and refinement and grandeur in building, such as we are incapable of furnishing.

It is said to be a style purely ecclesiastical; it was just as much civil. In fact, in its origin, it was the lay style of architecture, as distinguished from the religious or monastic.[1] That the monastic buildings in England and Scotland are frequently of pointed architecture, is due to the fact that the development of the monastic system took place later with us than in France, after the Gothic style was formed.

But is there anything in the Gothic style which makes it (as is often asserted) more suitable than any other for our modern houses? For this it is not sufficient that it appears to us more beautiful than any other. Our grandfathers thought Greek porticoes so beautiful, that they were willing to block up their window-light to have them. We see now that this

[1] See the evidence given by M. Viollet-le-Duc, 'Dictionnaire de l'Architecture.'

practice was absurd (though Mr. Ayrton has repeated it in his new Post Office) ; that it destroys not only the expression of truth in the houses, but the beauty of the portico, by using it where it has no meaning. No architecture can be satisfactory, even from an artistic point of view, whose forms are not founded on use.

The Gothic system of vaulting does not suit our ordinary domestic requirements. For great halls, where any amount of height can be given, the height occupied by the pointed vault is no disadvantage. But it is one, in a building divided into stories, as our houses are ; and if in special building we want fireproof construction, we can get it conveniently and cheaply by means of iron and brick, or concrete, in the usual thickness of a floor, without the loss of space which would be involved between the springing of the vault and a level floor over its crown.

In the modern revival of the style, however, in not one in a hundred of our churches,[1] and in houses still seldomer, has any attempt been made to revive vaulting. It is therefore hardly necessary to urge that a thing is unsuitable for us which we are never likely to use. Nor would the system of vaulting by flat arches be tolerated by us inside our houses. It would be thought prison-like and dismal, and, from its expense, it could never come into general use.

From the example of the practice of mediæval architects in domestic buildings, it is obvious that if we adopt Gothic architecture for our houses now, we ought to dispense with the use of the pointed arch.

Yet, as in all copying, it is the form, and not the spirit of the original, which is apt to be retained, our architects

---

[1] Modern French churches are often vaulted in stone; but even in restoring ancient buildings it appears to be too expensive for our use. Sir Gilbert Scott, after describing the vaulting of Nantwich Church in Cheshire, in his Lectures on Mediæval Architecture (vol. ii. p. 212), says, " I am imitating this to a certain extent in timber in the vaulting of the nave of Chester Cathedral, where, though the springers exist, the vaulting has never been completed."

and builders think they are working in the Gothic style when they put a pointed arch where it is not wanted, and means nothing—possibly an arch one brick thick on the face of a wall, supported by a wooden lintel inside—while the whole construction and details of the house follow the ordinary Classic traditions.

Old Gothic attempted honestly and fearlessly whatever use or necessity dictated. It has always the merit of truthful and apparent construction. But this to some extent unfits the style for modern use. It involves, unless when money could be lavished in decoration, an appearance of severity which does not accord with our modern feelings, and is least appreciated by the poorer and less educated, in whose houses, did we attempt really to carry out the principles of the style, it would be thoroughly disliked. Even in houses where no expense is spared, we should not like the appearance, however truthful it might be, of stone arches inside our rooms.

Moreover truthfulness of construction cannot be classed among the excellences of modern Gothic. The copiers of the style, after the manner of copyists, are very apt in their zeal for the form to neglect the spirit. Few better illustrations of this could be given than the polished oak boxes given as wedding presents, with magnificent brass hinges meandering over them, which make it seem as if no amount of wear or ill-usage could separate the lid. Unfortunately, those great hinges have no joint; the work is done by a little feeble one, which it is attempted to conceal, fastened by two minute screw-nails; so that, with all its appearance of massive strength, the lid could be prised open with a penknife. Of course a hinge is stronger if the tail is well fastened to the wood, and the old architects spread the hinges all over their church doors, in all sorts of playful, twisted forms; but they were always the strengthening of a real hinge. So different is the modern Gothic practice of ornamental door hinges, that the workmen's ordinary name for them is "the shams."

Again, why should Gothic grates have "fire dogs"? Before the forests were cut down, when people burnt wood, they were necessary in the great old open hearths, for resting the logs on, to let air under them to keep them burning; but it is sham Gothic to stick them on a grate for burning coals. And why should our gasaliers be made like the old coronas? These were great rings or hoops, suspended from the ceiling, with candles stuck round the circle. When the gasalier is very large, and the lights numerous, this may still be a convenient arrangement for gas-lights; but in a four-light dining-room gasalier, the brass hoop is perfectly useless, and it obstructs a great deal of light. Such a design, though a revival of a Gothic form, is contrary to the spirit of the style.

It is seldom that architecture has founded itself strictly on constructive necessities, using only such ornament as grew naturally out of the construction and thus explained and enforced it. The human mind moves so slowly, and clings to old habits so long, that for centuries after a nation has given up wood construction, we find it copying wooden forms in stone buildings. In the gateways of Hindoo Topes, of one of which there is a reproduction in the South Kensington Museum, enormous trouble and expense has been taken to procure posts and cross-bars of stones like long logs of wood; and of course the nail-heads, which in wooden construction fastened the logs, are carefully carved in the stone. Even in Greek architecture, the triglyphs which divide the frieze into spaces are said to be the reminiscence of the notched ends of the wooden beams of the roof. The decoration of Roman architecture has nothing to do with its construction, but is the artistic expression of a wholly different one. In fact, the history of all arts and ornament consists very much in tracing ornamental forms back to some long-forgotten use which gave rise to them. Illustrations without end might be given, but the following are as good as any. The holes arranged in waves and zigzags on the toe-caps of shooting-boots are a reminiscence of the old Highland brogues of untanned leather, which allowed the water to soak through them, and consequently had to be provided with little holes at the toes, where it squirted out again with the pressure of each step. Again, the bands on the backs of books have similarly now no constructive use, except in some of the best-bound books, in which they still cover the cords to which the pages are sewed. Such features in an art are not unnatural; on the contrary they are analogous to the imperfectly developed organs of animals, which performed functions in the ancestors of the species, now superseded from change of habit, and development of the organism.

In the later stages of Gothic architecture the same tendency shows itself. The Gothic house at Boppart, illustrated on the next page, shows a common mode of fortifying mediæval houses, by projecting turrets at the angles hung out on corbels, with openings at the bottom, from which stones and molten lead could be thrown down on assailants.

In the Nassauer House, at Nuremberg (fig. 50), there are similar turrets at the angles, which are useless for defence. They have no openings at the bottom through which missiles might be hurled. Nor do they fulfil any other purpose of use or convenience. They are purely ornamental; but I feel thankful to the architect for putting them there. Their beauty, and the character they give to the building, is to me sufficient justification for their existence.

Modern Gothic shows the same tendency. In the new Gothic Hotel at St. Pancras Station, which is a splendid example of the style, it cannot be said that the specially Gothic features, such as the pointed windows filled with

Fig. 49. GOTHIC HOUSE AT BOPPART ON THE RHINE.

tracery, are the outcome of any modern hotel requirements. Pointed windows are inconvenient for blinds and curtains and reduce the light at the top where it is of most value for lighting the room. The tracery still further obstructs

Fig. 50.   THE NASSAUER HOUSE AT NUREMBERG.

it, and it is scarcely sufficient justification for it that the circles in it are utilised as ventilators.

The beauty of the architecture may be sufficient compensation for the inconvenience and expense which the use of the style involves, but when applied to modern domestic use it has not the justification which has been claimed for it, that its features are the outcome of use and convenience.

To the earlier development of the old Gothic architecture belongs the almost singular merit of perfect truthfulness. When a form ceased to have meaning, it was frankly given up; people did not, as in most other styles, weakly cling to the dead carcass. Instead of the ignorance and darkness usually attributed to the Middle Ages, there is a freshness and independence of thought rare in the history of humanity, and a wealth of artistic conception employed in making every new necessity beautiful, which few races have possessed. If we could but do likewise, the result of working on the principles of Gothic architecture would be something very different from pointed Gothic. We should have no pointed windows, and quatrefoils, and buttresses which receive no thrust. We should not have in stone-work chamfer-stops, at the angles of windows, simulating wooden framed work; and all sorts of ugly and unmeaning notchings; and roofs so steep, that they endanger men's lives.[1] We should ruthlessly abandon unsuitable forms, not developed by our modern necessities, even though we admire them for their beauty. Can it be said that the Gothic revival has exhibited these signs of the true Gothic spirit? On the whole, certainly not; and we fear that such vices as appear in it are almost inseparable from the attempt to apply a thirteenth-century style to nineteenth-century use; that

[1] In old buildings these steep roofs had usually a parapet at the cornice, which saved any workman, slipping on them, from falling over the wall.

the Gothic style is, in fact, *the artistic expression of an obsolete mode of construction.*

As a matter of fact the attempt to introduce Gothic as the style for our domestic architecture has failed. The instances in which there has been any serious endeavour to build Gothic houses have been rare, and in these the style has shown itself as an external application of ornament not demanded by the necessities of convenience and construction. Under a pointed vault a pointed arch gives more light, but under a level ceiling it diminishes the light where it is of most value for lighting the room, not only by cutting away the corners at the top of the window and leaving useless spandrils (fig. 42 page 152), but by filling the window head with stone tracery, which not only blocks out light but is inconvenient for opening, and unsuitable for roller blinds. Hence pointed windows are not insisted on in modern Gothic, and when they are gone there is not much of the style left; for, in the mode of construction and the internal fittings of houses, the Gothic revival has had little or no influence. In most Gothic parsonages and mansions (except in some rare instances where the funds at command have permitted the expense of vaulted halls), walls and roofs, ceilings, floors, and windows are made in the ordinary way. Sometimes the architect, aiming at perfect truthfulness of construction, has left the brick-work unplastered, though that was not the practice in old Gothic; or has omitted the plaster ceiling of the rooms, leaving the joists visible, or substituting wooden boarding instead, making the floor less sound proof, and greatly increasing the risk from fire. But usually the common traditional construction is adopted, with Gothic details and ornament, wherever is opportunity of using them. These opportunities are rare; for the peculiarities of Gothic detail spring from stone construction, and it is difficult to express them in the wood and plaster fittings of our modern houses.

Plaster cornices and ornament, which give an air of finish to our commonest modern houses, were unknown in Gothic, as was also the modern system of wood panelling in doors and shutters, till the style had passed into its later forms. The Perpendicular style ornamented the surface of panels with patterns like folds of linen, but this was too expensive for common use. The modern system of ornamenting panels by moulded slips of wood planted round the edge grew up under Classic influence and took Classic forms, and its use takes away the Gothic character from the house. For churches and for the outside doors of halls the panelling could be dispensed with. These might be made simply of planks or boards, and hung like old Gothic ones on iron hooks fixed in the stone. But the better fitting, and the avoidance of warping and shrinking which panelling secures, could not be dispensed with for inside work. It was consequently used without mouldings, the edges of the styles or framework in which it was fixed being merely chamfered. Hence arises an appearance of coarseness and poverty in the interiors of modern Gothic houses, a want of finish, which even the cheaper Classic houses possess.

Our common sash windows, which open by the two sashes hung by cords and weights sliding one past the other, have proved a difficulty to modern Gothic, never rightly got over. This kind of window, which came to us, I believe, with Dutch William, is now a part of our English constitution, and, during the thirty years of the Gothic revival, architects have been trying to work it into the style. It was absurd in a pointed window to let the top sash down, for a pointed frame was an awkward shape to fit, and the air space left when the sash was pulled down was of a most unconstructional form for wood-work, something like an arrow head. Sometimes no attempt was made to fit it to the pointed forms. It was set well back from the face of the wall, and the Gothic shaft and tracery put in front of it for ornament, like the Classic porticos in last century houses. Sometimes it was kept close to the tracery, a stone transom concealing the meeting-bars of the stone sashes. In this case the different planes of the upper and lower sash gave an awkward look, which was got over by making the sashes half or a third of the usual thickness, of seasoned oak. But these attempts only prove that to use sliding sash windows simply and honestly makes the architecture something else than Gothic.

So far, therefore, as truth in architecture is concerned, we are forced to admit that Gothic architecture, however beautiful it may be, is not the outcome of our modern habits and requirements, nor of the traditions and modes of work of our workmen. These are practically unaffected by the thirty years' crusade waged by our best writers and architects and the highest culture at the universities, supported by the country's wealth. It seemed at one time as if the best talent in painting and sculpture had ranged itself on the side of Gothic. Beauties, which for three centuries had been unnoticed, were found in the painting of the schools before the time of Raphael. Sculptors tried to forget what the Greeks had done, and saw, behind the imperfect forms of mediæval sculpture, the intensity and earnestness which breathed through them.

In poetry the subject which fired genius was King Arthur's round table and the deeds of his knights, as they were seen reflected in mediæval tales.

The wave has gone back, but it has quickened and revivified art, making it a matter of interest to every one, not a dead body of Classic rules, interesting only to the learned. Sculptors have returned to their allegiance to Greek forms. Pre-Raphaelite pictures are no longer painted. The great masters of the Renaissance are again the highest models. But the artists see with their own eyes, as they would not have done if they had not worked in the same school as that from which the Renaissance painters sprung.

In domestic architecture the tide is turning. Since I wrote these sentences six years ago, the change in feeling has been rapid. But we cannot go back to the dead Classic, from which Gothic was a reaction. The spirit and life which it has left us need freer forms for their expression.

I say nothing here about the architecture of churches. Gothic may still be the best expression of their purposes, since it was developed in building them. If so, the problem is not solved of finding a style which, like old ones, might be universal. Architecture cannot reach its highest development in merely utilitarian buildings, when it lacks the force of religious enthusiasm. But the practical evil of having separate styles for churches and for houses is not serious. Gothic has not failed in churches, for it has perfect models to follow, and no new wants to satisfy.

Churches too are simpler in their purposes, and can more easily be superintended throughout by an architect. In the greater number of our houses we are dependent on the workman; his ideas and capacities must in many points limit our art. To get art on these terms in our houses is an advance and a gain, for hitherto our houses, unlike churches, have been almost wholly outside its domain.

What little influence Gothic has had on ordinary house architecture has been deleterious. When set free from the well established laws which regulate it in churches, it lends itself with fatal facility to the expression of ignorance and ostentation, and, instead of architecture governed by beauty and refinement, produces masses of crude forms inspired only by unrest, loudness, and vulgarity. Better far the monotony of Gower Street. That at least does not cry out continually, "Come look at me." If it is dull it is at least quiet and unobtrusive. If not clever it is sensible and practical, for the workmen understood what they were doing. It is plain prose, while "fast" Gothic is hysterical sensational poetry, bristling with vulgarity and bad grammar. It is not understood by those who have to work in it, and the more it spreads the more is this apparent. After thirty years of careful tending the plant has not taken root in the soil.

Fig. 51.   HOHENZOLLERN.

CHAPTER VI.

GREEK ARCHITECTURE.

AMONG the styles of architecture which remain after eliminating all which were unsuitable for our use, as neither understood nor practised, we included Greek.

Till lately Greek architecture was unknown. It was known that Greek buildings existed, but they were included along with Roman ones under the general designation of "Classic." The publication in the end of last century, of Stuart and Revett's careful measurements and delineations of Greek buildings, in their 'Antiquities of Athens,' made evident the great divergence in form, and the essential difference in spirit between the two styles of architecture, and the immense superiority in beauty of line of the mouldings and ornament and refinement of the Greek, of which it was seen that the Roman was only a bad copy. Our possession of the Elgin Marbles created an enthusiasm for Greek art, and about fifty years ago every new building of importance was designed in the style. The most notable attempts are St. Pancras Church; the unfinished National

Monument at Edinburgh, and St. George's Hall at Liverpool. But the influence of the style permeated all architecture, and in every builder's house of the period we find attempts at Greek mouldings in the wooden doors, and enfeebled copies of the ornaments of the Parthenon in the plaster work.

Fig. 52. GRECIAN DORIC.—TEMPLE OF THESEUS, ATHENS.

Greek architecture grew in building temples. These consisted of an enclosed shrine, the dwelling of the god—the naos or temple proper—and porticos or sheds surrounding it, for the accommodation of the worshippers, formed by prolonging the temple roof beyond the walls and supporting it on columns. As these porticos were the visible part of the building, they determined the nature of Greek architecture, which consisted of stone columns supporting a roof, on which rested the *architrave*, great stone lintels from column to column. On it were placed the beams of the roof. The triglyphs with their notched ends (fig. 52) are said to be a reminiscence in the stone construction of the older wooden beams. These with the spaces between them, which were generally ornamented with sculpture in relief, are called the *frieze*; above them is the *cornice*, the crowning member, projected to throw off the wet, the raindrops hanging from its underside, being still represented, petrified into stone.

The ground idea of Greek architecture is weight adequately supported. It is a very simple idea. Some, like Mr. Ruskin and Mr. William Morris, hardly allow it to be architecture at all. A child or a savage can set up two stones and rest a third on the top of them. This primitive idea the Greeks held to with religious veneration, retaining every traditional form of it as sacred, even copying in stone the ends of the wooden beams of the earlier temples. This gives no ground for imagining as is sometimes done that the columns and lintels were once of wood. One may have a roof of wood on a stone building, and the form of the Doric column is certainly a tradition of ruder stone form. The square stone slab or abacus, resting on the capital, is no imitation of anything wooden. Its earliest examples are the most massive, and they would not have been so had they been imitations of wooden buildings. The Ionic capital perhaps suggests a wooden origin; a corbel with its ends rounded, set across a post to receive the lintel (fig. 54).

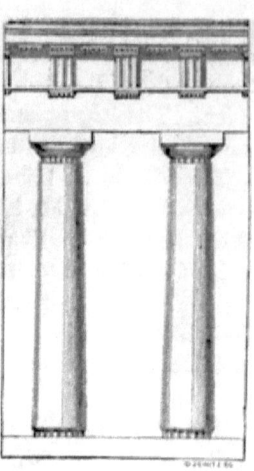

Fig. 53. GRECIAN DORIC.—TEMPLE OF APOLLO AT DELOS.

In Greek architecture there are three orders: the Doric, the Ionic, and the Corinthian.

The Doric (figs. 52, 53) was simple and massive, but, on account of its simplicity of form, it exhibits all the more clearly the proportion between the weight and its supports, which is perfectly adjusted. In the Parthenon the lines of every part are drawn with exquisite delicacy and refinement. None are quite straight, but all, not merely the columns but the walls and the steps, are gentle curves. There is no ornament in the architecture; nothing to interrupt the idea of great stones, each doing its work of supporting or being supported. Everything that might be called ornament is with a view to this end. The building stands on a platform of three steps so solid looking that the columns require no bases. The capitals are mere projections, their delicate curves indicating support of the mass above them. Their *entases* and flutings give them grace and ease in supporting the weight of the architrave, which remains merely a square stone. The triglyphs and the *guttæ*, or petrified raindrops, indicate the downward pressure of the entablature.

The temple at Paestum in the Greek colony of Magna Græcia, fig. 20, p. 56, is a magnificent specimen of the order. Whether because it is provincial work; or, possibly, because it is of earlier date, the style is ruder than at Athens; the capitals are more massive and have less refinement of line, but this does not detract from the grandeur of the architecture.

The Ionic (figs. 54 and 55) was lighter and more graceful in its proportions than the Doric, having the same relation to it in its proportions as a woman to a man. There is no doubt that, as its name implies, it is Asiatic in its origin, and that the spiral corners of the capital are a tradition of architectural forms of the ancient Asiatic monarchies. Representations of rude Ionic capitals are found in the Assyrian sculptures; and in ancient Persian architecture the capitals have Ionic volutes placed not across the top, but attached perpendicularly to the side.[1] The Greeks took the form and gave it new meaning and grace. These spiral curves of the Ionic capital may seem unmeaning. It is not the form which naturally suggests itself for support, but it is beautiful in itself, and it gives to the capital

[1] See Fergusson's 'History of Architecture,' vol. i. pp. 179, 196.

an impression of spring and elasticity. These two orders were used simultaneously by the Greeks. They are not successive developments of different ages, like the styles of Gothic architecture. Nor were they confined like national styles to districts of their own. One of the most splendid examples of the Corinthian order is the temple of Jupiter Olympus, at Athens, and one of the oldest and most

Fig. 54. ERECHTHEUM, ATHENS.   Fig. 55. TEMPLE ON THE ILISSUS.
GRECIAN IONIC.

remarkable examples of Doric is at Corinth, where no specimens of the Corinthian order now remain.

The proportions of these orders were not fixed by unalterable rules according to the "Classic" idea. The order of the Erechtheum (fig. 54) is about nine diameters high; that of the temple on the Ilissus (fig. 55), about seven and a half, the weight to be supported being more massive and simpler. Both are right, the various parts of the architecture being made to harmonise in their proportions.

The Corinthian is rather a Roman, than a Greek order, the examples of it which occur in Greece having been erected under its Roman masters. It is par-excellence the Roman order; they loved it for its magnificence and

Fig. 56. TEMPLE OF VESTA, TIVOLI.   *Fig.* 57. TEMPLE OF JUPITER OLYMPUS, ATHENS.

THE CORINTHIAN ORDER.

sumptuousness. In it spiral volutes, springing from a crown of acanthus leaves which surrounds the bell of the capital, mask the junction between the round bell and the corners of the abacus; which is not square in plan, as in the Doric, but hollowed in the centre and projecting at the angles.

We all know the story about the discovery of the Corinthian Capital, told in every treatise on the Orders, from

Vitruvius downwards, how a basket (shaped like those we use as waste-paper baskets), covered with a square tile or "abacus," having been left beside an acanthus plant, the plant climbed up the basket and turned round in spirals under the projecting angles of the tile.

The forms of architecture seemed to the ancients so immutable that any change in them seemed to them to need a special interposition.

But the Corinthian capital may be accounted for by the ordinary process of natural development. The capitals at the angles in the Ionic order (see figs. 54 and 55, page 189) had spirals on each face, unlike the intermediate capitals of the range, which had the spirals only on the front and back faces. The two meeting spirals at each corner of the capital coalesced into a horn supporting the corner of the abacus.

The ornament round the neck of the column seen in the order of the Erechtheum (fig. 54, page 189), which was at first merely painted, was afterwards carved in relief, as in this instance. With the desire for greater richness in Roman taste, it was merely a natural development to carve this ornament round the neck in richly cut leaves in high relief. This process is better seen in what is called the Composite order (fig. 58), from its being supposed to be a union of the Ionic and Corinthian. It is merely a ruder form of the latter, in which the spiral horns at the corner are more delicate and refined.

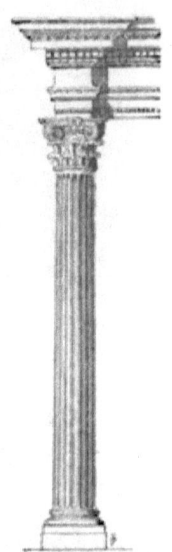

Fig. 58. THE COMPOSITE ORDER — ARCH OF SEPTIMIUS SEVERUS ROME.

There is no question that the Corinthian capital is more logical in form than either the Doric or Ionic. So far it is an advance and improvement. It is natural that the capital should expand to receive the weight; the Doric capital so expands, but leaves the corners of the abacus unsupported. The form of expansion in the Ionic is not that suggested by the function which it has to perform. But the Corinthian capital carries the line of support, in the simplest and most natural manner, from the round of the column up to the square of the abacus.

It has continued the normal type of capital ever since, through the Byzantine and Gothic styles; often beautifully modified; birds and animals being substituted for the spiral horns to support the corners of the abacus.

It may appear as if Greek architecture judged by the test of being at present understood and practised might have been passed over as unsuitable for our use; that the enthusiasm for the style among highly educated persons, which followed the publication of Stuart and Revett's 'Antiquities of Athens,' and our possession and appreciation of the Elgin Marbles, had passed away; that no one would think now of building a church like St. Pancras, or of attempting a reproduction of the Parthenon, like the unfinished National Monument on the Calton Hill in Edinburgh. The style required special knowledge and learning for understanding it, and was never generally appreciated. As practised with us, it was cold and formal; and, as there were very few specimens to copy from and only the most perfect of these were followed, there was a weary sameness in the results. The sculpture which had given life and interest to the original was omitted; colour was thought vulgar; and the general impression of one of those Doric porticos in our climate, in any weather, but especially in an east wind with sleet driving through it, was dismal and depressing.

The style had also the serious practical disadvantage for

our climate, that windows were supposed to be inadmissible. As it was impossible wholly to dispense with them, they were ignored, like vulgar intruders in good society, and treated as if no one was expected to look at them, as plain holes cut in the wall, without any ornament or moulding whatever. This of course, only made them more painfully conspicuous. Smuggled in between columns, and cutting up what should have been their solid background of wall, they became vulgar and objectionable.

These mistakes, however, do not prove that Greek architecture is unfitted for our domestic purposes; for they arose from too slavish adherence to a very limited number of copies, all of which were from temples built for purposes wholly different from our civil buildings or houses.

In Greek temples like the Parthenon, only about half the space under the roof is enclosed. All the rest is open, merely a roof supported on pillars; the object being to provide the worshippers with shade, shelter from cold not being needed. The enclosed part, the dwelling of the god, was more sacred; its solid walls a painted background for the white columns. To attempt to adapt forms resulting from an arrangement like this, to modern domestic or municipal purposes, could only result in failure. It showed little appreciation of Greek art to imagine that this was following it; but temples being the only buildings remaining, no other course was open to copiers, who as usual, in zeal for form, managed to miss the spirit. They could not see that for every different purpose the Greeks had a different form; that pains were taken to make buildings, whose uses were not the same, dissimilar; to place them on different levels, and even change the architecture, though they formed all part of the same group or even of the same building. All this they might have seen, had they only had eyes, in the Erechtheum (fig. 59, which is really more varied in its outline and more purposely irregular than any Gothic church. Being three temples, the architect did not see why he should make it look like one; and so he has made the architecture of each different. So also when two buildings were near one another, the Greeks avoided placing them at right angles or in right line. They saw no reason for destroying by

Fig. 59. THE ERECHTHEUM.

perpetual straight lines and right angles all variety and play of shadow, as we do in our modern streets.

Nor has Greek ornament the frigid dull cast-iron character which any one who had only seen the reproductions of it in modern work would suppose. It has the same free-hand irregularity and variety as Gothic ornament, but the copiers thought to improve on the original by reducing everything to dead sameness.

Some reproductions of Greek architecture, notably the High School at Edinburgh, appreciated this adaptability and variety of the style; but all are cold and formal, and rather depressing in their effect, and they must be utterly unlike in character to what, for lighter domestic purposes, the "merry Greeks" themselves produced.

Their domestic architecture has perished; from the remains of Pompeii, in the Greek colony of Magna Græcia, we have an idea of the decoration of their houses in the latest times, but of their external architecture few traces are left. It must be a libel on their taste to suppose that it at all resembled that which they employed in the temples, in form or solemn character, or in anything except grace and beauty, and suitableness to its own purpose.

There is an antique bass-relief in the British Museum representing the visit of Bacchus to Icarius. The background is formed by the house, which has simple windows with a square pillar in the centre of each, dividing it like a mullion; a low pitched roof covered with tiles, but no portico for mere ornament, in imitation of a temple, as in our Classic houses of last century.

The appreciation of this practical common sense, which characterised the domestic architecture of the old Greeks, has lately given rise in France to what is called the Neogrec or new Greek style, in which some houses and villas have been built in Paris, characterised by grace and elegance, the architects showing such a knowledge of Greek art that they dare use it with freedom.

Glasgow possesses some examples, due to the genius of the late Alexander Thomson, of a treatment of Greek architecture characterised by great freedom and originality, and appreciation of its severer beauties, if not of its playfulness and lighter elegancies. He had few chances of showing his power, but everything he designed, even common houses for building speculators, has an unmistakable stamp of genius and originality. His enthusiasm for art, and his unswerving allegiance to it, which made him reject any personal advantages at the cost of what he believed to be right, have left their influence, and have raised the character of the architecture of the city.

So far, therefore, as our second condition of FREEDOM is concerned, no exception can be taken to the use of Greek in domestic architecture. Symmetry and regularity were not thought essential. Irregularity is admissible, indeed is enjoined, when it arises naturally and truthfully from the purposes of the building. Windows may be large or small, as occasion requires; and the style is even flexible enough to adopt some mode of dividing windows, probably by means of slender pillars and cornices, which would serve the purposes of mullions and transom in carrying the architecture across wider openings.

Some hold that architecture, properly so called, did not exist for the Greeks; that it was first invented by the Romans, when they discovered the arch and developed it in vaulting; that before this it no more existed than the modern sciences did before the time of Bacon; that, though whatever the Greeks did they did well, their architecture is only a refinement of Stonehenge, setting up two long stones and laying a third on the top of them.

Certainly, now that we know the arch, it would be an impossible folly to reject the use of it in our houses, for it would deprive us of the use of bricks and small stones for bridging over openings, causing needless expense, and depriving us of many charming effects which those who have gone before us have taught us. But to adopt the arch in Greek architecture would be carrying freedom so far as to abolish the style altogether.

As regards our third condition—its SUITABLENESS TO OUR

HIGHEST ART—more could be said in its favour now than would have been possible a few years ago. Our sculpture, indeed, has always looked to Greek art as its highest model, and would easily adopt its forms. Of late years prominent artists like Leighton, Poynter, and Albert Moore, have painted Classical subjects in a Greek manner, and the tendency seems to be growing; but the great mass of our art is out of its influence, and it will probably continue to be admired and practised only by a few.

It cannot be objected to the style, that it would be impossible or even difficult to find suitable furnishing for it. Since Wedgwood's days, pottery and ornaments have affected its forms; and in general furnishing the style of the first French Empire, or the Classic delicacy of the time of Queen Anne, which still linger among us, are not unsuitable to it. But while we may expect to see Greek art crop out occasionally in architecture and painting, as well as in sculpture, there is no reasonable prospect of its ever being generally adopted in this country. It may be the highest and purest style, but Guinevere preferred Lancelot to the stainless Arthur, and it may be too high and pure for us. It has high merits, but most people cannot see them. It is not popular, and is even hated for its strangeness.

Nor would any one who really loved it wish to see it in the hands of ordinary builders, or of the mass of architects. The result would be even worse than the vulgarising of Gothic, for its beauties are more delicate and refined. It is as little a natural expression of our nature as of that of the Romans, who, though they professed to admire, and attempted to copy it, spoiled it in their reproductions. Its main influence on them was to delay them for some centuries in developing a true style for themselves, and the chances are that the attempt to adopt it would have a similar influence on us.

Although, therefore, its merits and its capacity of adaptation to our domestic wants are greater than in the specimens we have been accustomed to see, any attempts to revive it will be isolated and without general result. The nation must change before it can comply with our first test of suitableness—some prospect of its general adoption.

CHAPTER VII.

CLASSICAL OR RENAISSANCE ARCHITECTURE.

IN answering the question as to what style of architecture is best suited for our houses, it only remains for us to consider the various styles which are included under the general name of Classical architecture; all influenced more or less by the enthusiasm for Classical literature, and for old Roman art, which, under the name of the Renaissance or Revival (from the supposed darkness of the Middle Ages), sprung up in Italy in the fifteenth century, and has become part of all modern civilisation.

The memory of the old Roman Imperial power, which the barbarians destroyed, influenced the whole period of the Middle Ages. The law and order, and the civilisation which Charlemagne established was an attempt to revive the rule of the Roman Cæsar. The monasteries preserved the literature of Rome, and continued the traditions of its architecture.

In the thirteenth century there was an earlier Renaissance within the limits of the Middle Ages,[1] which showed itself

[1] See Pater's 'Studies in the History of the Renaissance.' London. Macmillan & Co. 1873.

in the Verse of Dante and of the Troubadours; and in Gothic architecture, which was the logical development of the Roman vault and arch.

"The word Renaissance," Mr. Pater says, "is now generally used to denote not merely that revival of classical antiquity which took place in the fifteenth century, and to which the word was first applied, but a whole complex movement, of which that revival of classical antiquity was but one element or symptom. For us the Renaissance is the name of a many-sided but yet united movement, in which the love of the things of the intellect and the imagination for their own sake, the desire for a more liberal and comely way of conceiving life, make themselves felt, prompting those who experience this desire to seek first one and then another means of intellectual or imaginative enjoyment, and directing them not merely to the discovery of old and forgotten sources of this enjoyment, but to divine new sources of it, new experiences, new subjects of poetry, new forms of art. Of this feeling there was a great outbreak in the end of the twelfth and the beginning of the following century."

In the fifteenth century when the Classic traditions, which had vegetated in the Eastern Empire since the time of Constantine, were driven by the conquest of Constantinople to the West, they burst into new life in the fresh soil of the vigorous Western nations. The new learning brought them light and life: their past efforts in literature and philosophy seemed gropings in the dark. Even the old pagan worship of Nature with its unrestrained enjoyment of life and beauty, which Christianity and asceticism had for centuries been suppressing, found sympathisers in cultivated minds and in the high places of the Church. Some enthusiasts even revived Roman manners, holding banquets lasting several days, reclining on couches, dressed like old Romans.

When such a spirit prevailed it was inevitable that

Classic architecture should revive. This Revival or Renaissance came first in Italy. As the intellectual centre of the world she was the first to be influenced by the new learning, and in architecture she had no vigorous native school of Gothic to oppose to the new spirit. For in Italy Gothic architecture had never properly taken root. It was there an exotic imported from the North; a copy of the form without the spirit. In the brighter Southern climate it developed a richness of colour and softness of form of its own, but it lost the nerve and vigour of the native Northern style. Italian Gothic always remained somewhat Classic in character. The capitals were a modification of Corinthian; the columns were generally cylinders, like Classic ones, not divided into a number of little shafts as in the true Northern style. In Italy the ancient Classic buildings, many of which remained—preserved from destruction as stone quarries by being utilised as churches and castles—and possibly also the old traditions of workmanship[1] kept alive the seeds of Classic architecture. In drawings by old masters, painters and architects, we have evidence that these Roman remains were studied and measured with the same interest and precision as Gothic churches have been in our own day by young architects.

Although it was Greek literature which supplied the chief force of the new learning, Greek architecture was unknown or at least unnoticed. In Raphael's picture of Paul preaching at Athens, the buildings of the Acropolis, which form the background, are Roman not Greek in style.

The architecture of old Rome was the representative of both Greek and Roman ideas in architecture. Hence it

[1] When Mr. Castellani revived old Etruscan gold work, he found in remote corners of the Abruzzi, workmen who inherited the tradition and the skill of executing the beautiful granulated surface of Etruscan gold ornaments. This effect is produced by the actual soldering together of innumerable minute points of gold.

became *Classic*, the standard of right; and buildings were admirable in proportion as they conformed to its rules. These rules were at first uncertain, for the ancient buildings themselves varied in their proportions, but they soon became systematised and absolutely fixed. Purity was conformity with these rules; aberrations from them were sins against art.

The Romans seem to have been unconscious of the artistic value of their own inventions in architectural construction. To them we owe the use of the arch, the inventions of vaulting and of the dome, and the practice of placing one story above another. These are such wonderful advances in architecture, that it may be fairly said the art did not previously exist. All that the Greeks had done in construction was to rest a long stone or lintel on the top of two upright supports. Whatever they did they did well, but it was no great thing to do. The arch revolutionised architecture. It created a new art, the name of which is derived from the new mode of construction. The *form* of the arch is found in primitive constructions, in which a space is covered over by successive layers of stones laid on a flat bed, each projecting beyond that below it, the top layers meeting and resting against each other, which prevents them toppling in. This mode of construction is a succession of corbels, not a true arch, in which the principle of stability is quite different. In the arch the stones, each cut into a wedge shape, are laid one above the other on a wooden ring or centering till the top stone, called the "closer" or "key stone," unites the stones rising from each side. The centering may then be removed, for the wedge-shape of each stone prevents it from falling in. But each stone by its weight and by the weight of any wall it carries acts like a wedge, tending to split the arch open; their united weight tending to thrust out the lowest stones or "springers" on each side, and the walls or pillars on which these rest, and also the arch stones immediately above the springers, for, as these rest partly on their sides, they do not act with the same force as wedges as the upper stones which press with their whole weight downwards. The arch will fall if it widens enough to let any one stone slip through. The springers and a few of the arch stones above them must therefore be kept in their places, which is done by placing against them a mass of masonry called the "abutment" of such weight that its resistance is greater than the outward thrust of the arch.

Wherever the arch was invented, the Romans were the first to see and make use of its enormous advantages in building construction. Lintel construction could span spaces only a few feet wide, and to do this required large stones difficult to procure. By the use of the arch the whole width of great buildings could be spanned by means of small stones, or even of bricks.

The Vault, which the Romans invented, is only a widened arch. An arch is the width of the wall it carries, a vault is an arched covering of a building. The Dome, which was also a Roman invention, is a vault covering a circular building. The springers instead of being straight in plan, as in the vault and arch, are each a portion of the circle which forms the circumference of the building. Each ring in a dome is an arch laid horizontal, and its arch-stones are wedge-shaped on four sides, not on two only as in the simple arch. It needs, therefore, no key-stone to complete it, but may be left off at the height of any completed ring, as in the Pantheon; whose only window is a circular opening thirty feet wide left in the apex.

The great civic buildings of the Romans under the empire gave splendid scope for the employment of these new inventions in arched construction. The Greeks had not needed such buildings. The assemblies of the people for politics and games, and even their courts of justice, were held in the open air. Their houses were simple. Their great buildings were their temples in which they adhered religiously to old forms. The Roman baths had great halls, the rendezvous of an idle people; which gave magnificent opportunity for vaulted and domed ceilings; and their courts of justice or basilicas, at first uncovered courts surrounded by arcades, were in later times covered in by vaults.

But when the Romans first began to carry out this arched construction which they had invented, they showed the mastery which the Greeks whom they had conquered had over them as artists. They seemed to feel that their arched buildings could have no place in art unless they possessed the essential features of Greek architecture — the columns with the mass of stone or lintel which they supported. They therefore added the Greek architecture as an ornament to their own, putting it as a covering or screen over their arched construction, which was seen through the spaces formed by the columns and lintel. The Arch of Hadrian at Athens (fig. 60) is an early example of this combination, in which, however, the parts are awkwardly put together.[1] The practice of later times especially of the Renaissance architects, produced more harmony between the parts, though the idea is at best a make-shift

Fig. 60. THE ARCH OF HADRIAN AT ATHENS.

---

[1] For the use of this and of the other illustrations of the Classic orders, taken from Rickman's 'Gothic Architecture,' I am indebted to the kindness of Mr. James Parker of Oxford.

Fig. 61.   CUSTOM HOUSE, KING'S LYNN.

and can never produce a result perfectly satisfactory. The Colosseum at Rome (fig. 21, page 59, in a former chapter) is a magnificent example of this treatment, though our drawing does not fully show this, as it is intended rather to give an idea of the mass and grandeur of the building than of its details.

The illustration of the old Roman gate called the Porta Nigra, or black gate, at Treves (fig. 62), gives some idea of this characteristic of Roman architecture. With the revival of Classic architecture this feature was revived, and to the present day it continues a favourite means of giving splendour to Classic buildings. It was employed in the Venetian palaces (see illustrations of the Vandramini palace, fig. 71, page 228, and of the

Fig. 62.   PORTA NIGRA, TREVES.

Cornaro and Pesaro palaces, figs. 72 and 74, pp. 230 and 234); frequently in France, as at Versailles; and in England, as in the lower story of the little building at King's Lynn, illustrated in fig. 61. But in this case as in many others, instead of round pillars against the wall, we have what are called *pilasters*, merely flat projections on the wall, with base and capital-like pillars. The pillars were ornamental, they did no work; they were expensive and necessitated great thickness of wall. A similar effect was obtained at much less cost by flat projections. The expedient had the sanction of ancient authority (see Roman capital carved in brick, fig. 63), and is a part of Classic architecture. Mr. Fergusson considers it the special curse of modern architecture; if he were Chancellor of the Exchequer he would put a tax on every pilaster. But it is a simple and ready means of giving proportion and effect to buildings, by supplying perpendicular lines, as cornices and strings give horizontal lines, and I do not see why we should be deprived of it.

Fig. 63. ROMAN CAPITAL, CARVED IN BRICK.

In another way the columns and lintels of Greek architecture were used to impart the element of art to Roman buildings. The gable-end of the Greek temple, which consists (see fig. 20, p. 56, Temple at Paestum, and fig. 52, page 186) of a portico formed of pillars supporting a flat triangular gable or pediment, was stuck on as an ornamental porch to a Roman building, as in the Pantheon at Rome. In England in the eighteenth century such porticos were stuck on the front of every house with any pretence to architecture, often on an upper story, where they could have no meaning as a porch. Fig. 64 shows an early specimen of this treatment in this country by Inigo Jones.

Such uses of the Greek sytsem of construction showed in the Romans a want of fine artistic perception; but it was the natural outcome of their character and circumstances, and it produced grand and magnificent results. It was eminently practical; and utilised admirably the capacities of the various nations who were under their rule and did their work. The walls and vaults and simple masses of their buildings could be constructed by ordinary slave labour properly directed, while the skill of the Greeks in art was employed to decorate them with mouldings and carved capitals and statues in marble. The result, though it had

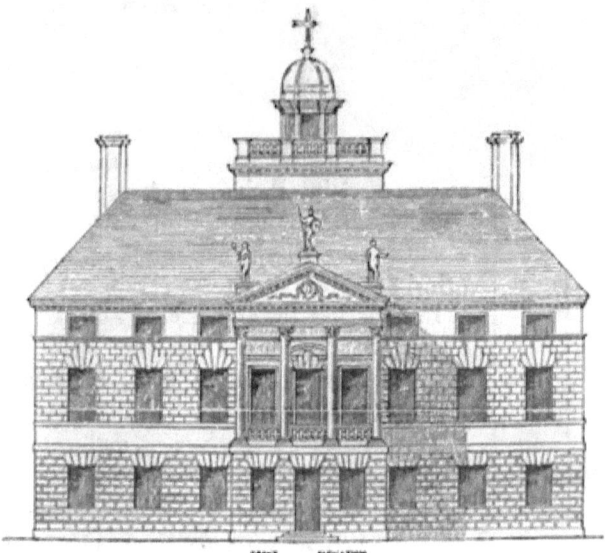

Fig. 64. AMRESBURY, PRINCIPAL FRONT.

not the perfect refinement of Greek art, was admirable in its own way. It is a different kind of glory from the glory of Greek architecture—a lower kind—sumptuous rather than refined.

Roman architecture tended to work itself clear of the extraneous ornaments of Greek columns and lintel. In engineering works, such as aqueducts, they had been from the first dispensed with. In Diocletian's great palace at Spalatro, where he retired when he resigned the empire, the arch becomes more prominent as an architectural feature. In the Church of St. Sophia at Constantinople, built by Justinian in the first half of the sixth century, all trace of Greek construction, and of "the orders," has disappeared. The architecture consists of arches, vaults, and domes

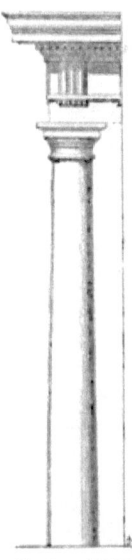

Fig. 65. ROMAN DORIC.—THEATRE OF MARCELLUS AT ROME.

appropriately decorated. But this natural development, which is a sign of life and truth in the architecture, has been counted degradation, the result of ignorance and error. After describing the splendid marble columns of St. Sophia, Gibbon, expressing the opinion of his time, adds, "but every order of architecture disclaims their fantastic capitals."[1] It was left to Gothic architecture under new conditions to give a new development to the principle of the arch.

In adopting the Greek orders the Romans altered and vulgarised them, bringing them better into harmony with their own feelings and the use they made of them, giving them greater richness and ornament, and less grace and delicacy of line. The delicate parabolic curve of the capital of the Grecian Doric, almost a straight line, became a segment of a circle. They omitted the flutings not from parsimony, but not perceiving their use and value, preferring instead of the white marbles of the Greeks, richly coloured marbles, whose surface the flutings would have spoilt. To the Doric order they added a base, the

---

[1] We have learnt to see such capitals now with different eyes. They are full of beauty and variety. The carving of their acanthus leaves is Greek, rather than Roman, in spirit and delicacy of line. A similar treatment of capitals is found in Gothic buildings of the thirteeth century, especially in France.

CLASSICAL OR RENAISSANCE ARCHITECTURE. 211

want of which is even painfully obvious in the illustration (fig. 65) from the Theatre of Marcellus at Rome, as the solid base is omitted on which, in Greek architecture, the Doric column rests. They lost the Greek proportions, elongating the columns, reducing the weight of the entablature or supported mass, and depriving the architecture of its dignity. In their hands the Ionic order was sub-

Fig. 66. AQUEDUCT OF HADRIAN, ATHENS. ROMAN IONIC.

Fig. 67. TEMPLE OF FORTUNA VIRILIS, ROME.

jected to a similar transformation. It is less severe, the columns are slenderer, the entablature of less depth, the shadow of the projecting cornice modified by a deep moulding supporting it.

The illustration from the Aqueduct of Hadrian at Athens (fig. 66) shows an invention of the Romans, in combining their own arched architecture with the Greek orders, which became a feature of Classic and especially of Renaissance architecture. This example is clumsy and imperfect in the combination of its parts. In adopting the idea the Renaissance architects carried the whole entablature and cornice over the two pillars, and rested the arch on the top of the cornice instead of, as in this instance, on the top of the architrave. They made the arch much lighter, only the width of the architrave.

In the buildings which the Romans left in Italy and elsewhere, the Renaissance architects believed they found five different orders of architecture, and therefore the science of architecture had five orders and no more. Besides the three orders of the Greeks they found the Tuscan, which, as Palladio says, "is the most plain and simple of all the orders of architecture, as it retains more of the old simplicity, and is devoid of all those ornaments which give so great a grace and beauty to the others."[1] "In it," he says, "the intercolumnations may be very wide, because the architraves are made of timber."

In old Roman practice the treatment and proportions of the Orders were by no means fixed, and in the modification of the Corinthian, which we have already described, which some Roman architect in the exercise of this liberty had produced, was found a new order, the Composite (see page 191, fig. 58). Palladio looks on these orders as ultimate facts of science. That a new order should be added was as impossible as the creation of a new animal. Freart, Sieur de Chambray, in Louis Quatorze's time in an interesting treatise, "made English for the benefit of builders," by John Evelyn, the author of the Diary, goes farther. He refuses to address himself to those who pretend that "the mind is

---

[1] Andrea Palladio's 'First Book of Architecture,' with all the plates exactly copied from the first Italian edition, printed in Venice. A.D. 1570. Revised by Colin Campbell, Esq., Author of 'Vitruvius Britannicus.'

free, not bound, and that we have as good right to invent and follow our own *Genius*, as the *Antients*, without rendering ourselves their slaves; since *Art* is an infinite thing, growing every day to more perfection." "The three orders which are derived to us from the Greeks, not only contain whatsoever is excellent, but likewise all that is necessary, of architecture; there being but three manners of *building:* the *solid*, the *mean* (or intermediate), and the *delicate*." He complains that, "we daily behold these orders so disfigured and ill-treated by the *workmen* of this age that, to speak seriously, there remains not so much as a single *member* which has not received some strange and monstrous alteration."

Yet Freart seems to have had no perception that the orders, as employed by the best authorities, differed in their character from Greek architecture; the faith in their authority was too strong for any such questioning. There was some doubt as to whether the Doric column should have a base; the authority of the order of the Theatre of Marcellus was against it, but the feeling of its necessity prevailed against authority. The principle of authority checked the free development of architecture, in a way unknown in the mediæval styles. The evil was not that the new architecture was derived from the old. It might have developed freely, as one language may develop freely which is derived from another. But the new forms of life which were constantly springing up were compelled to conform to dead rules: and under the force of this compulsion, the style was continually recurring to the original type. Instead of, as would have been the case in a natural growth, becoming less like the original, its aberrations were greatest at first; just as a school boy's Latin theme is marked at first by English idioms, which disappear with his more perfect knowledge of classic authorities.

The absolute authority of the five orders became

established about the time that the new opinions of the
Renaissance in religion were being crystallised into the
symbols and standards of the various churches.

There was an outburst of free thought and natural development, both in architecture and in religion, before this
result was attained. In both provinces it was condemned and
as far as possible suppressed by the decrees of the Council
of Trent and of Protestant synods, as at Dort; but, in the
early days of the Renaissance, architecture happily had free
course. The genius of the great Italians, when they revived
the ancient architecture, discovered, perhaps unconsciously,
new proportions. Alberti, Michael Angelo, Palladio, and
other architects, followed different proportions in the orders;
and in matters where the guidance of the ancients failed
them, and they had to trust to their own invention, they
worked out a new development of style.

The new learning crossed the Alps carrying with it the
new architecture, which was accepted as authoritative and
true. But the native Gothic styles had too much vitality
to be crushed out by it, and, like conquered peoples, mingled
with their conquerors. In each country a new style was
produced which united with the old native the features of
the new Classic style. The varieties of these styles almost
defy classification. Each country had its own, and in each
the style varied according to the strength of the Classical
knowledge or native habit. To the learned, like Freart or
Evelyn, they were all abominable; a corruption of pure
Classic by barbarous admixture. Such men could not see
that they were natural growths, inevitable in the circumstances, and worthy of study like any other natural
production. Even living writers have hardly realised this.
The advocates of Gothic and of Classic have alike abused
these styles; but their turn of appreciation has come.
Correct Classic, asphyxiated by its own rules, had, forty years

ago, become tiresome, almost dead, when a fresh rising of the Gothic spirit, the result of the Romantic revival, asserted freedom and common sense in architecture. This new spirit influenced all the leading thought of the day, and the authority of the orders was for ever broken. But the wave of the Romantic revival began to ebb. The spirit of the Renaissance reasserted itself as the basis of our modern ideas and life. Poets felt once more the meaning of the worship of Nature and of the old Gods.

In architecture those who had felt the enthusiasm for Gothic, who had drunk in its spirit and had made it a part of themselves, awoke to the consciousness that it was not the expression of modern ideas, or of the domestic requirements of modern life. But they could not return to the thraldom of the Orders, or give up for architecture the right of free development, which the Gothic movement had won. Trained and formed in Gothic, the spirit of the Renaissance coming to them with the force of new truth, they were under the same influences as the earliest Renaissance architects. They naturally produced work with the same characteristics, and found these styles the expression of their own state of feeling and models for their work. To this stream of tendency, I believe, it is due that these early Renaissance styles have again become interesting; the objects of study and the models for modern work. I believe it possible that, freed from the obligation to conform to the fixed Classic rules, a natural style, the growth of our modern wants, may be founded on them.

From the variety of influences under which these old styles were formed, the varieties of them almost defy classification. They cannot be arranged chronologically like the Mediæval Gothic styles, in which the growth is regular and the style of each century is similar in each country, for the force of the new spirit varied in different places at the same time. St. Peter's at Rome; the Spire of

Beauvais; King's College Chapel, Cambridge; and Renaissance buildings in France, were being built at the same time, and traces of Gothic continued in England, long after Inigo Jones had begun Whitehall.

It would be altogether beside our purpose to attempt a complete account or history of these styles. We shall content ourselves with describing some specimens, taken very much at random, as they appeared picturesque or interesting, or furnished some feature suitable for modern use. I have not given illustrations of palaces; those who wish to learn about them will find them treated of in Mr. Fergusson's book. Our interest is in houses on a scale that we might ourselves possibly live in. In such smaller houses, the new style had free development, for their builders, imperfectly learned in the Classic rules, continued old traditions and altered the Orders to suit themselves, sometimes with a true feeling and sense of art. Palaces were bound to conform to the strictest rules of Classic art and therefore have not the variety and suggestiveness of less important buildings.

CHAPTER VIII.

THE RENAISSANCE IN FLORENCE AND SIENNA.

IN the revival of Classic architecture in Italy, Rome was not the leader. Reduced in population and in wealth by the faction fights of her nobles, and by the absence of the Popes in Avignon, she did not recover sufficiently to erect new buildings till the beginning of the sixteenth century.

The first architects who were touched by the new spirit were Florentines. Brunelleschi, who was born in 1377, conceived the idea of covering with a dome the crossing of the nave and transepts of the cathedral of his native city which its Gothic architects had left unfinished, and he devoted his life to realise this idea. Going to Rome to study the dome of the Pantheon he learned Roman architecture and introduced it into his work. Returning to Florence he used the new style without a trace of Gothic admixture in the churches of San Lorenzo, commenced in 1425, and San Spirito.

Alberti, born about 1406, a scholar before he was an architect, advanced the movement greatly by his writings. He built several churches, as those of St. Francis at Rimini, and St. Andrew at Mantua, in perfectly pure Classic.

In domestic architecture the change was not so readily made, for the old style showed itself long afterwards in pointed arches and traceried windows and great rusticated stones, which the necessity for strong buildings for defence, as well as a feeling for picturesque grandeur, had made a characteristic of the old Gothic palaces of Florence.

In this, as in the recent Gothic movements, the new style was used for churches by people, who would never have thought of giving up the style for their dwelling-houses they had been accustomed to. In the Pitti Palace, commenced by Brunelleschi in 1435, the arches are all pointed, and the wall is composed of great stones, some of enormous size,[1] left rough on the surface, though carefully jointed.

In the Rucellai Palace[2] (which Alberti commenced in 1460), the roughness of the rustication is toned down, and the walls ornamented with pilasters between the arched windows, recalling the characteristic feature of the old Roman style; but though the arches have now become round, they are still filled with a form of tracery.

The Nicollini Palace, of which I give an illustration (fig. 68), shows an interesting mingling of Gothic and Classic features. The outside line of the arches is pointed while the opening is round, making the arch stones deepest at the top—a feature common in Italian Gothic work much commended by Mr. Ruskin. Inside these are Classic pilasters (not properly shown in the cut), supporting round and pointed arches. The cornices are Classic, though without strict adherence to ancient authority. The loggia at the top, a feature which gives much of its charm to Florentine architecture, has lent itself perfectly to Classic forms.

Mr. Fergusson thinks that this palace is of later date than the early period of the transition, and that Bramante may have been its architect. More likely it is of the time of

---

[1] I measured some between 20 and 30 feet long.
[2] A wood-cut of this palace is given by Mr. Fergusson, vol. iii. p. 86.

Brunelleschi, to whom it is usually attributed, who died the year Bramante was born (A.D. 1444), and whose style, as shown in the work which it is known he designed, like the palace of the Cancelleria at Rome, is quite different in character, being fully developed Classic. Judging from the

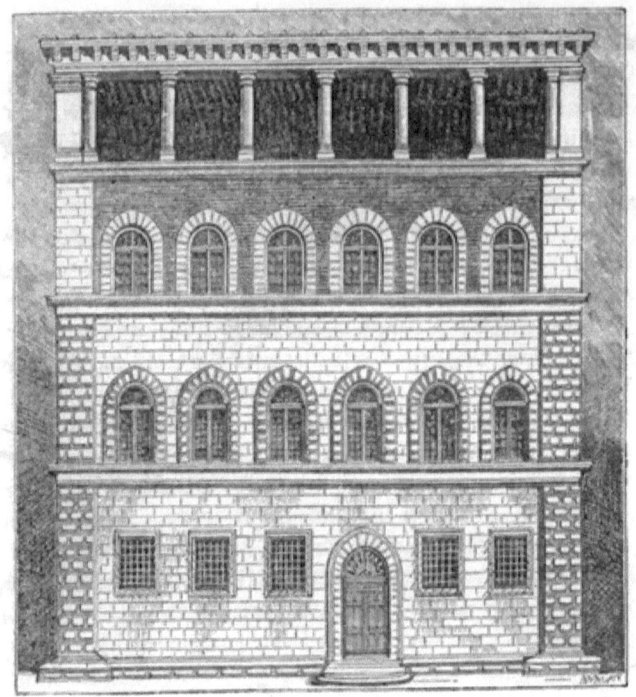

Fig. 68.   NICOLLINI PALACE, FLORENCE.

sections of its mouldings, given in Montigny and Famin's work on Florentine architecture, from which I have copied the illustration, the Nicollini Palace does not seem to me to have the lightness and elegance of detail which Mr. Fergusson attributes to it ('History of Architecture,' vol. iii.

chap. 87). The appearance of lightness from the want of the rustication of the wall surface, which might be supposed to indicate a later date, is due rather to part of the front being of brick, a common material in Italian Gothic. Making the whole of the rest of the surface of rough stones would have been incongruous, consequently the lower stories, which are of stone, have their stones hewn smooth on the surface; but the appearance of strength is retained by rusticating the angles and arches. The arches and angles beside the brickwork are also hewn smooth, from the same desire of avoiding too great contrast, while the piers of the loggia above them are in single stones. The angle piers of the building thus gradually get smoother as they rise; they are rusticated in the two lower stories, where the appearance of strength was desired, of hewn stone in the next, in the highest without any joint at all. The different surfaces of rough stone, hewn stone, and brick, are used together with great artistic skill; the Gothic and Classic features are combined without any sense of incongruity; and the result is a noble and artistic design in admirable harmony.

Like other Italian palaces, the Florentine have a great open central court surrounded by open arcades, which gives access to the rooms on each story; probably a tradition from the houses of Rome and Pompeii. In the architecture of these arcades we find no trace of Gothic. In some cases, because being usually the last part of the building to be finished, the Classic style may have come in by the time they were built, but even if built at the same time as the fronts, it may have been the fashion to use for them, as for churches, the purer Classic style, which was admirably fitted for them.

In the neighbouring city of Sienna, architecture, both in Mediæval and Renaissance times, was under the same influences as at Florence. In emerging from Gothic, her early Renaissance took similar forms and passed through the same stages. The Gothic towers overhanging the market-places in both cities are the same in form—an unadorned square shaft, with great straight corbels supporting little arches on which stand the battlements; with a smaller similar tower inside.

But the Sienna tower is of brick. Sienna had no quarries which could give her the magnificent stones of Florence. It is an unpractical criticism of Mr. Fergusson's (vol. iii. p. 89) that "the defect of the Sienna buildings is that the stones employed are too small to give effect to a design depending so much on rustication as the Tuscan palaces." There is no evidence that the Sienna architects aimed at the Florentine effect of rough wall.

In the Spanocchi Palace, commenced by Giorgio in 1472, the arches throughout, as in the Florentine palaces, have the outline of the arch stones pointed, while the arch openings are semi-circular. These are filled with tracery consisting of two round arches with a circle over them. This palace is built of tufa, a volcanic stone, the heads which look out between the corbels of the cornice being in terra-cotta.

The Piccolomini Palace, built by the same architect about thirty years later, is of travertine. It has the same kind of tracery, but the pointed form of the outside rim of the arch has disappeared. Montigny and Famin, the authors of the excellent series of measured drawings of Tuscan architecture (Paris 1866), to which I have already referred, give the following estimate of the artistic merit of this palace: "Dans son ensemble ce palais est d'un aspect grandiose et peut être considéré comme un des plus beaux de Toscane." This is different from Mr. Fergusson's estimate of the same palace quoted above. With such diversity of opinion among experts, what is the reader to believe? Such excathedra judgments are of little use. Art criticism seems to me to be of value only when it enables us to understand the meaning of a work of art, and the result which has been obtained under the conditions.

CHAPTER IX.

THE RENAISSANCE IN ROME.

THERE was little building in Rome till the beginning of the sixteenth century. Rome has no buildings showing the transition from Gothic to Renaissance, for she had no Gothic style of her own with which a compromise could have been made, or which could have resisted the influence of the splendid ancient Roman buildings she possessed.

The architects of her palaces were chiefly Florentines, called there by the sumptuous expenditure in building of her popes and nobles during the first half of the sixteenth century. It is not within my plan to give examples of palaces covering acres, of three great stories, each thirty feet high. The social state which rendered them possible has disappeared. I content myself with giving the elevation of a somewhat ordinary house with shops in the Via de' Bianchi (fig. 69) said to have been designed by Sansovino, the architect of the Library of St. Mark at Venice (born 1479, died 1570). Mr. Fergusson might consider it bad art, because it attempts to make two stories appear as if they were one.

Ordinary houses must have bedrooms and five or six stories of different heights, and to group two stories of windows together into one story by means of cornices, or by pilasters, or by putting them under the same arch, as in some old Gothic

Fig. 69.   HOUSE WITH SHOPS, VIA DE' BIANCHI, IN ROME.

examples, is a method by which architects in various ages and styles have given *proportion* to their buildings, thus raising them above the artistic level of cotton mills. It seems as legitimate as the grouping together of windows on the same story, a device which Mr. Fergusson frequently commends. In this example the grouping of the windows is simple and skilful. To remove the cornices which divide the floors, or to put a cornice to mark each floor, would take the dignity and meaning out of the elevation. This house shows the Italian style fully developed, and it is interesting as a prototype of the style which has become the commonplace of London builders. For its success it depends almost wholly on good proportion, which unfortunately the London builders have not always given us.

CHAPTER X.

VENETIAN RENAISSANCE.

VENICE had a flourishing style of Gothic of her own, which, of all forms of Gothic, supplies the examples best suited for modern use. It does not affect the gloomy grandeur of the Florentine palaces, or the small barred windows of French and English mediæval castles, for she was secure from foreign attack behind her "streak of silver sea;" while the strong hand of her oligarchy rendered fighting among the nobles, inside the town, impossible. Her palaces therefore were never castles or fortresses, but from the earliest times, in their fronts to the canals, had more window than wall. Her sea-girt position, like that of England, gave her colonies, and commerce, and wealth; in which others besides the great nobles were sharers, which she spent largely in building. Hence we find interesting specimens of architecture in moderately sized houses (fig. 70). Her Gothic style was not properly Italian, for Venice was not properly a part of Italy. Her people considered themselves Romans, and she continued the traditions of the Roman empire which had been transferred to the East, which influenced the eastern coast of Italy long after it had lost the West. The shape of the Doge's cap, and the use on state occasions of umbrellas like Eastern potentates, are traces of this Eastern influence. Her Gothic has an Eastern character. Her treatment of the pointed arch and her pointed domes, recall those of the Saracens in their mosques, or the Mohammedan tombs of India. It suggests a climate sunnier even than her own. When it has been introduced into this country, it shivers like a Hindoo in his white cotton dress in London streets. It is essentially a coloured architecture, delighting in broad surfaces bright with painting and coloured marble. The pointed arch was used more as a beautiful form than a necessity of construction; it was ornamented by coating it with marbles, not as in northern Gothic by cutting it into mouldings marking the lines of construction.

Fig. 10.   SMALL GOTHIC HOUSE AT VENICE.

Venetian Gothic was living and vigorous, and held its own against the Classic influence till the beginning of the sixteenth century, when it was still strong enough to force a compromise. The characteristic form of old Roman and

Fig. 71. VANDRAMINI PALACE, VENICE.

revived Classic architecture was adopted—the round arch behind a screen of columns and lintel—but the Gothic spirit asserted itself in filling these arches with tracery, in which Classic forms were used, similar to that which had been already adopted by Alberti in Florence, and Giorgio in Sienna (fig. 71, the Vandramini Palace). Though the compromise was natural in Italy, as is shown by its adoption in Sienna and Florence, it was not adopted north of the Alps. It is suited only for a round arch, and the northern Gothic, in giving up the pointed arch for its windows, had adopted not the round arch, but the straight lintel. In Italy, with the growing taste there for correct Classic, this tracery was felt to be unsatisfactory, and was soon abandoned. That it is an expression of the Gothic spirit, is shown by the fact that Sir Gilbert Scott has filled with it the windows of Sir Christopher Wren's Church of St. Michael's, Cornhill, which he has Gothicised. I dislike this form of tracery, and have never seen any modern example of it which seemed bearable; but I find some difficulty in giving my reasons for the feeling. It seems unmeaning, and without any beauty of line, such as genuine Gothic tracery has. Certainly it serves no practical need of modern architecture.

But every one admits the Vandramini Palace to be charming. The tracery looks well in it; and for once Mr. Fergusson pardons the introduction of the Orders as ornament and does not suggest an improvement by the substitution of panelling. The design is so admirably worked out, there is throughout such perfection of grace and harmony, that it is impossible to find fault with it. It is an instance of the old truth, that the artist is greater than his materials, and can express himself in any forms, if they are natural to him and he is used to them; while he will fail if he tries to fight with arms "which he has not proved."

By the middle of the sixteenth century, the architecture

had come under the same Classic influence in Venice as in the rest of Italy; San Michaeli was building several palaces, and Sansovino had begun his celebrated Library of St. Mark's. The great Cornaro Palace on the Grand Canal (fig. 72), commenced by the latter in 1532, gives some idea of his style. The main idea of the design is the same as that in old Roman architecture, ranges of arches behind a screen of columns and entablature, but it has a greater amount of opening than the Roman, in proportion to the wall. There is a variety of treatment in the lower and in the uppermost stories, and the two main stories are ornamented by balustrades, a charming invention of the Italian Renaissance. These and later architects who adorned the city were foreigners; but, whether they were inspired by the spirit of Venice or worked to please Venetian tastes, their buildings are characterised by an oriental magnificence unknown in other Italian cities. "The great defect," says Mr. Fergusson (vol. iii. p. 95), " in Sansovino's design of the Library of

Fig. 72. CORNARO PALACE, VENICE.

Fig. 73   STAIRCASE OF DUCAL PALACE, VENICE.

St. Mark, appears to be that the architectural ornament is not necessarily a part of the construction." "It is felt that it might be away, or another class of ornament used, and the building would not only stand, but might perhaps look as well, or better. More than this, there is a quantity of sculptured ornament, figures in the spandrils, boys and wreaths in the frieze, and foliage elsewhere, which not only is not construction, but does not even suggest it. If all this were omitted the building would be relieved from that confusion of parts which is one of its principal defects; or, if enrichment were necessary, more conventional ornament would have attained the same end, and if it could have been made to suggest construction, so much the better."

This is to suggest the substitution, for that which he criticises, of another wholly different design of Mr. Fergusson's own. Even if the Venetian architects could have followed Mr. Fergusson's instructions in designing their buildings, whatever the gain might have been, it would have lost us many charming bits of art, and interesting and characteristic varieties of style. It seems wiser to accept the productions of great artists as they left them, and to endeavour to understand their meaning.

The view of the Staircase of the Ducal Palace (fig. 73) is a striking example of this richness of ornament of the Venetian Renaissance. It is said to have been designed by Sansovino. Its peculiarities are more probably due to the skill and fancy of Venetian workmen. It reminds us rather of Gothic freedom and exuberance than of Classic purity, and though almost lost among the richness, we can trace the survival of Gothic forms in the central boss and ribs of the vaulting. It is an example of the same sumptuous taste and skill in carving which continued long afterwards to produce richly carved furniture and mirror frames in Venice and throughout Italy.

But all such irregularities were soon brought under strict

Classic rule. The old art might still have some scope in carved mirror frames and furniture, but, in building, the Orders were the only rule. The art of architecture often became a sort of puzzle of fitting together in the same building orders of different dimensions, but, of course, of exactly the same proportions. Palladio, in the Church of San Giorgio Maggiore, hit on an expedient which was much admired, of diminishing the size of the great order of the nave by raising

Fig. 74.   PESARO PALACE, VENICE.

it on pedestals, so as to lessen its disproportion to the lesser order of the aisles. The Orders sat upon Architecture like the old man of the mountain; they had to be carried about into positions where they were altogether out of place, and Architecture revenged the intrusion by reducing them to mere ornaments, and asserted her freedom in the sumptuous grandeur of the style of the Jesuits.

In the seventeenth century this spirit of rich magnificence showed itself in external architecture. The Pesaro Palace, of which the accompanying woodcut (fig. 74) gives an inadequate idea, designed by Longhena about 1650, is a mass of columns and sculpture, very rich and beautiful, and a fit outcome of the spirit which made Venice for a century later the gayest and most brilliant capital of Europe and the resort of all pleasure seekers.

In the Church of San Zenobio, built about 1680 (see woodcut in Mr. Fergusson's book), the façade is richly ornamented with statues, and the gables are curved and broken and tossed about with luxurious freedom.

The Church of Santa Maria della Salute, with its great scrolls with statues on them leading up to the dome, may, as Mr. Ruskin says, be bad architecture, but, with the Dogana with its great gilded ball as a foreground, if we may judge from the innumerable times it has been painted, it must seem to artists the most charming of architectural compositions. We cannot conceive of Venice without it; it seems to embody her colour and beauty.

The west side of St. Mark's Place is now occupied by a palace, built for their emperor by the Austrians, in this century while they held Venice. It is very correct in style; all extravagances have been carefully avoided, but it is dull and worthless as art, not worth criticism, and an example of the result to which criticism and fixed rules of art naturally lead.

The results worked out and embodied in the sixteenth century by the great Florentine architects in Roman palaces, by Palladio in Vicenza, and by Alessi in Genoa (1500–1570), have ever since remained the rule and standard for domestic architecture among all civilised nations. All departures from these rules, however charming, have been counted heresies, which it was the duty of all who aimed at perfection in architecture to discourage and suppress. The result has been the same as with fixed standards in other spheres of human thought and invention. The changes and developments natural among different peoples, or through individual genius, have been restrained, but only at the price of the loss of national freedom and life in domestic architecture.

A copy is apt to fall short of the original model, and in copying Italian palaces the builders on the other side of the Alps worked under a special disadvantage. The grandeur of the Italian palaces depends, in large measure, on the great mass of wall in proportion to the window openings. Each story is often thirty feet high, and the windows reach only halfway to the ceiling, leaving above them a great mass of unbroken wall. In the bright climate, windows of this size, in proportion to the size of the room, gave sufficient light. These lofty stories were built partly, no doubt, to obtain an effect of grandeur, but also for a practical purpose. In Italy, where there is great heat during the day and miasma at night, windows and all openings are kept carefully closed, except in the cool of the evening or in the morning when they are opened to renew the air. It was therefore necessary that the rooms should be of sufficient capacity to enclose enough air for a day's consumption. In England we can have constant ventilation, consequently our rooms need not be so lofty; and in our dark climate, windows reaching only halfway up the wall of the room would give an effect not of grandeur but of dismalness. We want all the light we can get, and from as high a point in the room as possible.

The conditions of building in the two countries are wholly different; and in merely copying Italian architecture for English use, our builders have lost its proportion and grandeur. In the different circumstances a different treatment was required.

In giving some account of Renaissance architecture

north of the Alps, we shall find interest and benefit not so much in great palaces designed by learned architects in imitation of those of Italy, as in smaller houses, where the builders felt themselves at liberty to modify the style, according to convenience and the old traditions of the country.

CHAPTER XI.

THE RENAISSANCE IN FRANCE.

FRANCE was the first country across the Alps whose architecture was influenced by the new revival. Even in the reign of Louis XII. (A.D. 1498–1515) there are indications of the change. Under his successor, Francis I., palaces and castles in the new style were built in every part of the country. The constant intercourse with Italy, the interest of the Court in art and its patronage of Italian artists, who were then acknowledged masters in all the arts, enriched the country, in the first half of the sixteenth century, with examples of the new style, of a completeness and correctness which was not seen in England and Germany till nearly a century later. There is some evidence which would almost make it appear as if the new style had grown up independently and simultaneously in France and Italy. There is said to be undoubted documentary evidence that the town hall of Orleans, in which there is a mingling of Classic features in a design otherwise Gothic, was built in the fifteenth century.

But French Gothic was a living and vigorous style. It

maintained a long struggle with its invader, and even when the new style was accepted without question, mediæval features continued to characterise it and were never wholly abandoned. By this union of the two styles the genius of the French in art produced one of the most charming forms of the Renaissance architecture, thoroughly worked out and finished, and admirably suited for modern domestic requirements.

One of the most marked characteristics which the French Renaissance inherited from the Gothic architecture of the country, was the tall pyramidal slated roofs, peculiar to it among the Renaissance styles of Europe. A few examples are found in Germany, due in part to French influence, but the true characteristic of German Renaissance and of German Gothic houses is, that the front is a great broad gable with several stories of windows in it.

Fig. 76.   CHÂTEAU DE THERY.

These tall pyramidal slate roofs are found chiefly in châteaux and mansions in the country; sometimes also in town houses. They are a legacy from the later Gothic style of the country, which it retains to the present day. It will be remembered that in attempting to give a rationale of Gothic architecture, I showed that, while in England the pointed arch had in later Gothic become flattened, and the roofs had been made flat in harmony with it, in France pointed vaulting and pointed windows having been retained, high steep roofs have been retained also. This habit was, no doubt, encouraged by the quarries of beautiful slates which almost every province of France possessed, durable and thin, capable of being cut into any forms or worked into any curves or angles and, when laid, forming a beautifully even surface. The excellence of the material led the builders to take a pride in their roofs and to make the most of them, and to prefer slate roofs to gables, sometimes even in their churches. In the treatment of the roofs lies the chief charm of the pretty little Gothic Château de Thery, which is here illustrated. It will be seen from this illustration that these sloping or "hipped" roofs, as they are technically called, are better suited than gables to the round and octagonal towers and to the machicolations—the parapets projected on corbels, which we see here, leaving openings for throwing stones and molten lead down on besiegers—of mediæval military architecture. In many French buildings (e.g. the new building of the Louvre) these pyramidal roofs are truncated so as to form a square platform on the top surrounded by an ornamental railing. Sometimes they terminated in a form like a chisel edge as in the entrance tower of Jacques Cœur's house at Bourges (fig. 44, p. 154).

These tall roofs have lately become very fashionable in England, partly because they express the Gothic tendency to height, with which most of the architects are imbued; no doubt also, because they give a good deal of show for the money. All about London now they break up the modest roof-lines of the older architecture. They are apt to look pretentious here, as there is neither tradition nor convenience to justify them, for they make the neighbouring chimneys smoke, and when stuck on the top of houses already of seven stories, they compel their chimneys to be carried so high that they cannot be swept. They are dangerous for fire. Constructed of wood and rising high above the party-walls separating the houses, the flames spread with the wind from one high roof to another. These high roofs were, it is said, a chief cause of the destructiveness of the great fire at Chicago, where this fashion apparently had been adopted. On houses in the country they make hard shiny black spots in the landscape, for our slates are not so beautiful as the French.

Another feature which French Renaissance inherited from the Gothic style of the country is, that the windows have mullions and transoms. From an early period French Gothic had given up the use of the pointed arch for domestic buildings. The little French château (fig. 75) illustrates this, as does also Jacques Cœur's house at Bourges (fig. 44, p. 154), in which all the windows are square-headed, except that of the chapel over the entrance, which is filled with tracery and pointed, thereby fitting better the vaulting of the chapel; also perhaps, because traceried windows had come to be considered specially ecclesiastical features.

Mullioned and transomed windows continued for some time a universal characteristic of French Renaissance. They formed part of the original design of the Tuileries, and of the Louvre, as we know from contemporary drawings in Du Cerceau's book on Architecture. The stone mullions and transoms are now removed, but a similar effect is obtained in these and other French buildings by broad divisions of wood occupying the same positions.

Another inheritance of French Renaissance from the

mediæval style was a castellated or semi-fortified character. Since the invention of cannon the nobles found that their castles had become useless as fortifications. They were dark and inconvenient as dwellings, consisting of massive towers at the angles with solid curtain-walls between, enclosing the great tower or keep; the only openings, except in the highest stories, being small narrow slits, which a man could not get through. Inside, the staircases and passages were narrow and tortuous, so as to puzzle an enemy if he got in.

With the new style came a new building impulse. King, nobles, and commoners re-housed themselves with larger accommodation, greater splendour, and above all, with abundance of window light. A desire for abundance of light in their dwellings characterised the style of this period in France as well as the contemporary Tudor style in England. It seems almost as if they expressed in their dwellings their delight in the light which they felt the new learning had brought them; possibly it was only a reaction from the darkness which the necessities of defence had hitherto compelled them to endure.

The castles being now useless as fortifications did not require a garrison. But in rebuilding them their accommodation was not lessened. Larger and more splendid rooms than the old ones were wanted, and the nobles did not much diminish the number of their retainers. They were a sign of power and importance, and the men-at-arms continued in the house, rendering the old sort of menial service of various kinds, in addition to their military duties, which were now dispensed with. The tradition remains to the present day; footmen and men-servants being kept in great houses for show rather than for use.

In most castles the solid curtain-walls between the angle-towers were pulled down, and on their sites ranges of well-lit buildings were built, giving greatly increased accommodation. But the angle towers were left. They gave some accommodation, one dark vaulted room on each story; while the curtain-walls gave none except by the sheds leant against them. It is a characteristic of almost every period of architecture but our own, that any work of predecessors which could be turned to use was never pulled down. Possibly also, the nobles kept the towers as the symbols of their former power.

These towers, thus left in the châteaux when they were rebuilt and fitted for modern use, gave them the look of

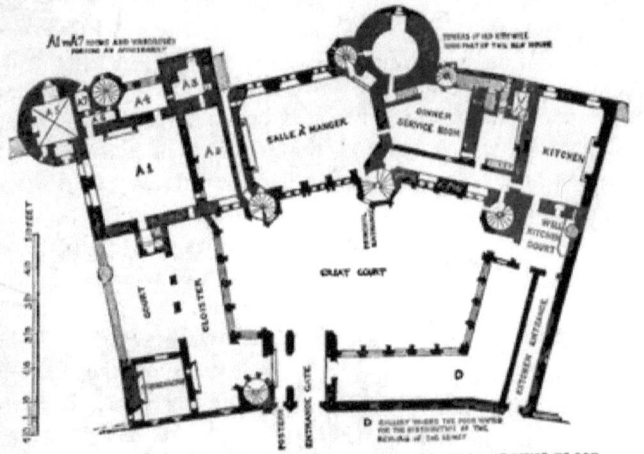

Fig. 76.   JACQUES CŒUR'S HOUSE AT BOURGES.—PLAN OF GROUND-FLOOR

fortified buildings, a character which was carried out in the parts which were rebuilt, and also in the new châteaux of the period. In both new and old, the moat or ditch of water round the castle was retained, though it had ceased to be useful for defence, from old habit or because it was a symbol of former power and importance. The possession of it was accounted a sign of signorial rights.

This process of remodelling old fortified places is well illustrated by the house of Jacques Cœur at Bourges (fig. 76).

R 2

He had bought for the site a portion of the old city walls which had become disused in consequence of the extension of the city. He pulled down the curtain-walls between the towers, and replaced them by ranges of elegant buildings. The towers he worked into the plan, remodelling them and making them fit for habitation by inserting larger windows. The greater thickness of the walls shown on the plan distinguishes the old from the new buildings.

The narrow windows or loop-holes in such towers, lighting each story, were usually in a tier, one above the other. Though the openings were small on the outside, they widened out inside into large deep bays in the thickness of the walls. It was therefore easy to cut a wide gash from top to bottom in the tower in which larger windows were inserted. These were built in the new style, flanked by pilasters which covered the junction of the new and old masonry. As the opening had been made from bottom to top, these pilasters were carried continuously through the whole height of the tower one above the other; there was no mass of plain wall dividing the rows of windows in the different stories as in Italian architecture.

These tiers of windows dividing the wall perpendicularly through all the stories became a feature of the French Renaissance. By enforcing perpendicular lines, they expressed the tendency to Gothic principles of design, which influenced the builders more than the principle of dwelling on the horizontal lines characteristic of Classic architecture. This arrangement was adopted in new buildings.

The Château d'Azy-le-Rideau, in the department of Indre-et-Loire (fig. 77), is one among innumerable examples of this mode of treatment, though the amount of window obtained is less than usual.

The spread of the new architecture in France was very rapid. There was a rage for building in the beginning of the sixteenth century. Architecture and the decorative arts

Fig. 11.   CHÂTEAU D'AZY-LE-RIDEAU, INDRE-ET-LOIRE.

were matters of interest to king and people, as we see from the wealth and favour given to Italian artists.

The palaces and châteaux then built are still the best in France. Only in towns decayed and deserted do we find houses older than this date, and however interesting archæologically these may be, they are poor dwelling-houses according to our notions. Châteaux and manor-houses were everywhere of a charming grace and kindliness of aspect, which does not suggest that oppression of the peasants for the next two hundred years, which in the Revolution sent so many of them up in flames.

In the earlier buildings of the reign of Francis I. Gothic details still prevail. In the Château of Nantouillet, built by his minister, Duprat, in 1520, the front is divided by Classic pilasters and mouldings not attempting Classic proportion, while the jambs and mullions of the windows have Gothic mouldings and bases. The staircase has pointed windows with tracery supported on mullions, which are shaped like Classic balusters, and has vaulting of the most intricate design, following the slope of the steps, the vaulting ribs being curved in two planes. There are the usual indications of an effete style; no crudeness, but an attempt to excite a sensation by intricate and wonderful workmanship.

The new style soon worked off all traces of Gothic form, and frankly accepted the Classic orders and details, but it was no slave to them. The spirit of freedom in which the practice of Gothic had trained the builders prevented this. The French genius in art used the materials of Italian architecture with a freedom and power of invention which formed out of them an original style. They did not restrict themselves to the five orthodox orders, with their fixed proportions and stereotyped capitals, which indeed was an idea of later growth, hardly formulated at this time even in Italy. They invented new forms of capitals almost as various as Gothic ones, and altered the proportions of the columns and cornices to suit their buildings. To do this well, implied genius and originality in art. A claim for freedom and doing as we like in architecture is justifiable only when we have a power to originate beauty, and taste to restrain us in its exercise. Otherwise, it is better to be content to copy.

French Renaissance long retained the Gothic feature of dividing the windows by stone mullions and transoms, along with the Classic feature of pilasters flanking their sides. The house so called of Agnes Sorel, and the Episcopal Palace at Sens (of which drawings are numerous),[1] as also the little house at Orleans (fig. 78), illustrate this treatment.

Fig. 78.   HOUSE WITH SHOP AT ORLEANS.

This house with its shop at Orleans which I have put into perspective from Sauvageot's drawing, is a fair specimen of the fully developed Renaissance of Francis I. Gothic detail has disappeared; there is a reminiscence of it only in the form of the

[1] See Fergusson, vol. iii. pp. 196, 197.

windows with their mullions and transoms, and in the slender shafts supporting the arches of the door-ways, though the arch mouldings are Classic. But the spirit of the design is Gothic. It has the effect of decoration spread over the surface rather than the opposition of solid and void which is the principle of Classic. Instead of void being placed over void, and solid over solid, which is an essential rule of Classic, the two upper stories are differently centred from the lower, but this suggests no idea of weakness. As in Gothic architecture the upper stories *spring from* the lower one, rather than *rest on* it. The pilasters spring from corbels; their weight is not carried down to the ground, as it would be in true Classic. The design is Gothic also in its irregularity and freedom, the windows are of any size, and placed not symmetrically, but in whatever position they are wanted. Symmetry is thought of, but it is not paramount. For the sake of it the large arch of the shop is drawn partly over the opening and partly over the solid wall at the corner, so as to bring it under the centre of the larger window, which is treated as one of the centres of the front, with two pilasters on each side of it. In all this there is more of Gothic than of Classic motive; a pleasing confusion—it would be too much to call mystery—which makes us feel there is more in the design than we see at first sight, and makes this building, though an unimportant one, a good example of the principle of the Renaissance—the Gothic spirit revealing itself in Classic forms.

The front of the Church of Saint-Étienne du Mont beside the Panthéon at Paris (fig. 23, p. 66) exhibits another and a later development of French Renaissance. I have already referred to it as a typical example of the union in Renaissance architecture of the Gothic spirit with Classic details. The front seems to have been added to the already existing church which shows itself through the traceried windows.

The church, said to have been begun in 1537, is in the interior one of the latest productions of Gothic. Though worked out with Classic mouldings and ornament, it illustrates Gothic lightness and aspiration better than many Gothic buildings.

I have chosen this front for illustration, as exhibiting the characteristics of the later Renaissance. There is no attempt at restraint or refinement of line in the design, but there is an effect of sumptuous picturesqueness, with an air of gaiety and aspiration, which may well atone for the incongruities for which Mr. Fergusson condemns it.

Some of the buildings at the commencement of the reign of Francis I. (A.D. 1513) are without trace of Classic admixture. Before the end of his reign in 1547, palaces such as Fontainebleau and the château of Madrid in the Bois de Boulogne, now destroyed, had been built, and the Louvre had been commenced, without a trace of Gothic in the details. For other important buildings, although Italian artists were employed to give designs, the native artists and workmen seem to have taken a good deal of their own way in carrying them out; while in less important buildings, of which they were the designers, they merely added to their old Gothic designs some touches of the new manner which they had learned from the Italian masters. They did this with such thorough knowledge of practical requirements and feeling for art as to create a new and beautiful variety of style, more interesting and more profitable for study than the correct Classic.

In the next century Roman infallibility in the province of architecture had crushed out national characteristics and individual freedom. But though this authority was formally acknowledged, it was not obeyed. Gallic liberties were asserted and maintained in architecture as in religion.

It is not within the scope of this book to give a complete history of French Renaissance architecture, or to refer, except briefly, to the forms which it assumed in succeeding reigns. Any one interested in the subject will find information in the volume of Mr. Fergusson's book on the Renaissance styles, especially in the woodcuts with which it is illustrated. I cannot, however, always agree with Mr. Fergusson in his criticisms on these styles.

The architecture of the time of Henry II. (1547-59) had the purer Classic forms of the later style of his father, covered with rich and beautiful ornament. A well-known example is the south buildings of the court of the Louvre, where Henry's initial is united on the carved panels with that of Diane de Poitiers.

The style of Charles IX. (1560-74) had many of the characteristics of our own contemporary Elizabethan, an outcome of the same spirit which delighted in quirks and fancies, which took Classic features such as the projected corner stones and carved them with bands and straps, made columns and pilasters tapering outwards instead of inwards, and finished them with grotesques for capitals. The world was young again and was playing itself.

But the authority of the Classic style was ever reasserting itself. The palace of the Tuileries, commenced by Catherine de Medici in 1564, from the designs of Phillibert de Lorme, is almost pure Classic, but French rather than Italian in character.

In Henry IV.'s reign (1589–1610) architecture became still more Classic. In the two great pavilions which he added at each end of the façade of the Louvre, he employed great pilasters running through two stories. In the designs of the gallery, which he commenced to connect the palace with the Louvre, this range of great pilasters is continued, surmounted by pediments alternately curved and straight-sided. The design is mere external ornament, the windows being placed alternately under the centre of these pediments, and in the spaces between them.

The architecture of the palace of the Luxembourg, designed about 1611 by De Brosse, is better, inasmuch as it accords with the internal arrangements. The order ranges with each story. It is said that Catherine de' Medici, for whom it was built, insisted that it should be a copy of the Pitti Palace at Florence—not evidently of its massive front of gigantic stones, but of the later buildings towards the Boboli gardens, which it resembles in the smaller and more orderly rustication with which its surface is covered. A French character is given to the building by the tall slated roofs, which are unknown in Italy.

During the long reign of Louis XIV. (1643-1715) the authority of the Classic orders was unquestioned, but an independent style grew up alongside of them, employed chiefly in internal decorations. We know it as the style of Louis Quatorze, and its influence on our upholstery has continued to our own time. Those strange twisted carvings like capital G's interlocked, which we find on chiffoniers at seaside lodgings, are the last dregs of it. Straight lines and rectangles are the natural forms for a panelled door. But in this style they were bent and curved and broke out in flourishes. In one instance which I have seen, even the window-bars which divided the window into small panes were curved in wavy lines, so as to give the panes ornamental forms, in sympathy with the decoration of the room. In French hands the style was graceful and elegant, but, like the morals of the court whose palaces it adorned, it was not pure. In religion, after due deference was paid to the authority of the Church, society felt unrestrained in luxury and morals; and, in the architecture of the time, "the Orders" having been duly acknowledged, usually in some outside part where they did not interfere with convenience, unrestrained liberty prevailed in the internal decorations, which, however, were always charming and gay. One feature of these decorations is the prevalence of white. We wonder now at finding oak carvings painted white, and think it due to the barbarism of a subsequent time; but in France, and in this country also, it was so intended from the first; our laborious and expensive scraping to show the surface of the oak being often quite opposed to the intention of the original design.

The exterior architecture is handsome and elegant, but dull. It is always on its good behaviour; its first essential is symmetry; carried out not only to the remotest corner of the building—the kitchen wing on one side the exact copy of the stable wing on the other—but to the bridges and summer-houses of the gardens, and miles away in the straight alleys through the woods. The orders are scrupulously correct. The decorations are strictly confined to Classical subjects; nymphs, gods and goddesses; the representation of a Frenchman of the period being permissible only on condition of its being in Roman costume.

This style continued during the earlier part of the reign of Louis XV. (1715-1774). A book of plans and designs for châteaux, "De la distribution des Maisons de plaisance et de la décoration des édifices en général," published by Jacques François Blondel (Paris, 1737-1738), an architect of this time, throws much light on the habits and ideas of the aristocracy. One of the most striking features to us is the absence of servants' accommodation. Occasionally, in explaining a plan, the author states that servants' rooms are provided in the roofs; but Classic authority had by this time succeeded in flattening the roofs to the low Italian pitch; the rooms are miserable in size, and, with only slates between them and the air, hot in summer, cold in winter. No windows in the elevations give indication of their existence; the dignity of the architecture was far too important a matter to be sacrificed for the sake of light and air for servants.

The space is quite inadequate for the numberless servants of a great French house. Doubtless, however, many of them lived not in the house, but in the village beside it, the near neighbourhood of which the seigneur no more felt an intrusion on his privacy than we do the servants' accommodation of our houses, for it belonged to him, and only his dependants lived in it. This custom of the servants of a great house living not in it but in the neighbourhood still survives in the colleges of Oxford and Cambridge.

The plans of these French châteaux indicate a life of which the aim was display and pleasure. On the ground-floor magnificent ranges of entertaining rooms; on the upper floor, the central feature is the lord's bedroom with its antechamber for those who attended his "levee," and sometimes a low rail like that across a chancel, making a sacred enclosure round the bed, within which the specially favoured were admitted while he was dressing. There is always a "*dégagement*" by which he could leave his room without encountering those waiting for him in the antechambers. The larger châteaux of this age had usually connected with them a building, called the Trianon after that at Versailles, the purpose of which was to allow a small select company to disembarrass themselves of the crowd of guests in the great house. It contained rooms for billiards and card playing, a small kitchen for private dinners, and a couple of bedrooms, one with a private cabinet for the lord. "All these little apartments," says Blondel, describing a "Trianon," of which he gives designs, "being for relaxation, nothing should be neglected to render the decoration joyful and gallant. Here genius may take a spring and abandon itself to the vivacity of its caprices, not as in the apartments of parade, where she should restrain herself within the most exact rules of propriety and good taste, and not fall into the unmeasured liberties of our modern sculpture and ornament, which ought to be banished from these all the more that true architects can scarcely tolerate them in places such as I am describing." "In the card-room Indian and Chinese plants and figures may form part of the decoration; they are naturally suited to it, and it is in this place only that in my view they should be admitted."

Such determined efforts at pleasure produce a saddening effect, which somehow seems to communicate itself to the architecture, which is dull, in spite of its unmeasured licence.

In the latter part of the reign of Louis XV. the style of architecture and decoration became simpler and more severe. The same influence showed itself at the time in England also, as in the refined and elegant forms of silverplate in the reigns of the early Georges. The appreciation of Classic form became more accurate and the attempts to imitate it more successful, if less interesting, as in the Church of St. Geneviève at Paris, better known as the Panthéon; the building of which occupied the latter part of the eighteenth century.

The troubles of the Revolution and the uncertainty which preceded it were not favourable to architecture; and, when the country again became settled under the empire, taste had become still more accurately Classic. The old Roman invention of inserting an arch between the columns was perceived to be a mistake. In the Madeleine and the Bourse at Paris the columns stand free, supporting the entablature, and forming a colonnade round the walls of the building as in a Greek temple.

The Gothic revival of our time has had little influence in France, compared with what it has had in England. A few churches have been built in the style which, though they have most of them the merit, which ours seldom have, of being vaulted, are generally poor and weak in design. Houses in the style are rare, and public buildings almost unknown. At the same time, France has produced excellent books on the old historical Gothic.

During the reign of Louis-Philippe, and in the earlier days of the second empire, some houses were designed in what is called the Néogrec style. Some of these are interesting and beautiful; not slavish copies of Greek remains, but a new form of the style suited to modern wants and showing invention and originality. But this fashion, too, has passed, and the tendency now seems to be to return to the earlier developments of the Renaissance style of the country. Tall steep roofs had never been wholly abandoned. They are a characteristic of the modern street architecture. The galleries by which Napoleon III. united the Tuileries to the Louvre exhibit this feature, with a great dormer window on each side, exuberant in decoration. Some of the hotels lately built near the Champs-Élysées exhibit still earlier forms of French Renaissance, occasionally even windows with stone mullions.

French architects generally show more knowledge and training in their work than ours, except when they attempt Gothic, in which their opportunities have been fewer and their skill is inferior. Their houses are more complete in style throughout than ours, for it is the custom there that the architect designs and superintends not only the building proper but the decorations and the furniture, which with us are often left to the upholsterer. The French workmen, too, are better-skilled than ours in art. Their Classic traditions have not been broken, and though they do not profess themselves "art workmen," they inherit a style, and give their work an artistic character naturally and without effort, and therefore cheaply.

It would be foolhardy to attempt to predict what will be

the future style of domestic architecture in France; for there, as with us, the style is determined in each instance by the taste and skill of the individual architects. The new buildings of the Palace of Justice at Paris, designed by M. Le Duc (not M. Viollet-le-Duc, the author of the excellent Dictionary of Gothic Architecture), exhibit an original treatment of Classic, refined and almost Greek in character. Other instances, especially some modern châteaux and hotels outvie the richest examples of the old Renaissance in exuberance of ornament and curved forms. There seems little prospect at present that a single style will prevail over the country at one time, gradually growing, or changing as new influences affect it, as was the case with the old historical styles. It seems more likely that we may see what has already happened in costume and ladies' dress, which are governed no longer by tradition, but by passing fashions. But the fashions in architecture, however frequently changing, will probably keep within the limits of the Classic style, which has for three centuries been the style of the country.

CHAPTER XII.

THE RENAISSANCE IN GERMANY AND THE LOW COUNTRIES.

THE new light of the Renaissance in art came to Germany later than to France. Its first glimmerings came through the painters, who crossed the Alps into the north of Italy to study the works of the great contemporary Italian school. The elder Holbein (b. 1498, d. 1559) was one of the earliest. Albert Dürer (b. 1471, d. 1528) was in Venice in the year 1506, but the Renaissance influence which these and others brought back extended no farther than their paintings, in which Classical backgrounds begin to appear.

Many years elapsed before the new spirit began to affect architecture. It showed itself first about 1520, in ecclesiastical palaces and bishops' monuments; for the bishops were naturally in constant communication with Italy and looked to it as a source of light in this as in other matters. The parts of Germany which remained Roman Catholic adopted the Renaissance architecture earlier than those which became Protestant.

The old part of the palace at Dresden was built in 1530.

By the middle of the century the new style had begun to spread rapidly.

Like other Renaissance styles the German inherited the features of the Gothic of the country. The special characteristic of German domestic Gothic was a tendency to give importance, by ornament and great size, to the gables. Sometimes they were covered with tracery worked on the surface in stone or in brick. The two gables from Nurem-

Fig. 79. Fig. 80.
GABLES AT NUREMBERG.

berg (figs. 79 and 80) show a pretty treatment in brick, by means of small projections or buttresses terminating in little Gothic arches. The chimney is placed not on the apex, but on the side, so as not to destroy the triangular form of the gable.

But the most usual form was the stept gable. Instead of the gable following the line of the roof and sloping with it to the apex, it was carried up above it, and diminished by several great steps or intakes. These steps were ornamented with tracery, sometimes pierced where they projected above the roof to give them greater lightness and play of light.

These gables had usually several stories in their height. They were the features in the building of most interest to the designers; the chief field for ornament; in towns they were towards the street. These characteristics the German Renaissance inherited, changing the Gothic ornaments and details into Classic ones.

This process is well illustrated by the accompanying drawing of part of a street in Münster (fig. 81), which has already been given, but is inserted here for convenience of reference. The taller house is a typical example of late Gothic, though it has lost something of its Gothic character, from the removal of the mullions and tracery of the windows. The lower part is without ornament, but from the cornice level the design springs upwards with true Gothic aspiration. The stepping of the gables is disguised somewhat by the ornamental pillars or pinnacles, as compared with the simple steps of the gable of the house farther off, part of which the drawing shows.

The Renaissance house is similar in design. The arcade of pointed arches probably belongs to an earlier building, of which this portion had been left when the house was rebuilt, as it is a portion of the continued arcade of the street. As in the Gothic house, the lower stories are plain, and the ornamentation commences at the cornice level. This gable also is stept, but the steps are disguised by being filled up with scrolls. The horizontal lines are more enforced; the chief characteristic of Classic architecture, as compared with Gothic. There is not the same impression of aspiration, though Gothic influence survives in the little spikes or pinnacles, but there is more ease and gaiety.

The general effect of this gabled architecture is shown by the accompanying drawing of one of the streets of Landshut (fig. 82). It contains both Classic and Gothic houses, but the effect of the two is so similar that we hardly distinguish them.

This mode of building a street, by setting the gable ends

Fig. 81. HOUSES AT MÜNSTER, WESTPHALIA.

Fig. 82.

STREET IN LANDSHUT, BAVARIA.

towards it, is unpractical and inconvenient. It necessitates a gutter between each house, which can have no overflow except at the ends, and, if it leaks, leaks into the houses. If the chimneys are in the party-walls, which is often the most convenient position for them, they must rise from this gutter to the height of the ridge, with a risk of smoking, and expensive to build. There is danger besides, of fire spreading from one roof to another, when there is no solid wall between the houses rising higher than the roof. For these reasons the practice has been gradually given up.

In the drawing of the Carolinen-Strasse, at Nuremberg (frontispiece), it will be seen that though some of the houses have their gables to the streets, in most of them the cornice is to the street, and the gable between the houses.

An effect of as great or even greater picturesqueness is obtained by this means. It gives the expanse of roof broken up by little windows, characteristic of the Nuremberg houses, as well as smaller gables or dormer windows, toward the street. These were indispensable to a German house, for the stories in these great roofs were used as store-places, and for the periodical washings of the family. The great stores of linen which each house possessed made the discomfort of a family washing necessary only about every three months. The same custom still prevails in Germany and Holland; the extensive floor space of the stories of the roof was used for washing, mangling, and drying; and to facilitate the last process, the little windows in the roofs were opened so as to create a through draft. Hence a derrick projecting over the street was necessary in each house, as may be seen in the drawing, for hoisting up or down the linen as well as the stores. Some part of the space was usually devoted to keep these. Other portions were occasionally used for drying apples, the produce of the family orchards.

Nuremberg, above all other cities, gives one the impression

of a city of the Middle Ages; yet this impression is produced by houses Classic in date and details. A Gothic city existed before the present one, as the two great Gothic churches testify, and the view in the Nuremberg Chronicle, in the year 1498. The Nassauer House (fig. 50, p. 177), and some others remain. But most of the streets have been rebuilt in Classic style, and so handsomely and conveniently that nothing would be gained by rebuilding it in the present day.

Here, as elsewhere in the early Renaissance, the essential spirit of the style is Gothic. It has Gothic freedom and picturesqueness and aspiration, though doubtless the good burghers thought they were carrying out true Classic. The words were Classic, but they were embodied in the old language. The builders were trained to familiarity with them, and used them as their natural mode of expression, but they had not changed their nature; the Classic words express Gothic feelings and ideas.

Fig. 83. HOUSES ON THE PEGNITZ, NUREMBERG.

It is this unconsciousness, this perfect naturalness, which gives the charm to these streets. They are the natural outcome of the circumstances, and are entitled to be considered examples of a true style. (Frontispiece.)

There is a character and picturesqueness about the Nuremberg houses which gives a charm even to those in the poorer districts, like those in my sketch beside the river, fig. 83.

In her Renaissance style Germany retained another characteristic of her Gothic architecture, the projecting bow windows, not rising from the ground, but hung out from the upper stories; which, as the illustrations show, occur so frequently in the houses. Almost every house in Nuremberg has one such, usually attached to the principal dwelling-room of the house. That at St. Sebald's Parsonage, opposite the church, is a beautiful Gothic example, well known from photographs and drawings. There is a pretty little one on the centre of the Nassauer House (fig. 50, page 177), facing St. Lawrence Church. In the Renaissance houses of Nuremberg they were usually square in plan, with a curved Classic pediment over them. This sketch from Freiburg in Breisgau (fig. 84), is a late Gothic example of a square projecting oriel. Sometimes they were continued through the several stories, as in the house to the right in the drawing of the Carolinen - Strasse, (Frontispiece, and the house at Würzburg, illustrated in page 273).

But the form of projecting windows, peculiarly characteristic of German house architecture, is the *Erker* or *Eckfenster*, a lantern or turret, pierced with windows all round, projecting from the corner of the house. The idea doubtless sprang from the angle turrets of Gothic fortification, of which the little house at Boppart (fig. 49, p. 176), is an illustration. The idea is fully developed in the beautiful example of late Gothic date at Augsburg (fig. 48, page 169). On the corner of the Bishop's house at Würzburg (fig. 86) there is a beautiful and picturesque example, dating from the last quarter of the sixteenth century. It has carved on

Fig 84. ORIEL AT FREIBURG IN BREISGAU.

it the arms of Bishop of Julius who founded the university about 1590. It is Classic in the detail of the cornices, but Gothic in its picturesqueness as well as in the mullions and transoms dividing the windows. The other windows of the house have Gothic interpenetrating mouldings, even that over the pretty little Classic doorway with its fluted Corinthian columns. The Classic architecture seems to have been employed on the parts intended to be specially beautiful and ornamental. Where use alone was aimed at, the familiar Gothic was thought good enough. The massive arched doorway, on the flank of the Bishop's house, seems an alteration of the eighteenth century.

Fig. 85. INN AT KRIEGSHABEN, NEAR AUGSBURG.

The drawing of the house opposite the Cathedral at Augsburg (fig. 9, page 40), gives a later example of these corner turret windows. The ogee form of the corbels supporting the turrets, as well as the flattened arches, seem to indicate that the building dates from the eighteenth century. Sometimes the builders made projections at the ground-level, as the little inn at Kriegshaben near Augsburg (fig. 85) shows. In date and details it is late Classic, but there is a picturesqueness, I must even say dodginess, in the arrangement of the structure which ought to charm the heart of a modern Gothic architect, and to convince him that the characteristics, which he loves so much, are not peculiar to his favourite style.

These projections from the general wall surface of the houses give great interest and picturesqueness to the streets of Nuremberg and other German towns. They relieve the

Fig. 86. BISHOP'S HOUSE, WÜRZBURG.

dull monotony, which is the chief characteristic of our modern towns, and they make the houses pleasanter to live in. Our modern building Acts forbid them, partly with a view to uniformity and regularity, which it seems their great object to encourage, partly because the encroachment they make on the street is supposed to be an evil, and partly perhaps because the framers of these Acts seem to have thought that the small amount of skill in building required for their construction was beyond what modern builders could with safety be allowed to attempt; for they are forbidden by the London building Acts, even where the house is set back from the street and they do not project over the roadway.

Another characteristic of the Renaissance architecture of Germany, which is also found in her Gothic, is the arrangement of the ground-floor in the houses, and the uses to which it was put. It was not generally used for living rooms or bed-rooms. As in Italy, people seem to have preferred to live not on the ground, but one story at least above it. So the ground-floor was left to be utilised as best it might. Sometimes it was occupied as cellars, or for storing farm produce. When, as is still frequently the case in German towns, the merchant's house was also his place of business, the ground-floor served as the magazine for storing and selling his goods. Sometimes it was unappropriated, left open to the street as in the Neu-Münsterhof at Würzburg (fig. 87), and provided with stone benches for public convenience; or the front part of it, as at Münster (fig. 81, page 261), appropriated as a covered arcade for foot passengers.

The picturesque house in the same city (fig. 88, page 273) shows a characteristic feature of south German house arrangement in the great door, wide and high enough to admit a loaded waggon to the court behind, with the smaller door beside it for access to the house. Sometimes almost the whole of this ground-floor was occupied with a large hall provided with stone benches, generally open to the public, from the inner end of which ascended the great staircase to the house proper, which occupied the floor above.

Fig. 87.   NEÜ-MUNSTERHOF, WÜRZBURG.

A special characteristic of German house architecture, is the imperfect development, and small importance of the chimneys, as compared with those in French and English houses. This arose from the use of close stoves instead of the great open fireplace, common in France and with us. This feature also is an inheritance from Gothic times, for stoves of Gothic date still exist in Germany. There is one such in the Castle of Landshut, another in the Castle of Coburg, made of cast-iron, and a very splendid one in the Rathhaus at Ochsenfurth formed of moulded tiles coloured and glazed.

Another feature of German house architecture is the frequency, especially in the northern provinces, of houses wholly constructed of wood. The house at Hildesheim, of which I give an illustration, for which I am indebted to the kindness of the

Fig. 89.   HOUSE AT WÜRZBURG.

proprietors of 'The Builder,' is a notable example (fig. 90). It has, I believe, been destroyed by fire, but others similar still exist in that city and in other towns in the neighbourhood. It was constructed entirely of chestnut—not like the usual post-and-pan houses of other parts of Germany, England, and northern France, of a wooden framework filled in with plaster panels—It dates probably from about the year 1620, and is similar in its construction and in the ornament of its carved panels to some houses in the Rue de la Grande Horloge at Rouen. But in the tendency the design shows to dwell on the gables and make the most of them, and in

Fig. 69. RATHHAUS, MANNHEIM.

the imperfect development of its chimneys it is thoroughly German; the great gable is peculiarly German in character. Except as an ornamental feature, the second small gable round the corner has no *raison d'être*.

This house exhibits another feature, which so far as I am aware is not found in houses of the period in any other district. The upper windows, as will be observed, have sliding sashes. These unmullioned windows are so completely part of the design that it is improbable that they are an alteration of later date, especially as sash windows are found in other houses of the date in the same district. Sliding sash windows, which have now become a British institution and an important element of English comfort, came to us, like our broad dining tables, with Dutch William from Holland. But they seem to have been in use in north Germany before the Dutch adopted them.

A feature of German architecture which strikes an Englishman at first as strange, are the bulbous protuberances formed of copper which occasionally occur on the

Fig. 90. WOODEN HOUSE AT HILDESHEIM.

roofs. The tower of the Rathhaus at Mannheim (fig. 89) terminates in one of these; the lower part of this roof, where the square gathers into the octagon, is of slate. The tower itself is late Classic, not unpicturesque. Much more marked examples are to be found; small spires blossoming into a string of them, like tulip bulbs stuck at intervals on a stick. They are not a peculiarly German feature: we all know the remarkable specimens on the Cathedral of Antwerp. They may not be correct architecture, probably they are not; but they are quaint and interesting and picturesque, and the green colour of the copper is always beautiful.

It has been impossible within my limits, to trace the successive developments of the Renaissance style in each province of Germany. Those who wish to gain this knowledge will find the information, if they can read German, in Wilhelm Lübke's excellent work, 'Die Neuere Baukunst in Deutschland,' published at Stuttgart in 1873, collected with true German thoroughness, and amply illustrated by excellent woodcuts. My aim has been merely to give some notion of the Renaissance style in Germany, and to show that here, as elsewhere, its peculiar development was influenced and determined by the native Gothic style of the country.

The Renaissance architecture of Germany has not usually been considered to have great artistic merit, or much interest. Mr. Fergusson says of it (vol. iii. p. 336): "The Germans were not more successful in their attempts at Secular architecture during the period of the Renaissance, than in their Ecclesiastical buildings. The architect wanders in vain through the capitals of Germany in hopes of finding something either so original or so grand that it should dwell on the memory, even if it does not satisfy the rules of taste." "Nothing (p. 341) can be more unsatisfactory or less interesting than the history of German architecture during the Renaissance period."

This is partly true if domestic architecture has no interest except in palaces where vast sums are expended. I think, however, that architecture may be interesting and worthy of study even in small houses for middle class people. The German nobles were not generally fortunate in their palace building. In the seventeenth century in their palaces, as in their government and their manners, they attempted clumsy imitations of the glory and elegance of the Court of Versailles, alien from the best characteristics of the people. But Mr. Fergusson's assertion (p. 341) that, "during the three centuries of the Renaissance period, the German nobles built no city palaces to be compared in any way with those which adorn every town in Italy, nor one single country residence that can match in grandeur the country seats that are found in every county in England," can be refuted by a number of examples. Lübke's book gives numerous examples of nobles' castles, and especially of town houses, which in their own way may fairly compare with those of other countries.

But the German race has never been remarkable for the display of the highest qualities of art, either in colour or in form. Even her greatest painters cannot properly be called colourists, like the great Italians. Nor is their work remarkable for beauty of form; their merit lay rather in depth of feeling and an elevated tone of truth and morality. The Renaissance architecture, which the Germans got from Italy, lost in their hands its beauty of line and perfection of proportion; nor did it, as in France, acquire a special grace and refinement of its own. It has a want of elegance, sometimes even an air of clumsiness. But it has a picturesqueness and variety, which make German towns more interesting than any others in Europe, and truth and common sense, which is always satisfactory.

These old German streets are certainly more interesting and beautiful than those which we are producing in our modern towns, and yet they contain no marvels of art, such as we should be incapable of producing. I have attempted in a former chapter to give some of the reasons why we do not produce such streets.

I have no intention of attempting to give an account and history of the Renaissance style in other countries of Europe, though in some of these, especially Belgium and the Low Countries, more artistic specimens of architecture are to be found than in Germany. Holland, though she produced a notable school of painters, seems to have expended little invention on domestic architecture. The houses are all of brick. The earlier ones have mullioned windows and simple stept gables; a type which prevails generally in the Low Countries. The later houses in Holland, as at Amsterdam, are all of one type, not unlike the older London red-brick houses, the idea of which seems to have been derived from them; but the variations in the Dutch houses though very slight, the life which the water and boats of the canals and the trees which line their sides give them, make the canals of Amsterdam much more interesting than London streets. The style of the interiors is a mild echo of that of Louis Quinze. They are roomy and the workmanship is excellent. In one I visited, the owner told me that the white paint of the drawing-room had not been renewed for a hundred years.

Belgium, perhaps in consequence of the Celtic blood of the people, had more art; this was evident in Gothic times, and still more during the Renaissance. The decorations, especially of the houses and churches, such as the hammered brass-work, or Dinanderie, so called from the town of Dinan, where it was largely made; the stamped leather for covering walls, and the ornamental sculpture in marble, rival those of Italy, whose type they followed.

Italian influence was strong and direct. It is difficult of some ornamental work to say, at first sight, whether it is Italian or from the Low Countries. But native genius also gives itself free scope. In the carved wood pulpits of the great churches it revelled in a freedom which sometimes exceeded the bounds of taste and the capacity of the material.

In Renaissance architecture the Low Countries produced a variety of their own, more refined and imaginative than the German. The town hall of Antwerp, erected by Cornelius de Vriendt in 1581, is a charming building; the open loggia under the roof gives interest and grandeur by its shadow, and reminds one of the similar feature in Florentine palaces.

To this building the town hall of Amsterdam is a melancholy contrast. No expense is spared; it is of gigantic size, and built of stone in a country where every stone had to be brought from a long distance; but the art to direct the expenditure was wanting. It is dull, heavy, and uninteresting. No fancy is displayed, and the proportions are bad. Amsterdam was rich, but not artistic; she did not care for art, and did not know it when she saw it. She spent the money for brag, not for art, and got what she wanted. In this, she much resembles ourselves. We are anxious to be artistic, because it is the proper thing, and are, therefore, quite willing to spend money on it, but we do not quite know how.

In Belgium the influence of its Spanish rulers gave greater sumptuousness and magnificence to architecture and the decorative arts; for the Spaniards, in those days, had amongst them artists as great as any in Europe, and they had lordly tastes. Under Spanish influence and to the order of Spaniards the most splended stampt-leather, the richest metal work, the most magnificent stained glass were executed.

The group of houses in the Market Place, Brussels (fig. 91),

Fig. 91.   HOUSES IN THE MARKET PLACE, BRUSSELS.

shows this Spanish influence. They exhibit, in a degree rarely attained, the qualities of richness and sumptuousness. There is a playfulness about them which is very charming. Every house has a character of its own. That built by some admiral, with its gable like the stern of his ship, is specially picturesque and interesting.

Great artistic skill is needed, when houses are mere tall narrow strips like these, to give them any artistic effect. We give up the attempt and make our houses by the foot run, and cut them off in lengths as required.

It was not always so with us, as we shall see in the next chapter.

Fig. 92.   OLD HOUSE AT LUCERNE.

CHAPTER XIII.

THE RENAISSANCE IN ENGLAND.

THE new architecture, in anything approaching the purity of the Italian style, took root in England as the accepted style for ordinary buildings later than in any of the countries I have already spoken of.

The English are a conservative people. The native style was strong and vigorous, sensible and suited to domestic wants, understood by the builders and liked by the people. They were proud of its achievements in buildings like King's College Chapel at Cambridge, and of the new magnificence which it had added to almost every church in the country, and they had no thought of such revolutionary change in their habits as the adoption of the new style would have involved. Till our own day, when the Great Exhibition of 1851 destroyed the last remnants of traditional art remaining in England, it survived still in some remote parts as the style of village tradesmen, for unimportant buildings such as cottages or barns.

Yet there exist still in England pure examples of Classic art, dating from an earlier period than any such in Germany

Fig. 94. LONGLEAT, WILTSHIRE. FROM AN OLD PRINT.

or even in France. The tomb of Henry VII. in his chapel at Westminster, dating from the first years of his successor's reign which began in 1509, is the work of the Italian Torrigiano, and bears no trace of English Gothic influence. In the Rolls Chapel, Chancery Lane, there is a monument by the same artist to Dr. John Young, Master of the Rolls, who preceded Sir Thomas More in that office.

The ornamental parts of the stained-glass windows of King's College Chapel at Cambridge, are Classic in design, but these also are foreign importations, and had no influence on the general architecture. The fittings of the chapel, the altar-screen and stalls are also Classic; but the old tradition of English art was too strong for such small and isolated examples to make any impression on it. They remained mere foreign importations. By the quarrel between the King and the Pope in 1533, when Cranmer pronounced the divorce of the marriage between Henry and Catherine, Italian ideas in this as in other spheres were deprived in England, as in the Protestant parts of Germany, of the influence they would otherwise have had.

The Classic style was first introduced into the architectural construction of buildings, apart from mere decorative adjuncts, in Elizabeth's reign (1558-1603), in Longleat in Wiltshire; it is said, by John of Padua, between 1567 and 1597.

The accompanying view of this house (fig. 93) I copied from an old print, for the purpose of showing the arrangement of the gardens, which are now destroyed. It does not accurately represent the present condition of the house. The square projecting bays are in reality wider and flatter than shown; their cornices are of pure Classic contour, without the corbels shown in the drawing, and the pilasters are broader and shorter in proportion. The aprons under the windows are different in form. The great door as it exists now is more purely Classic in character. It has only

one column on each side, a broken Italian pediment the full
width of the door, with a shield in the centre; but this
looks like a later alteration made when the terrace leading
to it was destroyed to give space for a carriage-drive to the
door, and the present great flight of steps made leading
directly to it. In its essential features the building is late
English Gothic, ornamented with a few Classic details, and
so little impression had these made, and so thoroughly did
the art of the country remain Gothic in principle that
this drawing of a much later date Gothicises even its Classic
features.

To the influence of an Italian designer we probably owe
the pilasters of the bays, with their entablature and cornice,
which are designed in the actual building in excellent Classic
proportions. In the spaces left between these are inserted,
instead of the round arch of Classic architecture, English
mullioned and transomed windows, obviously not due to the
suggestion of an Italian artist, but to the English master
mason of the period. This seems a scarcely adequate result
for the employment of an artist specially brought from
Italy. But in England as in France the Italian artists
found a sphere for their art in the fittings and sculpture of
the internal decorations. The external building was wisely
left to the skill of the native workmen, who knew how to
build to suit English habits and the English climate.

In the time of King James the authority of the Classic
orders had become an accepted article of faith, and a part of
the ordinary building style of the country. This was due
in some degree to the influence of the new literature. The
Classic orders were part of the new light which the Renaissance brought to mankind. The treatise of Vitruvius
became the Bible of architecture. In it, and other books,
and in buildings abroad, the new art was studied by many
gentlemen, who doubtless tried, as country gentlemen some-

times try now, to get their workmen to carry out their ideas. A great building like Longleat would train many workmen, who, regarding what they had there learned as the newest light on art, would repeat it on the first opportunity. These new ideas were adopted, as new or foreign words are taken into a language, of which the construction remains unchanged. So the principles and construction of the style remained English. The workmen accepted the Classic features of columns, entablature, and mouldings, but they did not catch the Classic spirit or ideas.

The process of development was irregular, being dependent on the knowledge of the new architecture which each designer happened to have attained, so that the greater or less purity of the Classic details in a building is no sure test of its date. The result in the Elizabethan and Jacobean styles is very different from pure Classic, and was shocking to those who regarded the five orders as the standard of truth. When Classic architecture became generally known and acknowledged in authority, the new style was ridiculed as King James' Gothic. But it was the natural development of the circumstances, and is fairly entitled to be called a national style.

It was full of the quirks and fancies, which, as the literature of the time shows, occupied the minds of people in that generation. It delighted in abundance of window light, as a reaction against the small narrow windows, hitherto rendered necessary by the conditions of defence, as if the builders wished to reproduce in their dwellings the new intellectual light.

The drawings (figs. 94 and 95), for which I am indebted to the kindness of the proprietors of 'The Graphic,' of an interior in Lime Street, pulled down by the Fishmongers' Company in 1876, show a fair example of the new style which was formed by the union of the Classic ideas with the old native architecture. The screen between the two rooms (fig. 94) is according to the common Classic recipe—the round arch inserted between the columns and lintel,[1] but the workman has carved it out in his own way and has put his own ideas into it, as in the consoles of the frieze, which are after no Classic model, but of English growth. But there is no Classic authority for the design of the great chimney-piece (fig. 95). Classic columns and mouldings are used, but instead of the Classic principle of column resting upon column, massive below and getting lighter as it rises, the design springs upwards in great corbels, and the two columns in the upper part are supported, and supported without any sense of weakness, by the single one below. This lower column is of a form for which there is no Classic authority. Instead of its weight pressing down on the ground it seems to spring from it. The form is similar to that of a baluster. It occurs in French architecture, but it is a special note of the Elizabethan and Jacobean styles.

Classic architecture in anything like purity of style was first introduced into England by Inigo Jones. An excellent life of him, which by careful research brings out many new facts, was published in 1848 by the Shakespeare Society, written by their Secretary, Mr. Peter Cunningham. From this I shall state briefly the main facts of his career as an architect. He was born in 1573, the son of Inigo Jones, Clothworker, living in the parish of St. Bartholomew-the-less, in West Smithfield, London. His father (a native, it is thought, of Wales) was badly off when Jones was a lad of sixteen, as there is record that he had difficulty in paying a debt of £80. He died in 1597, when Inigo was in his twenty-fourth year, leaving debts, but apparently little property. Inigo, it is said, had been bound apprentice to a joiner—Ben Jonson ridiculed him as a joiner—in any case

---

[1] The two arches in the screen were not of the same date, the one nearer the chimney-piece was a later addition, probably about Queen Anne's time. Its detail was more *Classical* than the earlier arch.

Fig. 94.—INTERIOR OF AN OLD HOUSE IN LIME STREET, LONDON.

Fig. 95.   CHIMNEY-PIECE IN OLD HOUSE IN LIME STREET, LONDON.

no bad training for an architect. He was early distinguished, his pupil Webb tells us, for his skill in drawing and designing and in landscape painting. He went to Italy while young, but at what time is uncertain. "Being naturally inclined," he says in his book on Stonehenge, "in my younger years to study the arts of design, I passed into foreign parts to converse with the great masters thereof in Italy, where I applied myself to search out the ruins of those ancient buildings which, in despite of time itself and violence of barbarians, are yet remaining. Having satisfied myself in these, and returning to my native country, I applied my mind more particularly to architecture." Christianus IV., King of Denmark, Webb tells us, sent for him out of Italy, where, especially at Venice, he had resided many years. His stay in Denmark, Webb says, was long. In 1604-5, when in his thirty-second year, he had returned to England, where he was employed by the Queen of James I., Anne of Denmark, the sister of Christianus, along with Ben Jonson, to produce a Masque at the Court at Whitehall.

During the succeeding years there are records of his being occasionally similarly employed, his share in the work being to design the scenery and dresses. Drawings still exist of the figures and characters which he prepared for these occasions.

In 1610, Prince Henry appointed him Surveyor of Works in his newly established household, in which year he employed him in devising the scenery of a masque. He held this office till the Prince's death in 1612, when he went again into Italy, as we know from an entry in his copy of 'Palladio,' dated "Vicenza, Mundaie the 23rd of September, 1613." Entries in his sketch-books show that he was at Rome, Naples, and Vicenza in 1614. In 1615 he returned to England to take possession of the office of Surveyor of the Works, the reversion of which the King had promised him. The office gave him sufficient employment in superintending the repairs of the King's numerous manor-houses and palaces, in arranging for royal progresses, and occasionally in devising scenes and machinery for masques and entertainments at Court, which were the occasion of a deadly quarrel between him and Ben Jonson.

In January 1629, the old Banqueting-house at Whitehall was burnt down, and Jones was commissioned to build a new one, the first stone of which was laid in June of the same year, and the building finished in March 1622. By an account preserved in the Audit Office, it appears that the basement was of Oxfordshire stone, cut into rustick on the outside; the upper part of Northamptonshire stone, and the balusters of Portland. As the whole of the present building is of Portland stone, it must have been refaced at a later period.

In 1620 he received the King's commands to investigate Stonehenge. From "some few undigested notes," which he had left, Webb published a treatise which declared that Stonehenge was a temple of the Tuscan order, raised by the Romans, and consecrated to the god Cœlus, the origin of all things; an idea possibly suggested to suit the views of "the wisest fool in Europe."

In 1618 he commenced the chapel at Lincoln's Inn, which was consecrated in 1623. The cloisters under it were intended as a place for the lawyers to meet their clients. This work is specially interesting, as showing the hold the old style still had, and the architect's knowledge of it. Notwithstanding its Doric columns and pilasters, from which the Gothic arches spring, it is able work. There was a rumour, I hope unfounded, that the Benchers actually proposed to destroy this piece of history, by "restoring" the chapel into correct Gothic.

About this time Jones[1] built the beautiful water-gate

---

[1] This has been doubted. There is a record that it was built by Stone, a builder at the time, but Jones may have given the designs. It looks like his work, and in style resembles the gate at the Botanical Gardens at Oxford, which he designed.

Fig. 96.   YORK GATE. A LANDING-PLACE ON THE THAMES.

to the town house of Villiers, Duke of Buckingham, still standing at the foot of Buckingham Street (fig. 96). The view shows it from the land side. A flight of steps under the centre arch descended to the water. On the river side the base has been buried under the new embankment. Perhaps some day the earth which conceals it might be removed, and a pond made before it, which, now that the river which once washed it is far removed, would suggest its original purpose. It is one of the few buildings which remains as it came from his hand; untouched save by time, which has given it colour and interest, and, if it has worn and softened the mouldings, still lets us trace his actual work. May it be spared from the restorer's or the destroyer's hand![1]

His next important works were the great west portico of old St. Paul's, and the Queen's house at Greenwich. St. Paul's was in a state of decay; the King and Laud wished him to rebuild it completely, and his portico was intended as an instalment of the new building. The nave of old St. Paul's had been long used as a lounge, for gossiping, for servants seeking places, and for people unable to afford a dinner, who were said to dine with Duke Humphrey, believed to have been buried there, though his tomb has since been identified at St. Albans. The new portico was intended to provide this public accommodation outside the church; and, to make room for it, Jones removed the Church of St. Gregory, which stood in front of it, in a somewhat high-handed manner, for which he had afterwards to answer.

The Queen's house at Greenwich was begun by Anne of Denmark, and completed by Henrietta Maria, whose name, and the date 1635, the period of its completion, are still on

[1] As I write, the Board of Works talk of raising its level, to form an entrance to Buckingham Street. Better let it remain as the old landmark of the river. Though it will stand if let alone, it will not bear reconstruction.

the front of the building. It is the central portion of the hospital, now the naval school. The present west side of the great square was built by Webb for Charles II., it is said from Jones' design.

In 1631 he commenced the Church of St. Paul's in Covent Garden, which was not finished till 1638. As he designed it it was of brick with a red tile roof, the columns of the portico and other parts of stone. Lord Burlington repaired it with care and reverence in 1727; and in 1795, on its total destruction by fire, it was rebuilt of stone, by the elder Hardwick, on the plan and proportions of the original structure. The piazza of Covent Garden was from his design—originally with stone columns on a red brick wall. These have been covered with paint and plaster, and are now being removed.

Few great architects have been so unlucky. Almost nothing that he planned was finished, and his works have been altered or rebuilt. In 1642 the Civil War broke out and stopped all building. He joined the King's party—he was a Roman Catholic, and was taken prisoner at the siege of Basing.[1] He died at Somerset House in June 1652, in his seventy-ninth year, and was buried beside his father and mother, in the church of St. Benet, Paul's Wharf.

Inigo Jones fell on evil times for art. Its quiet music was drowned in the noise of battles and the strife of parties. The nation had more important things to attend to. Had the King, Charles I., had his way; had he been allowed scope for his artistic tastes, by the help of the foreign painters whose works he admired, and with the genius of Inigo Jones and the trained workmen of the time to carry out their ideas in splendid buildings and works of art, England might have become a home of the arts. But to give absolute power to the Crown was too high a price for Englishmen to pay for this. Whitehall would have been

[1] Carlyle's 'Cromwell,' vol. ii. p. 259, 2nd edition.

one of the noblest palaces in Europe. Had it been built it would have settled for us, in a way we might have been proud of, the still unsettled question of Government buildings in Westminster, and would have given a higher tone to all the architecture of the country. There was skill in art, and an appreciation of it in the country at the time, sufficient to have realised a splendid palace both in details and decoration. But, seeing what its completion would have cost us politically, few Englishmen will regret that the conception was never realised. Is it too much to hope that the Government offices, which remain to be built, may have something of the beauty and refinement which Inigo Jones would have given us, with greater suitableness for our modern purposes than his great palace would have had?

The troubles which prevented the building of Whitehall prevented the carrying out of architectural works throughout the country. In some few cases Inigo Jones' designs were carried out, but for the most part they exist only on paper.

I have copied from the book of his designs published by Kent, the plans and elevation of a house for the Duke of Queensberry.[1] Mr. Fergusson decides, from what he thinks the inferior merit of the design (figs. 97 and 99, pp. 304, 305), that it is not Jones', but probably Webb's. I do not pretend to the same insight, but it is historically interesting, because it illustrates what was, till the Gothic revival, the general type of English country mansions. The distinctive feature is the portico in front. For the next hundred years no gentleman's mansion was complete without a portico.

It is true that this was an unmeaning decoration,—the feature is beautiful in itself, and it had been worked out by successive refinements to a high degree of perfection, but its proper use and purpose was gone. It is a " survival,"

---

[1] In Campbell's 'Vitruvius Britannicus' the same design is entitled Amresbury, Wiltshire.

like what is said to occur in the animal kingdom, of organs now useless which had served necessary functions in other circumstances in an earlier stage of the animal's development. In this case the portico is utilised as a covered balcony from the great hall on the first floor (fig. 100), an expedient which has been repeated in the buildings of University College, in London, but with unhappy results in our climate, so far as comfort and convenience go. Almost every great mansion built in England in the last century had such a portico, blocking out the light from bedroom windows, and making the house look cold and damp. Yet undoubtedly it gives grandeur to the design.

The back elevation in this design (fig. 99) is interesting, showing how a certain dignity of architectural effect can be produced by the simplest means without appearance of effort, for the position of the windows is determined, as may be seen by the plan, solely by the exigencies of the internal arrangement. The windows in the rooms E and K are kept in the centre, irrespective of any considerations of symmetry outside.

Short square windows, as in this design, in the upper story, or attic, as it is architecturally called, continued long a feature of Classic houses in this country. The horizontal band which they make gives a Classical effect, which would be destroyed by breaking them up through the cornice into the roof; while to increase the height of the building so as to make these windows taller, would spoil its proportions. But to have bedrooms dark and ill-ventilated, from the top of the windows being halfway down the wall inside is, perhaps, too high a price to pay for architectural proportion. The practice of the French Renaissance, of raising dormer windows above the line of the cornice, is more practical and better suited for our adoption.

The designs of Inigo Jones thoroughly carry out the Classic principle of symmetry. It is a principle of all forms

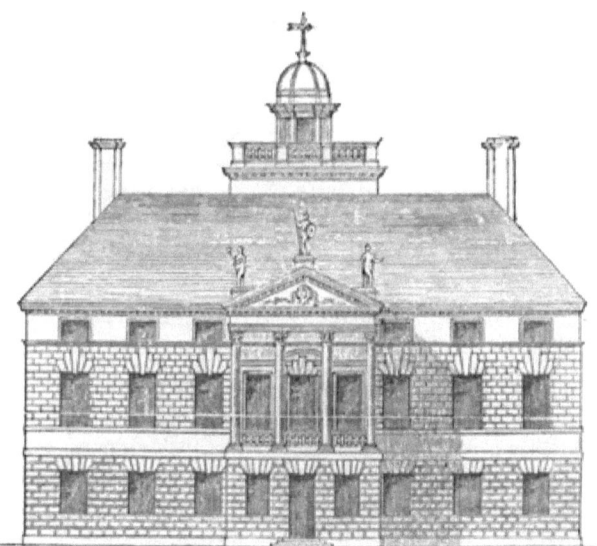

Fig. 97.   AMESBURY. FRONT ELEVATION.

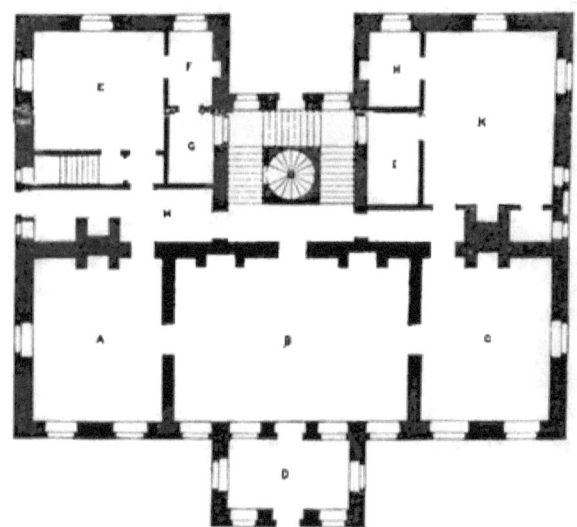

Fig. 98.   PLAN OF GROUND FLOOR.

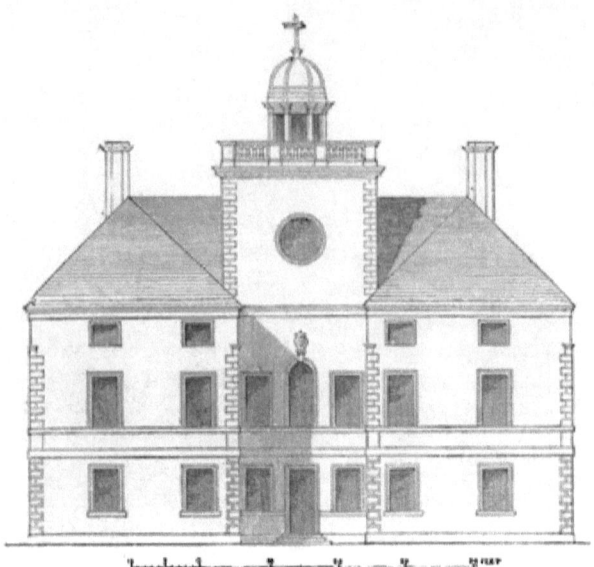

Fig. 99. AMRESBURY. BACK ELEVATION.

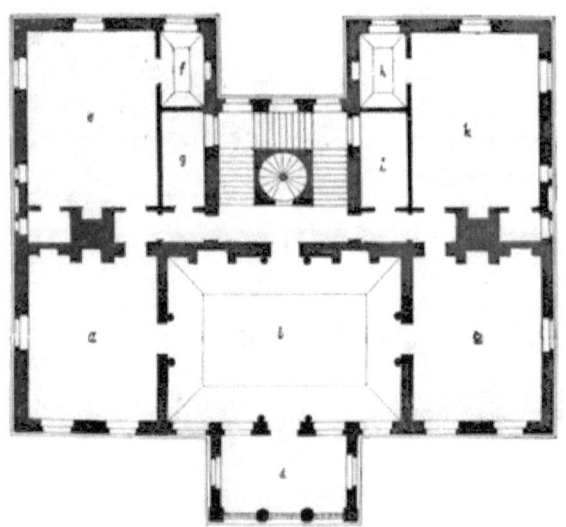

Fig. 100. PLAN OF UPPER FLOOR.

VOL. I. x

and types of architecture, as it is of animal organisation. It is essential to the highest dignity of great buildings, and it gives some even to small and simple ones. Among Jones' designs published by Kent there are some simple farmsteadings to which a really grand architectural effect is given by arranging the farm-buildings and enclosures with perfect symmetry on each side of the farmhouse.

It is an error to suppose that symmetry was not aimed at in Gothic buildings, though the architects felt that it was not essential in every case; as when of the two western towers of a cathedral which had originally been intended, they carried up only one, as at Strassburg, preferring the glory of height to symmetry, and feeling that two such high steeples would be absurd, as I fear that the two great steeples of Cologne may prove when they are finished. The old architects, if they had built both steeples, would have made them different in design.[1]

With our Gothic training we no longer consider symmetry essential, and think it even foolish to make the stables on one side of a house appear like a repetition of the kitchen offices on the other. The Gothic practice of allowing the internal arrangements to control the dispositions of the exterior architecture is a safer guide in house-planning, and more likely to attain satisfactory results in comfort and convenience than the Classic principle of making the internal arrangements fit in as best they may to the design of the outside.

The inner court of St. John's College at Oxford (fig. 101) is said to have been built by Inigo Jones. It was commenced in 1631, as we know from an entry in Laud's diary, "A.D. 1632, Julii 26. The first stone was laid of my building at St. John's." The next entry referring to the building

[1] Before the recent carrrying up of the *north* tower at Cologne, it was to be seen that the mediæval architects had given up all idea of making it similar to the south one, but the *restorers destroyed* the portions which varied in design from the opposite tower, and made both alike.

is on the 3rd of September, 1635, when he goes to St. John's from Cudsden, where he was staying, " to see my building there, and to give some directions for the last finishing of it." It is a charming building, happily still one of the few remaining in Oxford from which the colour and picturesqueness of age have not been removed by modern restoration. Its Gothic character is sometimes accounted for by supposing that it is an early work, before his second visit to Italy had taught him purer Classic. But dates disprove this supposition. He may have given a sketch for it, but when we know that before this date he had designed Whitehall and St. Paul's portico, it is impossible to believe that this building was carried out according to his ideas.[1]

It is true that, ten years earlier, he had designed the Gothic chapel of Lincoln's Inn. But that is not, like the Gothic parts of St. John's College, in the traditional style of the period, but an imitation of an older style mixed with correct Classic work.

The upper story of St. John's, with its Perpendicular windows and cornice and battlements, is clearly the production of the workman of the period, following the traditional style. The general design of the Classic central porch and arcade, may have been suggested by him, but the details, though effective, are too far removed from Classic correctness and elegance to have been designed by the same hand which drew those of the buildings we know to be his, or by any one who had studied to good purpose in Italy.

So long as there was a living style of architecture, this is what would naturally happen. Every workman, without any drawings, knew how to cut the ordinary traditional mouldings, and it would have required much trouble and

---

[1] Laud says nothing of any architect, nor does Anthony Wood in his elaborate account of the College in his History. In the notes to Wood by Gutch, about a century ago, the tradition appears ascribing it to Inigo Jones.

Fig. 101. SECOND QUAD OF ST. JOHN'S COLLEGE, OXFORD.

constant personal supervision to make him work in any other way.

In Wren's time there is a note of the change in the system of conducting architecture, by the architect supplying full-size drawings for the details, instead of following the old system and allowing the workmen to carry out these according to their traditions. In a letter, quoted by Elmes in his life of Wren, to the authorities of Trinity College, Cambridge, in explanation of the plans he had submitted for the new library, Wren says, "I suppose you have good masons, however, I would willingly take a farther pains to give all the mouldings in great, we are scrupulous in small matters; and, you must pardon us, the architects are as great pedants as critics or heralds." It almost seems as if Wren thought an apology needed for wishing to supply full-sized drawings, and thus interfering with the established custom of letting the masons cut the mouldings according to their own ideas.

Inigo Jones is said to have designed Heriot's Hospital in Edinburgh, commenced in 1628, and it is by no means improbable. Cunningham, in his Life, says the internal fittings of the council room are in his manner. But judging from their style they appear to me of later date, of the time of Charles II. and Grinling Gibbons. Jones may have furnished drawings for the general disposition and elevation of the buildings, but the Scotch workmen, who carried it out, have taken their own way, and built in their own traditional style.

The general idea of the design of St. John's College, Oxford, is found elsewhere in England, as in the interesting little market cross of Peterborough (fig. 102). And it may have been a natural development of architecture in the circumstances of the times. For the arcades, the builders would see no difficulty in adopting the new ideas. They had merely to substitute a round arch for a Tudor arch; but they might not see their way practically to manage the working of Classic windows without mullions. Just as Gothic architects at present find it impossible to get their style thoroughly carried out, because people will not give up the sliding sash windows, to which they have been accustomed.

During the Civil War and the Commonwealth (1642–60), there was little building. What was done was done in

Fig. 102.   MARKET-CROSS, PETERBOROUGH.

the traditional manner, people not troubling themselves with art or its professors. With the restoration of Charles II., and the return to power of an aristocracy, who considered themselves patrons of the arts, the interest in the new style revived. During his reign it became the accepted style of domestic architecture in London. In country parts, and occasionally at Oxford, long afterwards, the old style was still clung to. The Great Fire of London, in 1666, was a notable event in the history of architecture. It put an end to the building of wooden houses in the town, made brick the common building material of England, and spread the fashion of Classic houses. It gave to Sir Christopher Wren one of the finest opportunities any architect has ever had, and he proved himself not unworthy of it.

He was then thirty-four years old, having been born in 1632, at Knoyle in Wiltshire, where his father, who was in the same year made Dean of Windsor, was rector. The family were ardent Royalists. His uncle, Matthew Wren, Bishop of Ely, was charged before Parliament with High-church practices; turning to the east, and holding the consecrated bread over his head for the adoration of the people; with discouraging preaching in his diocese; and with encouraging sports on Sunday afternoons. He was not brought to trial, but remained twenty years in prison, till Cromwell's death, refusing the conditions on which he might have had his liberty.[1]

Wren, being delicate in health, was educated at home, excepting a short time at Westminster School. While a boy he was remarkable for his knowledge and invention in every branch of science. In his thirteenth year he invented a new mathematical instrument, which he dedicated to his father in a Latin address. In 1647, when he was fifteen, he was appointed demonstrating assistant by the Lecturer on Anatomy, at Surgeon's Hall. Anatomical drawings of his are extant, and he afterwards made discoveries in Anatomy. He made inventions in the use of the microscope, studied chemistry, and was an excellent mathematician. In his twenty-fifth year he was appointed Professor of Astronomy at Gresham College, and afterwards Savilian

[1] Parentalia: or, Memoirs of the Family of the Wrens; viz., of Mathew Bishop of Ely, Christopher Dean of Windsor, &c., but chiefly of Sir Christopher Wren, late Surveyor-General of the Royal Buildings, President of the Royal Society, &c. &c. In which is contained, besides his Works, A great number of Original Papers and Records; on Religion, Poloticks, Anatomy, Mathematicks, Architecture, Antiquities; and most branches of Polite Literature. Compiled by his Son Christopher; now published by his Grandson, Stephen Wren, Esq.; with the care of Joseph Ames, F.R.S., and Secretary to the Society of Antiquaries, London. London. Printed for T. Osborn, in Gray's-Inn; and R. Dodsley, in Pall-Mall. MDCCL.

Professor of Astronomy at Oxford. He was an active member and an early president of the Royal Society, founded immediately after the Restoration, and he was constantly bringing before it new inventions of his own in all branches of human knowledge.

Evelyn at Oxford, in 1654, says in his Diary: "After dinner I visited that miracle of a youth, Mr. Christopher Wren, nephew to the Bishop of Ely." In his Sculptura, he calls him "that rare and early prodigy of universal genius, Mr. Christopher Wren, our worthy and accomplished friend."

Wren's first employment as an architect seems to have been in 1661, when the King, on his Restoration, sent for him from Oxford to assist Sir John Denham, Surveyor-General of His Majesty's Works, in the repairs of St. Paul's and Windsor Castle, and in building a new palace at Greenwich. Denham had been promised the reversion of the post by Charles I., for his loyalty rather than his capacity, of which Evelyn, who speaks somewhat contemptuously of his proposals for Greenwich Hospital (Diary, Oct. 19th, 1661), "though he had Mr. Webb, Inigo Jones' man to assist him," had a low opinion.

There seems to be no record of how or where Wren got his practical knowledge of architecture. It was part of the polite learning of the day, and there is some evidence that his father, in 1634, designed a building for the Queen of Charles I., which apparently was not erected. It is not unreasonable to suppose that his father's interest in the art would give the son opportunities of which his enormous powers of acquisition and invention would make the most.

In 1663 he was appointed assistant Surveyor-General, to do Denham's work; and, having refused an offer to go to Tangier to fortify it and construct the mole there, of which Pepys speaks so frequently in his Diary, he was appointed to superintend the repairs of St. Paul's. The church was in a bad state, notwithstanding that Inigo Jones had cased a good part of it with Portland stone, and had rebuilt the north and south fronts, as well as the portico at the west end. The roof, as appears from an account of Wren's, was ruinous, the pillars bent from their "ill-building with small rubbish stones and much mortar, and cased only with small stones." But his proposals for its repair would not commend themselves to us. He wished, "by cutting off the corners of the cross, to reduce the middle part into a spacious dome or rotunda, with a cupola or hemispherical roof, and upon the cupola (for the outward ornament) a lantern with a spring top to rise proportionally, though not to that unnecessary height of the former spire of timber and lead, burnt by lightning." "I would not," he continues, "persuade the tower to be pulled down at first, but the new work to be built round it, partly because the expectations of people are to be kept up; for many unbelievers would bewail the loss of old Paul's steeple, and despond if they did not see a hopeful successor rise in its stead." Not much, apparently, would have been left us of old St. Paul's, even without the Great Fire.

In May, 1663, he exhibited a model for the Sheldonian Theatre at Oxford, not finished till 1669, the great roof of which of 90 feet span is still a marvel of construction; and in April the first stone was laid of the Chapel of Pembroke Hall, at Cambridge. Though this was Wren's first building; I believe it was actually in contemplation by the college authorities to pull it down, as they have done the old hall, and other most interesting parts of the College, replacing them by modern work by Mr. Waterhouse.

In the summer of 1665 he visited Paris, where he occupied himself, as he says in a letter to a friend,[1] "in surveying the most esteemed fabrics of the city and the country round." Versailles did not please him. "The women, as they make

[1] Parentalia, p. 261.

here the language and fashions, and meddle with politics
and philosophy, so they sway also in architecture; works of
Filgrand and little knacks are in great vogue, but building
certainly ought to have the attribute of eternal, and
therefore the only thing incapable of new fashions." He
seems unconscious that he was himself inventing new
fashions in architecture. "After the incomparable villas
of Vaux and Maisons, I shall but name Ruel, Couzance,
Chilly, Essoans, St. Maur, St. Mande, Issy, Meudon, Riney,
Chantilly, Verneul, Lioncour; all of which, and I might
add many others, I have surveyed; and that I might not
lose the impressions of them, I shall bring you almost all
France on paper, which I found, by some or other, ready
designed to my hand. Bernini's design for the Louvre I
would have given my skin for, but the old reserved Italian
gave me but a few minutes' view. I shall be able, by discourse and a crayon, to give you a tolerable account of it."[1]

He had returned to London in March 1666. He does not
seem to have thought of going to Italy. "The works going
on in Paris," he says, "make a school of architecture the
best probably at this day in Europe" (Parentalia, p. 261).
On August 27, he made a survey of St. Paul's, with Evelyn
and others of the commissioners, who reported in favour
of replacing it by Wren's cupola, though some wished to
reinstate the spire. On September 6th the Great Fire of
London, which had been burning since September 2nd,
settled the dispute by destroying St. Paul's.

The remainder of Wren's life, for the next fifty-seven
years, was spent in rebuilding what the fire had burnt.

Acting as surveyor-general, the duties of which office seem
to have included many of those at present exercised by the
Metropolitan Board of Works, he submitted to the King on
the 18th of the same month a plan for rebuilding the city.[2]

He proposed a "key" or embankment along the river,

[1] Parentalia.   [2] Given in Parentalia.

from the Temple to the Tower, lined with the Halls of the City Companies—the great lines of traffic widened and improved, with "piazzas" at their junctions. But the rights of individuals were too strong in England to make the scheme practicable.

Attempts were still made to patch up old St. Paul's. In 1668 parts of it threatened to fall, and Wren was sent for in great haste from Oxford to advise; but it was not till 1675 that the plan of the new church was decided on, Wren appointed architect, and the work commenced. The first service in the new church was held in 1698, twenty-four years afterwards and in 1710, when Wren was in his seventy-eighth year, the top stone of the lantern was laid in his presence by his son.

During this time, besides other works, he rebuilt fifty-two parish churches in London; many of the halls of the Merchant Companies; the hospitals at Greenwich and Chelsea; King William's Palace at Hampton Court; Marlborough House and a few private houses; among them the Earl of Orford's house at St. James's; the Duchess of Buckingham's, in St. James' Park, and the large mansion on the south side of Queen Square, Bloomsbury, for Lord Newcastle, the plans for which are among his drawings at All Souls' College, Oxford.

In 1718, the Court influence round George I. deprived him of his post. In February 1723, he died at the age of ninety-one.

Although Wren thought that "Building ought to have the attribute of eternal, and therefore the only thing incapable of new fashions," few architects have shown greater originality. The variety in the design of his steeples is marvellous. That of St. Magnus, London Bridge, built, according to Elmes, in Queen Anne's time in 1705, is a fair specimen of his style (fig. 103). With his age he accepted the authority of the Classic orders, but his irrepressible invention made a new architecture out of them. His skill in construction made him equal to the most difficult problems; his fecundity of invention in art was governed by a sense of proportion and beauty. We laugh at his Gothic. We can copy better old Gothic mouldings, but his Gothic towers are admirable in outline, which unhappily our modern ones seldom are. His Classic mouldings are always excellent; full and flowing in their contours, without the delicacy of the Greek. Many of the forms which he used, as for example, his windows, are those of the French architecture of his day—France, we saw, he thought the best school in Europe—but instead of their sometimes feeble elegance, he imparted to them an English masculine vigour.

In his works, there is a commonsense practicalness which render them always satisfactory. Merchant Taylors' School, lately destroyed, which he built immediately after the Great Fire, is an eminently sensible building. For the use of the illustrations of it I am indebted to the proprietors of 'The

Fig. 103. STEEPLE OF ST. MAGNUS, LONDON BRIDGE.

Graphic' (figs. 104, 105, 106). It was built cheaply; with no
expenditure on ornament except the Doric pilasters on the
street front (fig. 104) and a few mouldings and cornices, but
these were admirable in their contour. The interior (fig. 106),

Fig. 104.   OLD MERCHANT TAYLORS' SCHOOL, FRONT TO STREET.

though quite simple, is very dignified. The great door in
the end, which was of excellent design and well carved, and
the high panelling, give a feeling of art and comfort
different from the dreary interiors of most modern schools.

The mode of dividing the window-panes seems to me to be an alteration of a later date.[1]

Wren so trained a school of workmen that Classic became their traditional style, which they could carry out without drawings. This is the only practical method of producing art-workmen. The South Kensington system of trying to make each workman an artist, capable of invention, has hitherto produced only failure, and can never have any other result. The original inventors in any age must always be few. To produce good architecture generally, their inventions should be learnt and thoroughly understood by ordinary builders and workmen, so that they become part of their traditions and habits. The old system of apprenticeship accomplished this. Failing this, we are dependent on the modern system of architects directing the building to its minutest details by means of drawings, which presupposes

Fig. 105.
PLAYING COURT, MERCHANT TAYLORS' SCHOOL.

[1] I have since learned that they were altered in 1852.

Fig. 106.   SCHOOL-ROOM OF MERCHANT TAYLORS' SCHOOL.

that all architects are original inventors. If they are, this age is richer in originality than any previous one. The condition of modern architecture does not bear out this supposition.

Wren introduced Italians for sculpture and decoration, and developed a school of wood-carving under Grinling Gibbons.

The stone carving at St. Paul's is the work of a school of carvers, admirable in its style, full and rich, without the perfection of line of the Italian, or the graceful delicacy of the French. In time the carving lost this fulness, in striving after elegance, and became, as in the Church of St. Mary-le-Strand, somewhat thin and weedy.

The rich and splendid wood-carving was a special glory of the architecture of Wren's time. Grinling Gibbons was counted the best wood-carver of his day, though, as a part of architecture, his work seems to me too natural. Evelyn, then living at Deptford, discovered him, and Gibbons' work is so associated with the architecture of the time, that the story will not be thought out of place :

"This day," Evelyn says in his Diary for January 18th, 1671, " I first acquainted his Majesty with that incomparable young man Gibbons, whom I lately met with in an obscure place by mere accident as I was walking near a poor solitary thatched house, in a field in our parish, near Sayes Court.[1] I found him shut in ; but, looking in at the window, I perceived him carving that large cartoon or crucifix of Tintoretto, a copy of which I had myself brought from Venice, where the original painting remains. I asked if I might enter : he opened the door civilly to me, and I saw him about such a work as, for the curiosity of handling, drawing, and curious exactness, I never had before seen in all my travels. I questioned him why he worked in such an obscure and lonesome place ; he told me it was that he might apply himself to his profession without interruption, and wondered

[1] Evelyn's house at Deptford, which came to him through his wife.

not a little how I found him out. I asked if he was unwilling to be made known to some great man, for that I believed it might turn to his profit; he answered he was yet but a beginner, but would not be sorry to sell off that piece; on demanding the price, he said £100. In good earnest the very frame was worth the money, there being nothing in nature so tender and delicate as the flowers and festoons about it, and yet the work was very strong; in the piece were more than one hundred figures of men, &c. I found he was likewise musical, and very civil, sober, and discreet in his discourse. There was only an old woman in the house. So desiring leave to visit sometimes I went away.

"*19th. February.*—This day dined with me Mr. Surveyor, Dr. Christopher Wren, and Mr. Pepys' clerk of the Acts, two extraordinary, ingenious and knowing persons, and other friends. I carried them to see the piece of carving which I had recommended to the King.

"*1st. March.*—I caused Mr. Gibbons to bring to Whitehall his excellent piece of carving, where being come, I advertised his Majesty. * * * No sooner was he entered and cast his eyes on the work, but he was astonished at the curiosity of it, and having considered it a long time and discoursed with Mr. Gibbons, whom I brought to kiss his hand, he commanded it should be immediately carried to the Queen's side to show her. It was carried up to her bed-chamber, where she and the King looked on and admired it again; the King being called away, he left us with the Queen believing she would have bought it, it being a crucifix; but when his Majesty was gone, a French peddling woman, one Madame de Boord, who used to bring petticoats, and fans, and bauble out of France to the ladies, began to find fault with several things in the work; which she understood no more than an ass or a monkey, so as in a kind of indignation I caused the person who brought it to carry it back to the chamber finding the Queen so much governed by the ignorant French woman, and this incomparable artist had his labour only for his pains, which not a little displeased me; and he was fain to send it down to his cottage again; he not long after sold it for £80, though worth £100 without the frame, to Sir George Viner.

"His Majesty's surveyor, Mr. Wren faithfully promised me to employ him. I having also bespoke his Majesty for his work at Windsor, which my friend Mr. May, the architect there, was going to alter and repair universally; for on the next day I had a fair opportunity of talking to his Majesty about it in the lobby, next the Queen's side, where I presented him with some sheets of my history." The remainder of the entry, though it does not refer to art, is interesting: "I thence walked with him, when I both saw and heard a very familiar discourse between [him] and Mrs. Nelly, as they called an impudent comedian; she looking out of her garden on a terrace at the top of a wall" (where now is the Army and Navy Club), "and [he] standing on the green walk under it. I was heartily sorry at this scene. Thence the King walked to the Duchess of Cleveland, another lady of pleasure and curse of our nation."

The following letter, quoted by Evelyn's editor, shows how things are managed in much the same way in every age:—

HONRED

Sr I wold beg the faver wen you see Sr Josff Williams [Williamson] again you wold be pleased to speack to him that hee wold get me to Carve his Ladis sons hous my Lord Kildare for I onderstand it will [be] verry considerabell or If you haen Acquantains wich my Lord to speack to him hissealf and I shall for Evre be obliged to you I would speack to S^{ir} Josef mysealf but I knouw it would do better from you S^r youre Most umbell

"Sarvant

"G. GIBBONS.

"Lond 23 Mar 1682."

Gibbons had not had much advantage of education. Walpole says it is uncertain whether he was born in Holland or England. The errors in the letter are very English.

This digression may be pardoned for its own interest, and as bringing us into personal acquaintance with the times and the men whose works we are considering.

In Wren's day Classic architecture became the vernacular of the country; the mode which every workman understood, and in which he naturally worked. This result was caused partly by the abandonment of the old practice of building in wood and plaster, with which the Gothic modes of work were associated in England, from the exhaustion of the forests as well as the dread of fire; and partly from the new fashion, which had long been accepted by the rich and cultivated, descending in time to the people.

Gothic buildings were still erected. Wren built many himself, the Tom tower at Christ Church, Oxford, and Gothic towers to churches; as did Hawksmoor after him. But these were conscious revivals to harmonise with existing Gothic work, or to perpetuate a form which association had rendered dear. "Many unbelievers," as he said, "would bewail the loss of old Paul's steeple." But with these exceptions, which are of the kind that prove the rule, the architects and masons of the day all worked in the same style.

Old Bedlam, or Bethlehem Hospital, of the central block of which I give a drawing (fig. 107), is a fair specimen of the ordinary work of the day. I cannot find that it had any architect. It was begun in 1675, and finished in fifteen months, "which," says Maitland, in his history of London, "was considered wonderfully quick work," as well it might. Building is one of the arts in which mankind has not advanced. Its excellence depends on traditional skill, which

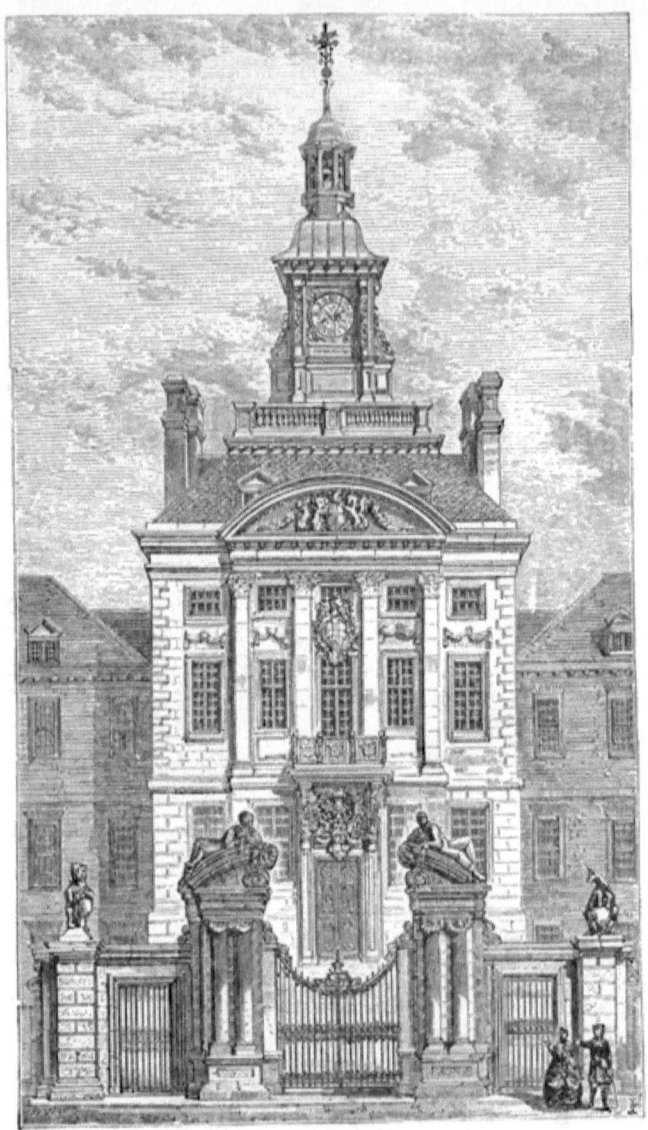

Fig. 107. BETHLEHEM HOSPITAL (CENTRAL BLOCK).

enables the whole body of workmen to work together in
concert; each, by the teaching of his apprenticeship, knowing his own trade, so that everything in the building, without special direction and without drawings, harmonises
perfectly in style. Our modern progress is destructive of
tradition. This building, now destroyed, was 540 feet long
and 40 feet wide, broken by the pavilion, which, with its
marked perpendicular lines, rose in the centre like a tower.
The gate,

"Where Cibber's brazen brainless brothers stand,"

was erected after the Union, as the supporters, representing
the lion and unicorn, show. It is a pity this gate could not
have been re-erected somewhere; for it is an admirable
design, and the statues of
raving and melancholy madness, though not the kind of
decoration for an asylum
which our kindlier treatment
of lunacy finds appropriate,
are powerful and interesting.
They are preserved in the
South Kensington Museum,
but, having been designed for
their position in the architecture, they lose their value
when removed from it.

Fig. 108.
ST. CATHARINE'S COLLEGE, CAMBRIDGE.

St. Catharine's Hall, or College, as the authorities call it,
at Cambridge, commenced in
1680, shows the same treatment of breaking the horizontal line of the building
by a taller Classic frontispiece. It is of brick with stone
dressings. Though later in date, it stills retains in its
mullioned windows some Gothic character; for here, as at

Oxford, old traditions continued. Till a few years ago St. Catharine's College was complete in style throughout, but its harmony was destroyed and its history falsified, by altering the chapel into quite incongruous Gothic. Its architecture may have been influenced by that of Clare

Fig. 109.   DRAPERS' ALMHOUSES, MARGATE.

College beside it, which was being built at the time, the design of which, though not fully carried out till 1715, dates from 1638, and shows mullions and other Gothic features, mingled with Classic, so as to produce a complete and characteristic English style.

Drapers' Hospital, near Margate, belonging to the Quakers (fig. 109), is a characteristic specimen of a type of English architecture which has lately acquired notoriety under the name of "Queen Anne." Whatever may be thought of its merits, it has claim, I think, to be called a true and national style. It is a builder's, not an architect's, style, the product of traditions naturally developing themselves. At the end of the seventeenth century brick had become the common building material of the country, and Classic forms and mouldings the vernacular of the workmen, who, following apparently their own instincts, formed the style out of these elements, without drawings from architects, who were too learned to tolerate its barbarism. In this instance, though the walls are of the usual flint building of the district, all the architectural parts are in brick, the grey and red making a beautiful contrast of colour. The style is common in the villages and cottages of the neighbourhood.

The shaping of the gables into various curves, which is one of the characteristics of the style, is a simple and natural and consequently cheap mode of producing an effect in brick. It is one of the many ways in which the builders in every country, still inspired by the old Gothic freedom, got rid of the trammels of Classic rule.

The later Italian architects, while not daring to alter the parts and proportions of the five orders, had, especially in the Jesuit churches, striven after richness and magnificence, by broken pediments and great curved scrolls. In France, in the style of Louis Quatorze, while the architecture under the dominion of orders continued correct and dull, the internal decoration revelled in a profusion of curved lines carried out into the forms of the panels and even of the window bars, where it was unconstructural and unmeaning.

The same tendency to free curves shows itself in the Queen Anne style, which, though Classic in all its details, has in it something of Gothic character. It avoids the deeply set windows and dark shadows of Classic, and gets the sense of continuous wall surface characteristic of Gothic by keeping the window frames flush with the walls, and making them part of the wall surface by covering them with thick sash bars. In this instance the windows are even more Gothic with their mullions and transoms and leaded lights.

This Gothic character seems to have impressed some architect, who has lately had this building through his hands, for, since this drawing was made, he has attempted to improve it by alterations in the Gothic taste. The Gothic canopied tops to the gate-piers show the commencement of his work. He has spoilt its character by traceried windows and the earthly vanity of shields for coats of arms, thinking these, I suppose, suitable historical adjuncts of an old Quaker establishment.

Kew Palace (fig. 110) is a more elaborate and architectural example of the Queen Anne style. It is probably not the work of an architect, else it would have been more correct, but one of those productions of a builder which were denounced by persons of taste and knowledge as aberrations from the standard of Classic purity. The orders are incorrect, and even clumsy. There is no Classic precedent for the curved gables of the roof; but it is a charming house, homely and yet dignified, built to live in, but yet pleasant to look on.

The two houses at Olney (fig. 111), in one of which the poet Cowper lived, have an air of neglect and squalor which make them less pleasant examples of the style. They date probably from early in the last century, the aprons under the windows being a common characteristic in Queen Anne's time. Though this and the key-stones give them some pretentions to architecture, they are probably the work of the builder of the period.

Fig. 110. KEW PALACE.

THE RENAISSANCE IN ENGLAND. 335

The old rectory at Redington (fig. 112) is a good example of a simpler and later form of Queen Anne architecture.

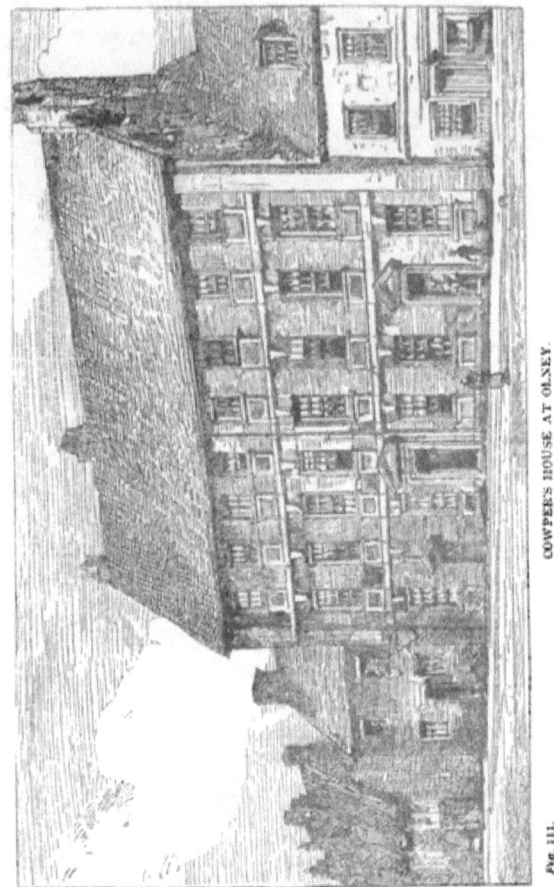

Fig. 111.   COWPER'S HOUSE AT OLNEY.

Such houses are common over all England. With their cheerful red brick fronts among the green, the windows with their broad white frames and small window panes twinkling in the light, they suggest all the pleasant associations of an English home. Inside, unless where modern taste has altered them, there are pleasant parlours lined with panelling painted white; roomy, comfortable bedrooms; ample cupboards and keeping places, and an excellent wine cellar. They do not come within the category of architectural buildings, according to our recent notions; Classic orders and Gothic ornament are alike unknown to them. They are the natural outcome of simple brick building, in an age when the work of every workman, and

Fig. 112.   RECTORY OF REDINGTON.

every moulding, however simple, was governed by traditions which secured it from offending against good taste.

A notable feature of the Queen Anne style is its use of cut brick for the mouldings and carving, which in Classic architecture are usually executed in stone. We have seen, that this was an old Roman practice (fig. 63, p. 208). A peculiar kind of brick is used for this kind of work, called "rubbers," granular and soft, but capable, as we see from some examples of carved capitals among the old buildings of the Temple, of standing several centuries of exposure without injury.

It may seem absurd and unreasonable to make up large blocks for mouldings and capitals out of such small materials as bricks, and it might appear better, if we cannot get stone, to mould them in large pieces of terra-cotta, as has been done with considerable success in the Albert Hall and other buildings at South Kensington. But cut brick produces a different and, I think, more charming effect. Large pieces of terra-cotta, and even moulded bricks, are apt to twist in burning, it is difficult to get their lines true, and the colour is often unsatisfactory. Yellow terra-cotta is often beautiful, but the red and the moulded bricks are usually of a livid purply hue. In cut brick work the lines are true and clean and the colour a charming orange red.

During the eighteenth century the Classic style became the style of the country—it was used in all kinds of buildings, domestic, civil, and ecclesiastical—it developed into a national variety, and assumed a distinctively English type.

By those who studied architecture and knew what Classic purity and elegance were, this process was considered mere degradation. The mouldings were not always given their proper parts and contours. The authorised proportions of the orders were not observed. English workmen gave the style a character in accordance with their own nature and common sense.

The Town Hall in the centre of the large market place of South Shields on the Tyne (fig. 113), a place which never advanced any pretensions to being æsthetic, is a fair specimen of this common English style. It has no pretensions to elegance; it is plain and even somewhat clumsy, but it is not without picturesqueness, and is an eminently common sense building The architecture is purely and naturally constructive; it has forgotten the orders and their proportions, it thinks for itself. Mr. Fergusson might think it ugly or beneath notice, but he could not criticise it as slavishly carrying out the rules of Classic, or using the unconstructional ornament of pilasters. It is interesting to compare it with another building, the Custom House at King's Lynn (fig. 114), of similar form and design, but of much greater beauty and elegance, of higher architec-

Fig 113.   TOWN HALL, SOUTH SHIELDS.

tural pretensions, and more in accordance with Classic rule.

In the lower story we have the Classic arrangement of filling in the space formed by the Greek column and architrave with the Roman arch, which is certainly less logical than the simple arcade in the Shields building. In the upper story Gothic influence appears in the similar space being filled in with a mullioned window. Over the entrance is a statue of Charles II., in whose reign the building was erected.

The general treatment recalls the Arundel Museum at Oxford, and the buildings of the later style of Francis I. in France.

The gradual progression towards greater simplicity in the English Renaissance, which can be traced especially in more ordinary buildings, was occasionally interrupted by the greater learning and better knowledge of some architect or even by the introduction of a foreign style.

The screen of Montague House, the old British Museum (fig. 115), is obviously French in its architecture. It occupied the site of

Fig. 114.   CUSTOM HOUSE, KING'S LYNN.

the present high railing which dwarfs the height of its Grecian successor, and shuts it up in a cage. This French character, shown specially in the tall slated roofs, is due to its architect having been a Frenchman, Peter Paget, of Marseilles. The fashion of these tall French roofs never took root in England till lately, in consequence, I believe, of the Gothic revival.

This English Renaissance style, to which accident has given the name of Queen Anne, but which commenced before her reign, and continued long after it, became the characteristic style of London.

The Great Fire destroyed old London with its "post and pan" houses of wood and plaster, whitewashed every three years; which had in old times given it the name of the White Town. That terrible lesson made peremptory the orders which had been frequently passed, but little observed, since the time of James I., that all houses should be of brick. London in its enormous growth, which began after the Restoration and has continued ever since, spread itself over the country, and absorbed outlying villages and towns. All the houses were built in the new style, which applied the rules of Classic, as far as they would conveniently go, to building in brick. This style continued in a process of natural change and growth till the time of George IV.

Fig. 115. MONTAGUE HOUSE—THE OLD BRITISH MUSEUM.

At first it retained something of Gothic picturesqueness, as appears in the old street (fig. 116), now destroyed, which led from the Strand to the river, near Waterloo Bridge. The narrow windows, at the corner of the house to the right, show a common feature of the style, due to the old Gothic ideas still influencing the builders, quite at variance with the Classic rule that all windows in a row should be equidistant and of equal size irrespective of the size of the apartment which they lit.

Gradually the style became more correct. The windows were made uniform, not only in the same house, but in the

Fig. 116.   OLD STREET IN LONDON.

whole row. As the houses were built by the yard for sale, there was no reason for making one different from another. They lost their individuality, and the process was encouraged by the foolish building conditions of ground landlords, insisting that streets should be built uniform, according to an elevation which they furnished; so that in time the style was degraded to the dreary uniformity of Gower Street.

Yet it is a true style, correct and in harmony, to the smallest particular. Every moulding is right in its own

Fig. 117.   Fig. 118.
DOORWAYS IN ESSEX STREET, STRAND.

way, and tells its place and date in the gradual progress. It avoided bad taste. The highest compliment that could be paid to art or ornament in that age, was that it should be "chaste," till architecture in fear of offending became absolutely dull and colourless.

In its dullest examples there is character and even dignity, as in the tall wrought-iron railings, the delicate balconies, and especially the entrance doors, on which was concentrated what little architectural ornament was expended on each house.

These doorways were different in every house, giving each house individuality, notwithstanding the general sameness of the street—and they were beautiful, sometimes even noble examples of design. In this respect these houses were better than those of our builders, which are ornamented all over—with stucco only, it is true—but

THE RENAISSANCE IN ENGLAND.

Fig. 119.   DOORWAY IN ESSEX STREET, STRAND.

all in the row absolutely alike, so that a man knows his own house only by the number on the door.

Of these doors I give three specimens, all from one little street, Cecil Street, Strand. They date from early in the eighteenth century, and very fairly illustrate the general character (figs. 117, 118, 119).

Except in some few more magnificent examples, these doorways in the old houses are always made of wood. This is forbidden now, by the London Building Act; somewhat needlessly, I think; the danger of their spreading fire not being obvious. The joiner work in the style, as in the internal fittings, is generally architectural, and more Classic than the brick and stone building. A universal feature in all these doors is the window above, lighting the passage, filled with delicate wooden tracery; always of playful and pretty design, and in many cases showing marvellous examples of delicate wood-work. These windows are part of the architecture of the door, and essential to its beauty. By a rule of the Portman estate, before a new lease was granted by the ground landlord, the tenant was compelled to improve the property, by clearing out this tracery and substituting a single sheet of plate glass—a curious instance of stupid destructiveness.

But the street architecture of the style was governed, to an extent Lord Bacon never meant, by his maxim that "houses are built to live in, not to look on." With the exception of the doorways (and when the style was dying out in the beginning of the century, no trouble was taken even with them), the fronts were absolutely plain. In the interiors neither trouble nor expense is spared in the design and ornament.

The ceilings are covered with delicately moulded plaster ornaments of leaves and sprays, and figures, specially designed for each room. The chimney-pieces are of marble inlaid in different colours, and excellently carved. The doors are of solid mahogany, the panel mouldings carved with egg and tongue, the architraves and cappings painted white like the other wood-work of the room, which brings out the contour of the mouldings. Every room is designed and treated architecturally, with a panelled surbase or dado round it, which was seen through the open carved backs of the chairs, and with an enriched and well-proportioned frieze and cornice. People cared more for these things then than they do now. They gave them thought and care, and spent their money on them. It was easier then than now to get them well-designed and all in keeping; for the style was a living one, understood by every workman, who worked as he had been trained, in harmony with his fellows. Some designers may have been better than others; acknowledged as masters of the style and setting new fashions, like the Brothers Adam. But the work which is not theirs is similar in style, and they could not have carried out the work they are credited with, all over the three kingdoms, so completely, unless the style had been everywhere familiar to the workmen. There are still in London many such interiors as I have described, some turned to base uses, in districts now unfashionable, while others, alas! have been improved by the modern builder, the surbase torn down, the delicate white marble chimney-piece replaced by one of enamelled slate, with a gigantic shelf and clumsy consoles; and a new cornice substituted, with coarse mouldings and vulgar ornament, for the old one which had been proportioned to the room.

The Adam style of interior decoration has of late become fashionable again. It is chaste and elegant, but rather feeble. The same attenuated ornament is used in every position and in every material; for plaster cornices and ceilings, the mantle-pieces and fire-grates and the wood-work of doors and surbases. In the modern revival of the style the examples frequently miss one chief merit of the older work, the consistency with which it was carried out into every detail of ornament and furniture.

During the Regency (1811-1819), there was a revival of street architecture; a part of that general awakening from eighteenth century dulness, which the French Revolution everywhere caused. By this time Greek architecture, which Stuart and Revett had discovered, had come to be understood, and was perceived to be different in principle and form from the Roman, with which, since the Renaissance, it had been supposed to be identical. It was seen to be more refined and beautiful; that it rejected the use of the arch, and of brick as a building material, and used great stone lintels as the only means of spanning openings. People had become tired of the meanness to which brick architecture had degenerated, and the wilderness of grey stocks which London had become. But stone, especially of the dimensions which Greek architecture required, was impossible in London houses; but the appearance of it could be got by *stucco*, for which there is Roman and even Greek authority. The brightness of the new white buildings charmed every one; and if, in looking at examples of them (such as the terraces round the Regent's Park or on the cliffs of Brighton, which were among the first fruits of the movement), we can divest ourselves for the moment of our present ideas and forget that they are shams, we must admit that they exhibit something of the brightness, and even of the grandeur of Classic architecture. The builders, as usual, followed the fashion, and carried out the new style, in their rows of houses, in worse architecture and meaner design. Ground landlords, in letting their land for building, insisted on its adoption in the new streets, and for the next thirty or forty years it was the common London style.

One element of grandeur was sought for by designing a row of houses as if it were one single great building, with a great pediment in the centre and symmetrical wings on each side flanked by *propylæa*. This grand design was apportioned equally among the several houses, the division giving perhaps to one house two windows out of the wings, and another under a corner of the pediment. To prevent this absurdity being apparent, which would have spoiled the effect of the architecture, a clause was inserted in each lease that the owners should all use the same colour in painting their houses. But the workman was not always successful in matching the colour, or the houses being painted in different years the various degrees of dirtiness made the deception obvious.

This palatial style was carried out with better effect in the squares and crescents of Edinburgh, which were built about the same time. Greek architecture was studied there with enthusiasm, and reproduced with knowledge and invention in adapting it to modern use. The splendid quarries of Craigleith furnished blocks of stone large enough for the columns and lintels of an order occupying the height of two stories. The result, as in Moray Place, has nothing of the meanness which their material gives to the London examples, but there is an air of gloomy aristocratic grandeur which the present age has found depressing. Even here a difference in the colour of the window-blinds exposed the deception of the design. Internally the requirements of the architecture were inconvenient, restricting the apparent number of stories, and making the windows of the upper floors look out on a gutter and blank parapet wall in order to conceal them.

In London, the brightness of the clean white-painted fronts of the new architecture was an improvement on the dinginess of the mean fronts of grey stock bricks. But the obligation on the owners to paint the outside of their houses once in every three years (for which there was precedent in a similar rule in old white-washed London) was found onerous. The stucco or cement occasionally fell off in great flakes, and was expensive to repair.

Of late the builders have got over this difficulty, still keeping the houses white, which was supposed to be the only proper colour for architecture, by facing the walls with white bricks and limiting the stucco to the architrave mouldings round the windows, the cornices, the corners, and the Classic columns of the porticos. The ingenuity of man has never produced a form of architecture more dismal and contrary to common sense; for the bricks, white at first, soon become a dirty grey, like dirty linen; and the meaning of architraves and cornices in architecture is, that being the exposed parts, they should be of harder and better materials than the walls of the building. But stucco is meaner than brick, and more easily chipped. The right arrangement of the materials would be to cover the walls with stucco, where it is useful to keep out the damp, and to make the corners and cornices of brick or stone. Some noble buildings, like the Palace of the Uffizzi, at Florence, have been designed on this principle.

The Gothic revival of the last twenty years, though a whole generation of architects have been trained in it and practised it, has had no appreciable influence on street architecture. The builders would not risk building Gothic houses for sale, and, I think they were right. Artistic publicans have occasionally adopted it for public-houses; but the result has not been gratifying to the lovers of the style.

Within the last year or two there has been a revival of the "Queen Anne" style for town houses, and even for streets. The fashion seems to be spreading. It has received some accession of force from the schools of the London School Board, planted in every district of London, having been mostly built in that style. For the architecture of a few of the earliest of these I am responsible, having found by the practical experience of a house I built for myself in this manner, that the style adapts itself to every modern necessity and convenience. In that case I made no attempt to follow any particular style, the style grew naturally from using the ordinary materials and modes of work, and trying to give them character and interest. It is as pliable as Gothic, having inherited its freedom. Large windows or small, wide or narrow, with mullions or without them, arched or square-headed, with sliding sashes or hinged casements, with sash-bars or leaded glazing may be used in it as convenience or fancy dictates.

Though some of its forms are adapted for stone, it is properly a brick style, and therefore specially suited for London houses. Ground landlords have favoured it and encouraged its adoption, insisting that the new houses on their estates should be built in red brick. But red brick is by no means essential. Great masses of it, especially when pointed with black mortar which gives the building a purple hue, almost hurt the eyes with their glare. Pleasant colour, I think, is got by dark brown stock bricks for the walls, and red bricks for the angles and cornices. The addition of black completes the harmony. But there is no need to use black bricks for the purpose, as the London atmosphere may be trusted to supply it. The black does not give an impression of dirt, for it is not, as Lord Palmerston defined dirt: "Matter in the wrong place," and an effect of cleanness and brightness is given to the building by the white window frames and sash-bars, which can be re-painted at trifling cost, their whole surface being small.

It is a first condition of good architecture that the building should weather well, that the effects on it of the atmosphere it is placed in should improve rather than spoil it. It should be like a part of its natural surroundings. Weather-worn stones, moss and grey lichens give many an old building a beauty which it had not when first built, and which it loses when it is restored. Even in towns, where smoke kills the lichens, it is possible to design so that it shall improve the building. St. Paul's is grander in the rich black of its base and the more than marble whiteness into which the weather has bleached it where it towers above the houses than it can have been when fresh and new. Polished granite or marble is soon dimmed and looks dirty. To keep them right they should be cleaned as often as the windows, which is impossible.

I do not claim for this style that it is perfect, or that it expresses greatness and nobleness as some of the great styles of the world have done. It is rather simple and homely,

> "not too great or good,
> For human nature's daily food."

CHAPTER XIV.

THE RENAISSANCE IN SCOTLAND.

IT was a remarkable series of historical accidents which made the northern portion of our island a separate country from England, and its people a separate nation with a different national character, different laws, and a different form of religion. This was not caused by difference of race. The differences between Celts and Saxons within Scotland in race and character, and, what is even of more importance, in language, were far greater than those between the English and the Lowland Scots, who were in reality one people. The boundaries of the countries were long undefined. During the Heptarchy, the kingdom of Bernicia extended from the Humber to the Forth, and included Edinburgh. The Scottish crown in King Stephen's time had nearly acquired Northumberland and Cumberland. After the Norman Conquest, many barons held land in both countries, and did fealty to both kings. By a strange fatality, the project common in these days of uniting the whole island under one crown by a royal marriage was never realised.

The wisdom of such a union was evident to statesmen, especially to one of the greatest, Edward I. But he took the wrong way to accomplish it; the title on his tomb is *Malleus Scotorum*; his attacks on Scotland, and the centuries of war they gave rise to, were the chief instruments which welded by hard blows the different races of the country into one nation.

The names of its mountains and rivers show that Scotland had at some early period been overspread, like England and other countries, by the wave of Celtic immigration which passed over Europe. The ancient kingdom of Strath Clyde extended over Cumberland, and had relations, from community of race and language, with Cornwall and Brittany. From another branch of the Celtic race, the Scots of Ireland, who conquered it about the sixth century, the country has its name. The name is now lost to its original land; but to Bede Scotland means Ireland. Duns Scotus was an Irishman. The Scots of Ireland established themselves on the coast of Argyll, at the island fortress of Dunstaffnage, where, it is said, was first placed the stone seat on which the kings were crowned; afterwards removed, as they pushed their conquests, to Scone, and by Edward I. to Westminster, in token of the transferrence to England of the royal power.

The invasion of the Saxons only partially overspread the country. They did not readily amalgamate with the Celts. The boundaries of the two races were often sharply defined; neighbouring villages spoke different languages, and did not understand each other. In Nairn, till lately, English was spoken in one half and Gaelic in the other half of the town.

In Orkney and Sutherland—the southern land from Norway—the population was Norse, and on the west coast there were constant inroads of Norsemen.

To these marked varieties of race, which are still apparent, is due the marked diversity of Scotch character. The Saxon steadiness and perseverance fostered by the struggles against a rugged soil and hard climate, which has conquered good positions everywhere, shows itself at times in the matter-of-factness, which cannot understand a joke, but oftener in a perfervid intensity of character which unites Teuton depth and toughness with Celtic fire.

Left to themselves, without the pressure of foreign attacks, these discordant elements of the population would

Fig. 120.   TILQUHILLIE CASTLE, ABERDEENSHIRE.

have split asunder or been successively absorbed into the stronger kingdom of the south. That the attempts to subdue Scotland called out the resistance it did indicated a strength, even a grimness, which found expression in her religion, her art, and especially in her architecture.

This severity of national character has generally been attributed to Calvinism and the Shorter Catechism. It would be truer to attribute the adoption of these to the national character, formed by the influence of a rugged land, by the struggles against a bleak climate, and grim centuries of fighting for national existence, which forged light-hearted Celt and stolid Saxon into one stern nation.

Scotch architecture gives the impression of grimness and severity which is usually credited to the character of the people. We see it in the solid windowless walls of this

Fig. 121. COURTYARD OF HOUSE AT LINLITHGOW.

old castle (fig. 120), and even the squalor of the back yard of a town slum (fig. 121) has a character and dignity which redeem it from vulgarity. Though they are full of windows, the walls like precipice cliffs of old Edinburgh houses—of which the sketch in fig. 130, p. 374, shows a fragment—somehow produce the same impression. They are not ugly like Manchester cotton-mills, though quite as plain and devoid of ornament.

Arrange their buildings as they would, plain as a cotton-mill or elaborate in ornament, the walls unbroken masses of stone or riddled with windows, in lord's castle or in back street, they all expressed the same national character.

The form which the national Scotch style of architecture adopted was determined by political circumstances. The natural course would have been that the style should have spread over to Scotland from her richer and more civilised neighbours in the south, and for a time this was the case. The Norman style in the two countries is identical. The nave of Dunfermline Abbey is a copy of Durham Cathedral. The Norman castles in England and in Scotland are alike in plan and style. But the wars of England against both France and Scotland threw these two countries into an alliance, which would otherwise have been unnatural. The first evidence of a treaty between them is in 1326, twelve years after the battle of Bannockburn, but friendly communications had been commenced by Wallace, and it was fondly believed that the "ancient league" had originated in the time of Charlemagne.

Before the time of Edward there are traces in the early Gothic architecture of Scotland of a sympathy with France rather than with England. In the groined roof of the crypt of Glasgow Cathedral, the filling-in of the vaulting is in the French, not in the English manner.

A special peculiarity of Scotch architecture—the steps running up the sides of the gables, forming their sky line into a series of nicks called "crow steps," in Scotch "corbie" steps—has probably a French origin. The name seems French. It is possible that Scotland may have invented this feature for herself, but I have seen an earlier instance of it in France than any I know in Scotland. In

France it was soon given up; French domestic architecture, as we have seen, abandoning gables and preferring high conical slated roofs. In Scotland it continued and became a feature of her Renaissance style. Almost all the drawings which I give of Scotch buildings illustrate this feature. (See the gable in fig. 128, p. 369, of the first court of Glasgow College.) The courses of stone are left square at the ends, forming a row of steps up the side of the gable instead of being cut to its slope. It is a feature which could only have been developed in a stone country, where stone in courses was used for the commonest buildings in which no refinement was attempted, and the gables were left ragged in their outline without the finish of a "water-table," as it is called, of large flat stones, covering the top of the wall to protect it from wet.

Like many other peculiarities of architecture, springing at first from mere rude workmanship, it became a feature of the style carried out at times with expense and elaboration, as when a projecting moulding is worked on each stone following the sky line of the gable. In this form of stept gable each step is a single stone, the outside stone of a course, differing therein from the steps of German gables which are larger, each being a piece of wall covered in with a flat water-table.

In French architecture, gables, as we have seen, were superseded by slated roofs. But in Scotland a strong preference was always shown for them. Even when (as in Tilquhillie Castle, fig. 120, p. 352) the angles are rounded for defence, they are corbelled out to the square at the top to allow their being roofed with a gable.

The gables with eaves projected over the face of the wall, to defend them from the wet, a special characteristic of wooden construction, were almost unknown in Scotland. The country was being perpetually harried and burnt, generally by the Scotch themselves, as a means of defence. Bruce's advice was, not to give battle to the English invaders, but to burn the country before them, so as to starve them out. The houses therefore were built of stones without lime, and a thatched roof, like highland cottages now, and burning them was little loss. The towers of the gentry, being built for defence, were stronger, but they were constructed so that, when burnt, little harm was done, the floors, resting on corbels independent of the wall, being easily replaced, and the roofs being sometimes of solid stone, which would not burn. Ecclesiastical buildings were considered sacred from such destruction, and though they were not always safe from the wild fury of the times, they were made as splendid as the poverty of the country could afford.

In the later development of her Gothic architecture, Scotland, from the circumstances which determined her growth and existence as a nation, followed France rather than England. No great divergence is observable in the earlier varieties of Gothic. In all the northern countries of Europe, including Norway even, as shown by Drondheim Cathedral, the styles are similar, but as soon as the peculiarly national styles became formed, Scotch Gothic becomes Flamboyant like the French, ruder perhaps and less elegant, with more of strength and severity.

In both countries the high pointed vaulting was retained so long as the Gothic style lasted. In the shapes of the arch openings we find occasional examples of the flattened arch and depressed gable of the English Perpendicular, as was unavoidable from the proximity and occasional peace and friendship between the two countries; but they are exceptions. The prevailing form of the gable is moderately steep, not so sharp as the tall slated roofs of France. The arch openings are usually sharp-pointed as in the contemporary French style, and the tracery has the flowing lines of the Flamboyant, not the straight bars of the Perpendicular.

In Scotland, as in France, the east end of the churches was frequently terminated by an apse. Both in church and castle the style retained its mediæval character of height and aspiration. For churches it was not subjected to the influence which in England flattened the roofs and arches. The castles, from the unsettled state of the country, could not become manor-houses, spread out over the ground, but continued lofty towers capable of defence.

Late Scotch Gothic has a characteristic peculiar, I think, to itself in the frequent use of round arched openings, especially for doorways. Mr. Billings thinks this is a remaining trace of Norman. But that style had been abandoned centuries before, and revivals were not thought of in these days. It probably arose from the perception that, when the necessities of vaulting did not require a pointed arch, the semicircular form, especially for a door, was stronger and more suitable, more easily closed by bars, and avoided the high point hanging above the hinge.

Another peculiarity of Scotch Gothic is the prevalence of square-headed windows without mullions, sometimes of fair width, without any attempt to disguise the straight lintel, as was usual in the Gothic of other countries, by cutting on it an ornamental pointed arch. These square-lintelled windows are found in monastic buildings and also in churches, though naturally they are more common in the castles. Borthwick Castle (fig. 122, p. 358), about thirteen miles from Edinburgh, was built in accordance with a licence obtained from James I. in 1430. It is a Gothic building, the roof of the great hall is a pointed waggon vault, and the details of the interior are late Gothic in character. The openings are not pointed, but square-headed and without mullions, and where an arch is needed, it is round.

In Scotland, as in other countries, the characteristics of her Gothic style were inherited by her Renaissance. Some

358   HOUSE ARCHITECTURE.

of them were already steps in the direction of the forms of classic, and they tended to make its adoption easier. The mullions, which are not a classic feature, were only gradually got rid of in France and England, as the classic tyranny

Fig. 122.   BORTHWICK CASTLE.

became established and the styles lost something of their national character; but, as they were dispensed with in Scotch Gothic, there was no question of introducing them into her Renaissance. We find them occasionally, but they are not a characteristic of the style.

The want of mullions in the style deprived it of the

effect of continuous surface characteristic of Gothic, especially of late English Gothic, in which wall was carried over window by mullions and tracery, and these mullions and tracery again carried over the wall, so that the whole building was one continuous surface. In Scotland, on the contrary, the windows are deeply recessed. The effect of the architecture is obtained by their contrast with the walls, which is the principle of classic.

This sketch (fig. 123), of an old house in Glasgow High Street, illustrates this treatment of the windows in the style, while at the same time the charming irregularity of their arrangement is thoroughly Gothic.

Fig. 123. OLD HOUSE IN GLASGOW HIGH STREET.

The Renaissance in Scotland, though we can trace in it many features of her Gothic style, was an importation from France of the Renaissance style of Francis I., after it had cast out Gothic features.

Scotland had remained barbarous longer than other parts of Europe, and when at last the new light of the Renaissance reached her it came to her in French form.

During the sixteenth century there was constant intercourse between the two countries, of which the marriage of James V. to the daughter of Francis I. and afterwards to Mary of Guise; the upbringing of Mary Queen of Scots in France, and her marriage to the Dauphin was as much consequence as cause.

In other spheres than architecture, Scotland was indebted to France for her civilisation; she had not, like England, a common law the growth of old rights and customs; this was prevented by the difference of race and language in her inhabitants, the Gaelic portion having their own tribal customs; and by the barbarism consequent on the continual state of war with England, and the arbitrary power which this gave to the nobles as military leaders, who had too frequently the vices as well as the virtues of savages; so that the country was kept almost in a state of anarchy. When at length she got laws, the complete system of Roman civil law was adopted as in France.

In the Scotch language there are many traces of French influence, especially for articles of civilisation and luxury, and for terms of building. I have heard a Scotch workman call the clock-face in a steeple, the "orledge," evidently from the French "horloge."

The Scotch "Baronial" architecture, as it is called, resembles that of the Renaissance châteaux of France, and we are frequently told that such a noble built his castle in the French manner, or even employed a French architect. Newark Castle, on the Clyde, near Port Glasgow, is a fair example of the style. It dates probably from the end of the sixteenth or beginning of the seventeenth century, as the initials of the laird who held it at that time are introduced into its architecture. The round pepper-box turrets with conical roofs are common features in French Renaissance. In both styles there is the same semblance of fortification, useless against cannon or even against the war engines of mediæval times, though capable of withstanding a sudden attack from a hostile neighbour or a rising of the peasantry. The machicolations and the angle turrets have no openings at the bottom for throwing molten lead and missiles on assailants. The windows of the turrets are on the outer angle, not where they could enfilade the walls. It is a dwelling-house with large windows, unlike the mediæval fortress. The lower part, being used for cellarage,

is a solid base with only a few small openings, which is a
chief element in the character and dignity of the style; but
this is as much from old habit and from a preference for
upper rooms for living in, as for defence.

Fig. 124.   NEWARK CASTLE, ON THE CLYDE.

The details of the building are classic, treated with
considerable freedom, and are but a rude reminiscence of
French work; but in its general character, in the pleasing
irregularity of its windows, and in its effect of springing
from the ground and expanding as it grows upwards, there
are evident traces of the old Gothic influence, possibly

borrowed anew from the French Renaissance, though more probably a remaining tradition of the country.

The castle, illustrated in fig. 125, shows small trace of French Renaissance influence. It is eminently Scotch in character. The prominence of the perpendicular lines over the horizontal give it the growth and aspiration of Gothic. It is not a fortress; the angle turrets are merely ornaments, a reminiscence or tradition which gives castellated dignity

Fig. 125.   SCOTCH CASTLE.

to a dwelling-house. The style has features of its own, not borrowed from the French Renaissance. It did not adopt its tall pyramidal roofs, but retained stone gables and crow-steps, and it has a sternness and grandeur impressed on it by the country and the race, very different from the grace and elegance of the French style.

It was during the seventeenth century that the greater number of the houses in the Scotch castellated style were built, the union of the crowns under James I. (1603) having at length given the country some repose and

Fig. 128.

OLD GLASGOW UNIVERSITY: NORTH SIDE OF INNER COURT.

Fig. 127. OLD GLASGOW UNIVERSITY: SOUTH AND WEST SIDES OF INNER COURT.

opportunity of cultivating the amenities of life, and notwithstanding their suggestions of feudalism and appearance of fortification, the Scotch castles are really the signs of security and peace.

The old buildings of Glasgow University were a characteristic example of the Scotch civil and domestic architecture of the seventeenth century, specially interesting from the fact that the dates of the several portions are known from the muniments of the University; and the progress of the style can thus be traced.

The earliest portion of the buildings was the north side of the inner court, or "Close," as it was called, shown in fig. 126, p. 363, which was commenced in 1632, and with the eastern side appears to have been completed before 1639, when the civil troubles put a stop to the building. The eastern side was destroyed in the beginning of this century, and replaced by the commonplace building, part of which appears in the corner of the view. The old building had in the centre a large projecting oriel with mullions.

When under the Commonwealth political and ecclesiastical affairs got settled to the satisfaction of the Scotch, the works were commenced again, under Principal Gillespie, who showed indefatigable energy in collecting funds from all quarters, from the Lord Protector downwards. "Our gallant building," says Robert Baillie, one of the professors, writing in 1656, "goes on vigorously; above £26,000 [pounds Scots only, let it be remembered] are already spent on it, Mr. Patrick Gillespie, with a very great care, industry, and dexterity, managing it himself as good as alone." About this year (1656), with the aid of a splendid legacy from Zachary Boyd and a large subscription from Thomas Hutcheson, the south and west sides of the inner court, shown in fig. 127, p. 366, were completed. The bust of Zachary Boyd was placed in a niche inserted in the tower over the entrance, apparently after the tower had been so far built, from its partly blocking up one of the windows. The money was given on condition that the university should print the donor's metrical paraphrase of the Bible in doggerel metre. The authorities thought the publication would not do credit to themselves, or the author. They kept the money, however, and complied with the behest by printing two copies only.

The tower was partly erected by a contribution from Mr. Snell, the founder of the exhibitions to Balliol College, Oxford, which bear his name. It will be noticed that while the turret staircases and general features of the architecture are the same as on the opposite side of the court shown in the previous illustration, the pediments of the dormer windows have lost their classic simplicity of form, and have assumed the ornamental form characteristic of the Scotch style.

This form of ornamental pediment is better shown in the next illustration (fig. 128, p. 369), which shows the corner of the outer court and part of the inner side of the beautiful hall which formed the front of the university buildings towards the High Street. These buildings were the next proceeded with; their design dating probably from about 1657. At the Restoration in 1660, Principal Gillespie was deprived of his office, without the satisfaction of being allowed to complete the great work which he had carried on so far with so much success. Not till 1690 was the great staircase leading to the Fore Hall completed by "a rail of stone balusters with a lion and a unicorn upon the first turn. The cost was £12 sterling, the College furnishing stone, lime, and materials."

The design of this building is interesting from the manner in which the national style asserts itself in it over classic influence. The cloister is an example of Roman

Fig. 128.   OLD GLASGOW UNIVERSITY: STAIR TO FORE HALL.

Fig. 122.

FORE HALL, OLD GLASGOW COLLEGE.

Doric faithfully conformed to classic rules. Its object being chiefly ornamental, it could afford to be foreign and fine. But for the parts that were to be lived in the common style of the builders was adhered to, being made, however, more splendid and ornamental than usual.

Fig. 129, p. 372, shows the interior of the Fore Hall, as it was called, to which this great staircase led, though the illustration scarcely does the design justice, a charming large low room, panelled up to the cornice with dark oak. Instead of the cornice being placed as high as it might, the ceiling above it is coved, as if the aim of the designer had been to produce an impression of comfort rather than of height.

The troubles which in Scotland followed the Restoration prevented anything more being done to the building till about the time of the Revolution of 1688. The steeple was provided with a clock, and was probably raised and the upper clock face built at that time (see fig. 127, p. 366). The square balusters on the tower are of the same character as those on the great stair which, as stated, were set up at this time.

It is to be regretted that within the last few years these most interesting buildings have been destroyed. The progress of the city westwards made the site unsuitable, and it was sold for a railway station. But I thought at the time and endeavoured, ineffectually, to persuade others that, the removal of the college being decided on, it would not be impossible to remove the Fore Hall, with its staircase and cloisters and its noble front to the High Street, to the new site. I was informed, however, that the college authorities were advised that the architecture of the building was of a degraded character. The destruction of the tower, which was one of the land-marks of the city, seems needless. Railway stations need a clock-tower, and a little ingenuity could have made it a part of a new building.

Old Glasgow University was a most characteristic example

of Scotch architecture. It was without any semblance of fortification, which, though found in country houses of later date, was felt, no doubt, to be incongruous with the nature and purpose of the building. Though the details are Classic, or at least a modification of it of native growth, the building is more truly Gothic in the character of its architecture, in the charming irregularity and various sizes of its

Fig. 130. IN THE HIGH STREET, EDINBURGH.

windows, placed as convenience demanded; and to me more interesting than the more splendid and expensive building which has replaced it, notwithstanding the elaboration and the correctness of its Gothic details.

In most towns of Scotland examples of the style are found, dating, some from the seventeenth, but more commonly from the eighteenth, century. In some of the earlier examples we find angle turrets and projected corbel courses, the reminiscences of fortification, but these were abandoned after a time. Among the most remarkable and the best known examples are the tall houses of the High Street of Edinburgh, some of them a dozen stories high. A small part of one of them is illustrated in fig. 130. In these each separate floor is a separate dwelling-house, which could not only be let, but sold, without the other floors. In this mode of living, Scotch and French habits are alike, and it is probably an instance of the influence on Scotland of French customs. It arose as much, perhaps, from the habit common to the architecture of both countries of building high as from scarcity of room or necessity of defence. In any case, having become a habit in Scotland, it was continued when it had neither justification, even in villages and houses standing alone in the country.

These Edinburgh High Street houses illustrate also a method of building common in Scotland, and almost peculiar to it, which arose from the peculiar character of the sites which were chosen. Scotch castles were usually placed on the edge of a steep hill, enclosing a courtyard on the top of it. The side of the building to the court was of moderate height, but that to the outside founded down the steep hill had as many stories looking out to the open, under the level of the inner court, as it had above it. It is this practice which gives to many Scotch castles their appearance of height and grandeur, the lower stories to the outside, used frequently merely as cellars and showing outside as solid walls forming a grand base for the building.

The same practice was followed in building towns. They were commonly built along the ridge of a hill, the street running along the top of the ridge, with the houses on each side. The High Street in Edinburgh is built in this way. The entrance of each building, or "land," as it is called, was at the level of the street from which the stair descended to as many floors below as there were above.

It is to be regretted, I think, that this feature of Scotch architecture was not followed in the new buildings of Glasgow University. These occupy the summit of a hill, of which the top was cut down to make a level platform for a long low building, the height of which is further lessened by a wide terrace in front, which buries a great height of foundation wall. Had the old Scotch plan been followed, all this useless under building would have been available for admirably lighted rooms, commanding an extended view; the hill, instead of being flattened, would have gained in height and the building would have been grander.

An attempt was made, not many years ago, to introduce into London this system of making houses of many stories, each of which was a single dwelling. Old habit long opposed the innovation, but at length the convenience and common sense of the arrangement has conquered. The toil of long stairs for approaching the house is obviated by lifts, while once in the house all is on one level. Houses convenient and of moderate size can thus be had in good situations, and on sites where land is valuable we may expect to see an extensive adoption of the system. It has of late had a new development in the system of

Fig. 131.   ORDINARY CLASSIC HOUSE.

what are called "Mansions," like the old one of the Inns of Court, with the difference that the "laundresses" are on the premises and supposed to be at the call of the bell.

It has its advantages for many people, but for families, especially with children, it has not always been found suitable. Probably something more might be done than has yet been accomplished to make such houses pleasant and suited to English habits.

During the eighteenth century the Scotch style underwent considerable modifications, mainly in the direction of mere practical convenience and commonplaceness. Angle turrets disappeared, crow-steps ceased to ornament the gables, the only ornaments were dull classic door-pieces and window-frames. This common-looking house, illustrated in fig. 131, shows what the style had come to in the early part of this century. It is common builders' architecture, the result of old traditions, and its commonplaceness is of a different type from that of the English houses of the same date. Yet there is an air of practical good sense in it, more satisfactory perhaps than the more ambitious attempts of many modern architects.

When the mediæval revival began to influence architecture, the old national Scotch style of domestic architecture was felt to be Gothic in spirit and an adequate expression of the new movement. Some even called it Gothic, and Mr. Kerr, in his 'Gentleman's House,' considers that the details should be of a rude Gothic character. Had this been so, it would not have been adopted, as it has been, as the common style for country houses for the last twenty or thirty years.

But "features" enough could be found in old Scotch to satisfy the most romantic imagination. In the old buildings these had always some reason in necessity or tradition, and were used with a moderation which makes the buildings look sensible and quiet. But the wonderful productions of modern Scotch "Baronial" seem composed wholly of corbels and towers, arrow-slits and pepper-boxes. They are all mustard with no beef. The enthusiasts for Scotch nationality have recently erected, as a monument to Wallace, a tower which alters, and some think destroys, the contour of a beautiful hill near Stirling. Corbelling has run mad in it, making marvellous protuberances where one does not expect them; corners are hacked out of it, and the pieces stuck on somewhere else. The design seems to aim at being wild.

Scarcely less wonderful is a monument lately erected to Burns at Kilmarnock, something between a steeple and castle and a shrine to hold a statue, made up of Scotch corbels and turrets, and Gothic buttresses and mouldings.

Such productions are not true expressions of national feeling. National peculiarities and differences have of late become softened down and assimilated by more frequent intercommunication with England and the influence of common culture. We should therefore expect that the architecture of the two countries should become assimilated, as in fact has happened, except in this revival of Scotch "Baronial," which has exaggerated the peculiarities of the old national style. It is like the wild spasmodic effects of galvanism rather than the natural outcome of life.

The old Scotch style, when such extravagances are avoided, is well fitted for modern houses. Its details and its forms are classic, its use involves no necessity of changing the existing habits of the inmates, or the workmen's methods of building, such as was involved in the attempt to reintroduce her national style of Gothic into England.

In the Scotch style, mullions and narrow windows were not essential, and ordinary sash windows could still be used. Crow-steps, though an addition to the expense, did not affect internal arrangements, and projected angle turrets, adopted for the sake of appearance, could be fitted up as water-closets or wardrobes. It must, however, be confessed that recent attempts to revive the old style have too often failed in reproducing its artistic character. There is no lack in them of turrets and towers and great projections of corbels, but somehow these fail to produce the sternness of the old buildings, or the appearance of strength that would defy attacks. Our modern custom in country houses of placing the public rooms with their large windows on the ground floor renders this impossible. These modern Scotch castles look like what they are, the mansions of rich modern merchants with useless extraneous features, put up for ornament and show. I cannot help thinking that the later Scotch styles of the last Stuarts and the first Georges, when the country had become finally settled and all idea of even the appearance of fortification had been abandoned, when windows as large as were needed were used on the ground-floor or wherever they were wanted, when the buildings were spread out in long level lines, instead of being piled up in great towers, as if intended to command the country, a style such as we saw in the old buildings of Glasgow University would have been a more sensible model on which to found a revival.

CHAPTER XV.

CONCLUSION.

THE Renaissance styles of architecture in Europe, some of which I have attempted—I know how inadequately—to describe, had long been considered productions of mere ignorance and barbarism; offences against classic purity and good taste, like vulgarisms or bad grammar in language.

But, as in language, words and expressions once thought vulgar have been found, on investigation, to be the natural outcome of historical development, I think I have shown that these so-called debased styles had a natural growth, and are subjects of historical interest. It is true they arose from the ignorance of correct Classic architecture in the builders, but this ignorance left room for the workings of old traditions and the natural development of new forms, which are more interesting and instructive than the dry rules of the learned.

I have endeavoured to show how these styles grew out of the old Gothic traditions in each country modifying Classic architecture which all were compelled to adopt, to remove from them the reproach of being merely the aberrations of ignorance and stupidity, and to restore them to the dignity of true and natural styles of architecture.

The state of architecture in the present day is similar to that which produced these national Renaissance styles. For thirty years we have been trained in the principles and the freedom of Gothic. The world can never again accept the dominion of classic rules; a dominion founded on an ignorance which recognised no difference between the Greek and Roman orders, and considered the clumsy Roman expedient of amalgamating the Greek orders and the Roman arch to be the ultimate outcome of architecture. We accept with knowledge and consciousness the freedom from classic restraint which the Renaissance builders took unconsciously; while Classic details and Classic forms are the basis of our style, as they were of theirs. The attempt of the last thirty years to introduce the Gothic style into domestic and civil architecture has failed. In churches the case is different; their associations and traditions are to a great extent mediæval, but the traditional habits of our daily life are too deep-seated to be altered, and Classic has still remained the domestic style of the country. Let us accept it as the basis, the material of our style, but infuse into it the Gothic spirit and freedom which we have lately learned.

The foregoing attempt to describe the genesis and character of the principal Renaissance styles of architecture was undertaken, it may be remembered, in answer to the question,—"What style of architecture is best suited to our use?"

It is a good many years now since I commenced this book, with the object chiefly of answering that enquiry. The short intervals which the practice of an architect has permitted me to devote to it, and the desire (which I have had at last to give up in despair) to make it as perfect as

I could, have delayed its appearance till the advocacy of my views has become useless, for the world has come round to them. Architects, even of the staunchest Gothic principles, are attempting the new style; builders are adopting it with enthusiasm, and more houses have been built in it during the last few years than the Gothic style produced in a generation.

Is this merely the fashion of a day, to disappear as rapidly as it has arisen, an outcome of our restlessness, which must every year have new fashions? I fear there is some risk of this. Its very popularity is its danger. Being freed from classic rules, there is no curb on the vulgarity or ignorance of those who practise it; while in the old Renaissance styles the classic rules were modified only by deep-seated Gothic traditions. The style, especially in the form known as "Queen Anne," and in the "Scotch Baronial," gives great facilities for the expression of clumsiness, crude form, and vulgarity, which may make even good examples of it seem disgusting, and put it out of fashion.

No style of architecture nowadays can continue and gradually develop like the old natural styles; for in architecture, as in ladies' dress, we have emancipated ourselves from tradition, and to keep up our interest in either we must have perpetual variety. Instead of a development so slow that it was inappreciable to those who lived in it, and could only be measured over centuries, we must have obvious change every year or two. We may expect therefore in architecture, as in dress, a recurrence at intervals to fashions lately discarded; each, as it is taken up again, receiving some new form of treatment. The present fashion of "Queen Anne" may become so associated in our minds with bulbous curves and ugly forms as to cause a revulsion to the dignity of Italian Renaissance or to the purity and refinement of Greek art. When we get tired of these, when we find that an Italian style is unsuited to our climate, that Greek architecture becomes in our hands cold and insipid, and gets misunderstood and vulgarised, when we find from experience that Englishmen are not Italians or Greeks in their tastes or their artistic powers, we may turn again with new pleasure to the cheery comfort of an English red-brick house.

But any such changes of fashion, if their authority is to be acknowledged as binding, if they are anything more than the whims of a small knot of enthusiasts, must be like the fashions in dress; changes within certain limits, the limits of our domestic habits and the traditions of the building trades. And these traditions are Classic. We cannot renounce, if we would, the inheritance of Roman forms which the Renaissance has bequeathed to us and to modern civilisation. Unwillingly, or not, we must bow to

> "Those dread unsceptred sovereigns who rule
> Our spirits from their urns."

END OF VOL. I.

LONDON: PRINTED BY WILLIAM CLOWES AND SONS, STAMFORD STREET
AND CHARING CROSS.

www.ingramcontent.com/pod-product-compliance
Lightning Source LLC
Chambersburg PA
CBHW032013220426
43664CB00006B/230